P9-DIW-558

How *One* of You Can Bring the *Two* of You *Together*

ALSO BY SUSAN PAGE

If I'm So Wonderful, Why Am I Still Single?

Eight Essential Traits of Couples Who Thrive

How *One* of You Can Bring the *Two* of You *Together*

BREAKTHROUGH STRATEGIES TO RESOLVE YOUR CONFLICTS AND REIGNITE YOUR LOVE

SUSAN PAGE

BROADWAY BOOKS • NEW YORK

HOW ONE OF YOU CAN BRING THE TWO OF YOU TOGETHER.

Broadway Books titles may be purchased for business or promotional use or for special sales. For information, please write to: Special Markets Department, Bantam Doubleday Dell Publishing Group, Inc., 1540 Broadway, New York, NY 10036.

Library of Congress Cataloging-in-Publication Data

Page, Susan.
How one of you can bring the two of you together : breakthrough strategies to resolve your conflicts and reignite your love / by Susan Page. — 1st ed.
p. cm.
Includes bibliographical references and index.
ISBN 0-553-06730-3 (hc)
1. Marriage. 2. Marital conflict. 3. Married people—Psychology.
4. Self-help techniques. I. Title.
HQ734.P15 1997
646.7'008655—dc20 96-24092
CIP

FIRST EDITION

Designed by Fearn Cutler
Illustration by James Hammock

97 98 99 00 01 10 9 8 7 6 5 4 3 2 1

This book is dedicated with gratitude and love

to my mother-in-law,

Florence Shacter,

who lived this book decades before it was written.

(On her ninetieth birthday, she did her usual hour of yoga.)

Contents

Acknowledgments ix
Introduction xi

PART ONE: IS THIS IDEA FOR YOU?

1. How to Work Alone on a Two-Person Relationship 3

PART TWO: PUTTING YOURSELF IN CHARGE

2. Give Away the Booby Prize and Go for the Gold 29
3. Learn ERAP (Emergency Resentment Abatement Procedure) 50

PART THREE: SHORT-TERM STRATEGIES FOR CREATING A THRIVING RELATIONSHIP BY YOURSELF

4. Create Harmony in Your Home 87
5. Resolve Your Most Upsetting Problems—by Yourself 115
6. Discover How One of You Can Bring the Two of You *Very* Close Together: Intimacy and Companionship 163

PART FOUR: LONG-TERM STRATEGIES FOR KEEPING YOUR RELATIONSHIP ROBUST

7. Practice Taking Care of Yourself 187
8. Cultivate Good Will 213
9. Loving Leadership: Self-Care and Good Will As a Blend 246

PART FIVE: WHEN YOU SET CHANGE IN MOTION, ANYTHING CAN HAPPEN

10. Evaluating Your Relationship 263
11. The Good Marriage, The Good Self 279

Bibliography 291
Index 293

Acknowledgments

To all the members of my audiences who have asked me, "What if my spouse won't go for counseling?" I owe my first debt of gratitude. Also, to the people I've interviewed, coached, and guided through workshops, my heartfelt appreciation for your hard work and your willingness to talk so openly with me. This book wouldn't be possible without your stories.

If you like this book, you owe a huge thank-you to my parents, Helen and Edwin Hammock. I learned from them how to do a good marriage, and it was they who helped me become the person who could write this book. They are both extraordinary people. (And thank-you to them for correcting my grammar all those years too. It sank in!)

My sterling literary agent, Sandra Dijkstra, encouraged this book idea and has been an invaluable partner throughout every stage of the project. She is a master at what she does.

See that halo over literary agent Patti Breitman? "Brightwoman" that she is, she generously steered publisher Bill Shinker in my direction and then wouldn't even let me take her out to dinner! Here's my thank-you, Patti. I'm beholden forever.

I'm extremely grateful to Bill Shinker at Broadway Books, the person who brought this book to life. Working with him has been a special pleasure.

Every author knows the agonizing search for the perfect title. This time I was rescued by marketing genius David Garfinkel. The title fell out of his mouth one day while we were talking—and it was he who had the brilliance to notice it! David has been a great support throughout the project.

Psychotherapists Janet Kirk and Harriet Sage and editor Amanita Rosenbush read early versions of the first few chapters. Their encouragement was important. Fellow relationship author Azriela Jaffe was a wonderful resource, faxing me relevant articles and turning me on to useful books or chapters.

My writing buddy, Bob Davidson, and I had long conversations about the philosophy that permeates these pages. He took a special interest in each step of the book's development and offered his relentless optimism and support.

I feel a special debt to style consultant Susan Schwartz who dresses me for my public appearances, and has contributed valuable ideas to this book—and to my life. She is a gem!

Numerous friends have offered critical insights or special help. They include Rebecca Beardsley, Ida Centoni, Ilene Dillon, Naomi Epel, Robin Everest, Bob Fink, Anita Goldstein, Gail Henningson, Jane Hunter, Jerome Kirk, Malcolm Lubliner, Melinda Marmer, Joanne Mendez, Jim Mittleberger, Annie Mudge, Diane Ohlssen, Roseanne Packard, Ruth Pritchard, and Chris Reeg.

My fabulous sister, Bonnie Davis, carefully combed through late versions of several chapters, coming up with insightful nuances.

Alice Vdovin, my resourceful, imaginative, and generous assistant, has provided relentless support for many years now. I can never thank her enough. I would be lost without her.

Janet Goldstein, my editor at Broadway Books, is a true professional and pure joy to work with. Her assistant, Betsy Thorpe, has also been extremely helpful.

Mayer Shacter is an amazing husband. He's talked over every aspect of this work with me, endured the "I can't write!" days, and helped to celebrate all the excitement this project has been for both of us. He is a model of the ideas in this book, and has contributed some very important thinking to it. And he takes absolutely wonderful care of me.

I also want to acknowledge my son, Gabe, and my brand new daughter-in-law, Kim, who will have been married about six months when this book is first published. They have brought immeasurable joy to my life, and I want to say out loud how much I love them!

Susan Page
Berkeley, California

Introduction

***Radio talk show caller:** "I know our marriage has great potential, but my partner doesn't think there is anything wrong and doesn't want to work with me on making any changes, so I feel totally stuck and frustrated."*

One historic moment during a radio talk show, it dawned on me that I was answering this question from a caller for the thousandth time, and that I ought to become a bit more organized about how I responded. After the program, I thought I'd jot down a few notes to guide me in the future. When the scribbled notes became three pages and I was just getting started, I realized I had to write this book.

A belief is a powerful thing! It can limit or expand your life to a staggering degree. The belief that both partners have to be available to work on a relationship or else nothing can happen is widely held—and completely erroneous. I couldn't wait to demonstrate this, to give that caller and thousands of men and women like him the news that you don't have to wait for your partner to come around. You can act on your own with gratifying results.

Immediately, I began offering and honing my theories in workshops, and gathering information through in-depth interviews with couples. The results are in your hands.

This book is closely related to the last one I wrote, entitled *Eight Essential Traits of Couples Who Thrive*; in fact, I view the two books as companion volumes. I worked hard to avoid repeating in this work the information I put in that book, which describes the qualities that happy, thriving couples have in common. Both books rise out of the same fundamental philosophy about marriage, that an inner shift to "good will" is a critical factor that makes the difference between couples who thrive and couples who don't.

My work is deeply rooted in personal experience. With a background in both theology and psychology, I have been working with singles and couples for more than twenty-five years, beginning in 1970 when my colleague and I founded one of the first university-based human sexuality programs in the country at the University of California, Berkeley. After extensive training in both gestalt and bioenergetic therapies, in my work as a Protestant minister and in my relationship workshops, I have been refining the strategies you will find in this book.

I was married for eight years, single for six, and have been the happy, well-nourished wife of Mayer—whom you will hear more about in these pages—since 1981. When I find something that works, I have a strong inclination to organize it into a useful tool and pass it along to others. So my work is undeniably autobiographical. The ideas emanate from my own carefully observed experiences and are embellished by hardworking workshop participants and thoughtful, wise interviewees.

WHO CAN BENEFIT FROM THIS BOOK?

The tools in this book are appropriate for individuals in a wide range of relationships. Even the happiest and most stable of couples face challenges and harbor *some* unfulfilled desires. I know of no couples who wouldn't love to have a magic wand to change certain little pet peeves in their relationship. This book is the magic wand you've been seeking but thought couldn't possibly exist, and I'm willing to bet it is an approach you haven't tried before—largely because it never quite occurred to you.

Perhaps you are feeling disillusioned or disconnected from each other. You are confident the phase will pass; but you are finding it most unpleasant and worrisome. Or, you may be in the transition from infatuation to enduring, everyday love. This passage can begin on your wedding day or even three or four years later, but whenever it comes it is disorienting. Maybe you are in a crisis, caused by a sudden event or by a long, slow buildup of resentments and unresolved problems. You may even feel on the verge of divorce—that your relationship is beyond hope.

If any of these descriptions fits you, the ideas in this book can be, as one workshop participant described it, a "love potion" for you. They can create significant changes in your household overnight—without elaborate, time-consuming "exercises" or "dialogues." No matter what the present status of your relationship, you will find an approach in this book that is refreshingly different from all the two-way "discussions," "communication skills," and "listening" exercises you've heard about and maybe tried before. Many people have found that working alone is both less hassle and more effective than trying to work together.

To be sure, some relationships really are toxic and even destructive for both people involved, and everyone would be better off if they did end. If your relationship is so unpleasant or difficult that you wonder whether you should put time and effort into it at all, or whether now may be the time to gather up your courage to get out of it, the program in this book will be an enormous help to you in making a decision. Indeed, after you have given the program a try, Chapter Ten will take you through a step-by-step evaluation that will give you factual, concrete help in deciding whether to stay in the relationship or leave it.

The book is addressed to individuals who are in a committed, long-term relationship or who are considering such a commitment. It matters not whether you are actually married, and I have used terms like partner, spouse, and mate interchangeably.

Most of the examples I use in this book are about individuals who are *not* in therapy or marriage counseling. I have found that people tend to discount progress made by couples who are in therapy by saying, "Well, that could happen for them because they are in therapy. But it won't work for us because my partner will never go to therapy." So I have deliberately drawn my examples from workshop participants who were working alone, and from individuals I have interviewed or coached.

I don't discount the value of marriage counseling. Far from it. When both partners want help with their relationship, counseling can be most effective. The strategies in this book will be equally useful for any couple in therapy.

But I aim to demonstrate that one person working alone can create momentous changes, and that therapy is not an essential part of the mix. The "working alone" approach is very different from the types of activities that go on in therapy.

The strategies will also work for the other relationships in your life. You will have great success using them with co-workers, family members, and friends, as well as your intimate partner. Once you learn them, you'll find you will apply them widely.

Couples Welcome!

Everything I suggest in this book is designed for use by one individual in a relationship. However, be assured that it will all work just as beautifully if both partners are working on their relationship together. The book will also be a lot of fun if used in that way!

THE EXPERIMENTS

Throughout the book, I have suggested "experiments." They are optional. *You do not have to do the experiments in order to get full value from the book!*

But I strongly encourage you to *read* the experiments, even if you do not choose to do them. They often summarize or even add a dimension to ideas in the preceding section. They may offer you an idea that will be useful to you at some time, even if you don't use it right then.

I quite deliberately call my action suggestions "experiments." The sole purpose of an experiment is to gather data, so no matter what its outcome you can never fail; you will have gathered some kind of data! If your result is not what you wanted or expected, that is important information for you. It doesn't mean you failed; it means you succeeded in eliminating one strategy because it isn't going to bring expected results. So you will go on to a different experiment.

This is actually an important philosophy for life in general. If you keep on doing what you have always done, you will keep on getting the same results. Many couples go on doing what they have always done for many years, and can't figure out why nothing changes. An experiment offers you a low-risk opportunity to try something new. I predict that you will often be surprised at the results of your experiments.

OPTIONS FOR USING THIS BOOK

You can use the book in any one of the following ways:

1. Read the book for its general ideas. Read the experiments, but don't feel any pressure to do them. The general concepts being discussed can, by themselves, make a major impact on your marriage. You will get a *feel* for the message in the book. Working on your relationship by yourself is a "gestalt," that is, while we must break it into its component parts to present it, it comes together at the end as one giant shift in your entire approach to your relationship. You can get this overall picture without doing any of the experiments.

2. As you come to experiments that can be done casually, maybe even in your head, pause to do them before you read on. You may want to keep paper and pen with your book, so you are ready to make the little list suggested in an experiment, or jot down the sentence requested. Some of the experiments are quite simple, and you will be tempted to see what happens for you when you do them.

3. As you read, keep track of the experiments that you would like to try at some later time, after you have read the entire book. Keep an A list for the ones you are most interested in, a B list for your second favorites, and a C list for your third priorities. It is unlikely you will want to do all the experiments, in any case, because some will be far more relevant to your own situation than others.

4. Use this book as a personal workshop for yourself, a program you will work through systematically over a period of weeks, just as I do with the participants in my workshops. In this case, you may still want to read the book through first, or, you may choose to do the experiments as you come to them in the book. Choose the experiments that interest you most; they won't all be appropriate for your relationship.

If you decide to use the book as a personal workshop, you will need to acquire two basic pieces of equipment before you get started. You will need a journal and a support person.

The value of a supportive friend who agrees either to do this program with you, or to support you as you do it yourself, cannot be overemphasized. For one thing, some of the experiments require an assistant. Also, a support person will keep you on track and completing what you set out to do. Your friend can remind you that you are not alone in what you want in your marriage, can reassure you that what you want is valid, and can help you see progress you are making when you might be missing it yourself. Often, talking with a friend will give you an insight that you simply won't see if you work only with yourself and your own journal.

You have behaviors and attitudes you will never see on your own because you are so immersed in your own experience. An honest friend can gently point out some of these factors to you, especially in the safe context of a specific, limited experiment.

EXPERIMENT #1

(If you are planning to use this book as a personal workshop)

1. Purchase a notebook or blank bound book that is easy for you to write in. Whenever you make an entry, be sure to date it. One of the most educational ways to use an experiment is to repeat it after several months and compare your results to your previous effort.

2. From your friends, select one whom you trust and enjoy and who is likely to support what you are setting out to do. It is ideal if you can find a friend who wants to work on this program along with you. The two of you can exchange support and learn from each other as you go. But a friend who is not doing the program will work too, as long as the person is interested and genuinely wants to help and support you.

Do not select a friend who is also close to your spouse, or who is part of a couple whom you and your partner see socially. This may complicate your efforts unnecessarily, and could create a conflict for your friend.

Your support person will need to spend about an hour a week with you, sometimes more, sometimes less. Some of the work can be done on the phone if necessary.

3. Identify the person you want, and invite him or her to consider supporting you or entering into a mutual support program with you. If for any reason, you aren't successful with the first person, ask another. If you want to treat this book as a personal workshop, your chances of enjoyment and success will be greatly increased if you are not trying to do it completely alone. The program requires you, your journal, and your support person.

THE STRUCTURE OF THE BOOK

Many books begin with a general theory and an attempt to persuade you that its philosophy is a useful one. In the final chapters, you get down to practical strategies you can put to use.

I've chosen to organize this book in the opposite way. Very early, I will offer you practical strategies you can put to immediate use and see results. Only then, when you have a context in which to better understand it, will I discuss the general philosophy that underlies the practical strategies.

But there is overlap, too. You will glean the general philosophy by reading through the practical strategies; and the general philosophy at the end is also presented in extremely practical terms. Practical and usable is the standard I insist on when I write.

In Part One, I will alleviate the skepticism you may have about the very idea of working alone, and answer some of your questions. In Parts Two and Three, I will offer you specific strategies for shifting your viewpoint, managing your anger or resentment, creating a harmonious atmosphere in your relationship, and actually solving the most annoying problems you and your partner have. Part Three will also offer you a magical idea for increasing the intimate flow between you, an idea that arises out of the general principles we will have discussed.

Part Four will reveal the general principle behind working alone, a concept I call Loving Leadership.

Finally, in Part Five, I will give you the opportunity to evaluate your relationship and its potential in the light of all that you will have tried or considered as you read through the book.

AN ENCOURAGING WORD

"The significant problems we face cannot be solved at the same level of thinking we were at when we created them," Einstein pointed out. Conversely, sometimes moving to a new level of thinking will do a great deal to reveal the solution to a problem.

We have been trying to solve our relationship problems at the same level of thinking at which we created them. Two people create relationship problems; perhaps the idea that one person can solve them may be the new level we seek.

A well-timed idea can be extraordinarily powerful. I have seen the ideas in this book transform relationships. I hope you smile as you read this book. I believe that it will help you feel more powerful and more loving—and ultimately more loved—than you do now.

Enjoy the journey!

Part One

Is This Idea for You?

CHAPTER ONE

How to Work Alone on a Two-Person Relationship

Whenever I mention one person bringing two people together, skeptics tell me, even with a touch of irritation bordering on anger, "I object to the whole idea of working alone to improve my relationship," giving reasons like these:

1. It won't work in principle. A good relationship requires two willing participants.
2. I've already been working alone for years, and it hasn't worked.
3. My relationship is in awful shape. And my spouse won't cooperate. I'm afraid my marriage isn't worth working on.
4. Working alone isn't fair.
5. What about intimacy and soul connection? Don't both people have to be present and available for that?
6. One more time, the entire burden for change falls on women. This program perpetuates the outdated idea that it is women's job to take care of the relationship.
7. Taking all the responsibility by yourself is codependent, something I'm striving to eliminate altogether in my life.
8. Exactly how do I work alone? I can't even imagine what that would be like. Doesn't my partner have to be involved in some way?

I understand these worries; they are valid concerns. Let me respond.

Q: WORKING ALONE WON'T WORK IN PRINCIPLE! A GOOD RELATIONSHIP REQUIRES TWO WILLING PARTICIPANTS, DOESN'T IT?

A: This popular belief is understandable, but it is simply not true. Your spouse's disinclination to "work on the relationship" is not an indication of a special problem and not a handicap of any kind. Working alone will *not* negatively affect the outcome of your efforts. In fact, as you will see, working alone to improve your relationship can be both easier and more effective than working together.

Your spouse may have any number of *valid* reasons for not wanting to "work on the relationship." Often, it is the man who doesn't want to talk or to go to a counselor. What might be his reasons? Maybe he is afraid that your problems will become worse if you start to delve. Maybe he fears that you are more unhappy than you seem, and you really want to leave him. Maybe he is vaguely aware of some painful memories or regrets, and he doesn't want to dredge them up. Maybe he resents the time counseling will take. Maybe he carries around the belief that you don't ask for help unless your marriage is really on the rocks. Maybe he fears that he can't change in the ways you want him to, and he sees no alternatives. Maybe his best friend had a bad experience with a counselor. He may think that the problems are all your fault, but that you will expect him to make all the changes. He probably has no vision of what your relationship could be. Or maybe in his experience, the relationship has no problems. If he does see problems, he probably has absolutely no idea that he is doing anything to contribute to them.

Who knows? Whatever his reason, you must realize, it is a valid reason *for him,* and the best thing you can do is to respect it.

There are probably many traits you would change about your partner if you could wave a magic wand. Save your wand for something more significant than your spouse's reluctance to go for counseling.

Working on your relationship by yourself does *not* mean that you have less potential for happiness with your partner than a couple who are working together. A marriage's potential for success might be measured by other factors—like the nature of the problem and the level of commitment present—but whether one or two people are working on change is not one of those factors.

Your motivation is the key to your success. If *you* want you and your spouse to be closer and experience more pleasure together, no matter what your problems are, you are far more likely to succeed than a couple who go for help *together* but who are not highly motivated to improve their marriage.

The reason one person acting alone can make a major impact is that a relationship between two people is a single unit with two parts. When one person acts, the other is affected. Your behaviors and attitudes have an impact on your spouse. Right now, you may not be consciously choosing exactly what impact you want to make. If you decide to start improving your relationship, you have to make deliberate choices about the results you want to achieve.

Using an example, let's look at the difference between working together to solve a problem and working alone.

Like many couples, Mary and John have fallen into a pattern of interacting with each other. Mary reminds John of his household tasks; John expresses anger at being "controlled" by not doing the tasks. It's a perfect plot. She nags; he leaves the scene. Both have been playing their parts for so long that their response has become automatic. Mary is completely unaware that her nagging is actually *triggering* John's escapes. John is unaware that his escapes are *triggering* Mary's nagging.

Both Mary and John have a valid point of view. Mary is right that John escapes and doesn't help enough. John is right that Mary tries to control him and won't leave him alone.

Suppose Mary were to decide she wanted the two of them to work on their problem together. First, she'd have to convince John that this was a good idea. John would see this as one more attempt to control him. Now they would have a new topic for their drama! Same script, just a new problem inserted. "Mary keeps trying to get me to go to therapy. I don't think we need it!"

But let's say John eventually agrees to go to a counselor. The counselor may, quite appropriately, want to know what went on in the families John and Mary grew up in. She would work on getting John and Mary to talk with each other, to hear each other's point of view. Since John and Mary are both invested in being right, and since they have been avoiding understanding each other's point of view for years, learning to listen to each other would take time and would itself present problems and frustrations. Meantime, Mary would still be trying to get John to help around the house, and John would still be escaping.

I don't mean to disparage the counselor's methods. Exploring together and listening to each other are valuable. But deciding to work together and then actually doing the work together more than doubles the size of the task of "fixing" the marriage. Moreover, it depends on the continuing cooperation and progress of both parties, something that may or may not occur.

Now suppose either Mary or John decided to work on the relationship alone. Let's take Mary first. She doesn't have to get John to agree to anything. All she has to do is figure out one simple behavior or attitude that she, by herself, can do differently. For the sake of this example, let's say she decides that for fourteen days, she is going to say nothing to John about his lack of cooperation. She cannot know ahead of time what the result will be; but because she is making a unilateral change in the script, the drama will, by definition, change. John may continue his role as before and continue to avoid his household tasks; or he may appreciate Mary's lack of nagging and respond by working more; or he may become very uncomfortable without her nagging and stay away from home more. Mary may think she knows how he will respond, but she doesn't know until she actually experiments. And when she finds out, she can make some new choices. She will be making changes in their relationship all by herself, quickly and easily, and in a way that increases her own self-esteem, inner strength, and power.

Suppose John were the one to decide to make a change by himself. Since he knows quite clearly what Mary wants, he could try doing it once without being asked. Or, he could announce to Mary that he no longer wants to do that thing and offer to do something else instead. Or he could tell Mary he will take her out to dinner if she will refrain from making requests of him for one full week. Or he could decide to tell Mary every day one thing that he especially loves about her. His choices go on and on. The point is, by acting alone, he will be making a change in their relationship, the impact of which can be far-reaching.

A marriage is like a seesaw. Even when one partner acts alone, it affects the other.

When you make a change in your behavior or your attitude entirely on your own, you can work a miracle in your marriage. Hundreds of marriage partners have already discovered this. Listen to several participants in my groups or interviews:

> JANICE: The very idea that I could work alone on my marriage problems made me feel incredibly hopeful because suddenly, I wasn't dependent on anyone else! The changes I made gave me a feeling of power I have never felt before.

ALEX: The change I made was so subtle! I just stopped expecting my wife to "take care of our relationship." It took me awhile to realize that that is what I was expecting! But when I was able to let go of it, a barrier was gone, and we became closer than we had been for a long time. Maybe ever.

PEG: I was happy with my husband, but I had the feeling for a long time that we could be closer. Of course, I thought he needed to make all the changes. I wanted him to be more romantic, to talk with me more. What I discovered is that it was the way I saw our marriage, the expectations I was superimposing on it, that was really screwing us up. It is still completely amazing to me that by changing the way I was viewing things, I now have everything I want in my marriage. My husband hasn't changed at all, and we are definitely closer now. It's like I went searching all over the planet for diamonds, and all the while there was a diamond mine in my own backyard.

GEORGE: I was in despair. I really thought Julia didn't love me anymore, and we were fighting all the time. I tried everything—or so I thought. I now see that all I was doing to win her back just made the problems worse. I was pleading and making myself into her victim. When I saw an altogether different path and began to do the *right* things, everything changed. I will tell you, no marriage is too far gone to benefit from this system! Julia jokes with me now that I am her hero because I singlehandedly saved our marriage.

DIANE: You know how when an airplane makes a tiny adjustment in its course in Los Angeles, it can make the difference in whether it ends up in New York or Miami? Well, that's our marriage. I made a tiny change, and it led to a huge difference. All I did was to stop cleaning up Peter's messes. This led to other changes which led to a revolution in our marriage. If you have an hour, I'll tell you the whole story.

(We will hear Diane and Peter's story later on.)

Many marriage partners feel completely stuck and utterly frustrated when they report to me, "My spouse won't go for counseling. My spouse won't work on our problems and work on the relationship." But in fact, having an uncooperative spouse is not the worst of all possible problems. If he or she is a good person with many qualities you like, don't be excessively alarmed about this particular reluctance.

Q: I'VE BEEN WORKING ALONE FOREVER ALREADY, AND IT HASN'T WORKED. WHY SHOULD THIS METHOD BE ANY DIFFERENT?

A: It isn't the fact of working alone that works magic in relationships; it's what you do when you work alone that makes all the difference. All attempts at change are not the same.

Many of us have spent years in well-intentioned efforts to improve our relationships—to no avail. Because in spite of all our best efforts, we were doing the *wrong things.*

Unfortunately, often the most natural and automatic response to a difficult situation is precisely the one that is not only ineffective but actually counterproductive. A simple example is when Mary, in a moment of frustration, says to John, "You never help around the house!" John is likely to respond, "Yes I do! I cleaned out the whole garage last weekend." This is a natural, quite reasonable response. But it is not productive. If John could say, "You must be feeling extra frustrated right now. Is there anything I can do to help?" this wouldn't be a natural response, but it would be far more effective and relationship-enhancing. Mary's original comment wasn't effective either, of course. But she was feeling it right then, so she blurted it out. Quite normal and understandable.

This book will not ask you to make superhuman changes or to give up natural responses to the things you don't like. But it will introduce you to a new approach that has been effective for other couples.

Participants in my workshops discuss the futile attempts they have made over the years to improve their relationships by themselves. You may recognize some of these strategies. Most of us use them because we know of no alternatives.

Let's be clear at the outset that the following attempts at problem solving create more problems than they solve. They don't work! After you read this book, you will never need to use them again, as you will have a whole set of new strategies—that will work.

1. *Asking for what you want.* Although we will discuss in a later chapter a method of asking for what you want that is likely to be effective, most of the time, this method fails. This is usually because you are asking for something your partner genuinely doesn't understand, isn't able to give you, or doesn't want to give you. Women ask men to be more communicative, to be more romantic, to be more emotionally available. Men ask women to be less critical and more accepting of them. The pattern of asking for what you want and not getting it goes on for years, even in quite healthy relationships, simply because the partners are not aware that they have alternatives and especially because they don't know how to get the results they want.

Another reason asking for what you want is counterproductive is that when you ask for what you want, your partner may hear your request as criticism. For example, John says to Mary, "I wish you were in the mood to make love more often." Mary hears, "He isn't satisfied with me as a sexual partner." Whereas John was trying to bring the two of them closer together, Mary's response was to withdraw from John, to feel criticized and therefore more distant and self-protective. This is an honest effort gone awry because of an innocent mistake, and it is another reason that asking for what you want often fails to get results.

2. *Not asking for what you want.* Most couples continue asking for what they want and not getting it for many years. But occasionally, they realize it isn't working, so they consciously decide to stop asking. Often there is either a martyrlike attitude of, "Oh, I'll just learn to do without," or an angry resignation, "I'll never get blood out of this turnip. I just give up!" Not asking for what you want may relieve the surface conflict, but it buries your anger deep underground, where it grows and festers and will eventually emerge again, either in a volcanic eruption or a still, stagnant pool of depression.

3. *Emotional bribery.* Many people try to get what they want by becoming so generous that their partner will feel shamed or at least reminded into giving back. Larry told me he felt his wife, Bev, drifting away from him and desperately wanted her back. He surprised her by staying home from work one day, repainting their daughter's room, and fixing a lovely dinner for them all. But since Bev's complaint was that Larry was always busy with projects and not emotionally available to her, she saw his efforts as more of the same, and actually left to spend some time with her sister that very week. Larry told me, "I thought surely this surprise would make her see how much I love her. How could she distance herself even more after all I did?" He expected love as a return for his own loving generosity, and he felt betrayed. But in fact, his giving had a kind of hook in it. "If I give you this, you should love me back." Bev detected this, and was all the more annoyed. Generosity is a natural behavior toward someone you love. But giving with the hope of getting something in return will virtually always backfire.

4. *Advising, assisting.* Cheryl honestly believed that Donald would be happier if he could get over his money anxiety. She kept trying to persuade him that there was no reason to worry, and that worrying never helped anyway. But the more she tried to "help" Donald, the more criticized and misunderstood he felt. The extreme form of advising and assisting is, of course, nagging. Nagging creates nothing but conflict, hard feelings, and distance between two people. Yet it remains one of the most common of all single-handed efforts to "bring the two of you together."

5. *Denying your needs.* Sharon pleaded with her husband for years to take his share of responsibility with the house and children. Nothing worked. At last she figured out a way to make their lives work even if he didn't help. By going to graduate school and waitressing, she could actually be home with the children more than with her demanding job. The arguing diminished for a few years, but Sharon told me that in retrospect, she can see that she sacrificed herself and her own needs just to keep peace. Graduate school is not what she actually wanted for her life. It was just an elaborate scheme to make the family work, even if she could not get what she wanted from her husband. It took years for her real self and her real desires to reemerge.

A love relationship works only when it empowers both partners to become more their true selves, not less. Denying your needs to keep peace is one of the worst ways you can work alone to improve your marriage, and it is the most insidious, because it is, by definition, unconscious. (If you are aware of what you are denying, then you aren't denying it!) The method we will learn in this book is especially effective at preventing you from denying your needs. You will be encouraged not to adapt to your marriage, but to enrich it.

If working alone on your marriage has not worked for you in the past, perhaps it is because, although you were sincere, you did not work in ways that were effective. So don't give up on working alone because it hasn't worked in the past; the strategies in this book are different.

Q: MY RELATIONSHIP IS IN AWFUL SHAPE. AND MY SPOUSE WON'T COOPERATE. IS MY MARRIAGE EVEN WORTH WORKING ON?

A: The answer, almost without exception, is yes.

As we've seen, your spouse's reluctance to work with you is not an insurmountable problem. And even the most troubled relationships have responded to enlightened efforts on the part of one partner.

So that we can begin to work with your specific relationship, as we shall do throughout the book, take a moment to think about your own situation, however mild or severe you feel your problems are.

EXPERIMENT #2

Taking Inventory

In your journal, first make a list of all the qualities you like about your partner and your relationship.

On a fresh page, list your complaints, the changes you would make if you had a magic wand. What are the problem areas that you see?

Now list your problems again in what you believe to be their order of importance. Put the biggest, most overarching problem at the top, and the corollaries or additional, smaller problems under that one. If you have several main problems, list them side by side.

Keep these lists handy in the front of your journal as you will be using them in future experiments.

When participants introduce themselves at the beginning of a workshop, while they mention highly individual problems, we often hear comments along these lines:

- We have a great relationship. There are just one or two areas that continue to be a problem.
- Things my mate does annoy me, worry me, upset me.
- I don't have enough power. I can't be myself.
- We've lost our spark.

- We fight so much. I hate all the arguing.
- He's too distant. I don't feel intimate anymore.
- She nags me too much. She wants to change me.
- He takes me for granted.
- It's too late for us. Our problems have been the same for years.
- I don't feel my love anymore.
- There are too many differences between us.
- My needs are not getting met. I want more ________________.
- This is not what I wanted or expected.
- We've grown apart. We have no common interests.
- We have already tried everything and nothing has worked. I don't think our problems will ever change.

Amazingly, it doesn't matter what your marital problems are or how serious you believe them to be. The chances are still very good that your marriage is renewable and therefore very much worth working on. Consider the following evidence in favor of throwing yourself wholeheartedly into reviving your relationship, whether the problems you want to fix are mild or severe. Hundreds and hundreds of couples, some of them extremely unhappy, have turned their relationships completely around using suggestions like the ones in this book. Marriage "miracles" are occurring every day, fully documented by a wide variety of relationship experts:

> I've grown increasingly convinced that most marriages are worth saving simply because most problems are solvable. . . . I don't believe in "saving marriages," I believe in divorcing the old marriage and beginning a new one—with the same partner. (Michelle Weiner-Davis, Brief Therapy practitioner and author of *Divorce Busting*)

> Every day I receive mail from couples who tell me they have renewed hope, that they feel in love again. Then five years later, they send me pictures of themselves with their kids. (John Gray, Ph.D., therapist, workshop leader, and author of *Men Are from Mars, Women Are from Venus*)

> A great deal of powerful change can occur when one person in a relationship breaks free. Don't fall into the trap of waiting to change until your partner is ready. (Gay Hendricks, Ph.D.,

> and Kathlyn Hendricks, Ph.D., marriage therapists and authors of *Conscious Loving*)

> Fortunately, we have found that one person can change a two-person relationship by changing his or her part of . . . their interactions. . . . Changing your point of view can lift you out of the rut you are stuck in and give you the power to make a difference in your relationship. (Bill O'Hanlon and Pat Hudson, marriage therapists and authors of *Love Is a Verb*)

> No matter how alienated from your partner you may feel, it is possible to release your resentments and reestablish the flow of caring between you. It is possible to renew your loving bonds with one another . . . (Larry A. Bugen, Ph.D., marriage therapist and author of *Love and Renewal*)

All this "evidence" may not seem very persuasive to you right now if you are feeling drained and haven't seen progress in your relationship for some time. Change may feel impossible to you.

That's okay. A feeling of hopelessness may be quite appropriate for you right now, and it won't affect the results you will get if you follow the suggestions in this book. It is quite natural that you cannot imagine your relationship any different from the way it is now. When you are deep in the middle of one feeling, you can't feel, or even get a picture of how it will feel, to be deep in the middle of a completely different feeling. But that doesn't mean such a change can't happen.

So trust the evidence. Proceed on blind faith and see what happens. As Kierkegaard said, "To dare is to lose your footing temporarily. To not dare is to lose your life."

The feeling of hopelessness is painful and depressing. It feels like a downward spiral, and it is. The more you try to change things, the more entrenched you can become in the belief that your marriage is hopeless—because everything you try fails.

But wait. Maybe it is the other way around. Maybe everything you try fails only because you believe your marriage is hopeless. It is likely that "our marriage is hopeless" has become a self-fulfilling prophecy for you. When you view your marriage through the our-marriage-is-hopeless lens, you are able to accumulate a great deal of evidence to prove your point. It is true that making any changes, small or large, while retaining your present view of your marriage will not result in any meaningful change.

This book will suggest a completely different approach. What has to change is your belief about your marriage. This is an inner shift, a change of heart, a mental flip to a new "story" about your marriage.

Don't worry about shifting your belief now. I simply want to make the point here that all solutions are not the same and that there are in fact solutions that you have not yet tried. You may feel that your marriage is hopeless, but in truth, it almost certainly has every chance of becoming fulfilling for you again. If you try the suggestions in the chapters that follow and you still feel hopeless, only then will you be ready for the guidelines in Chapter Ten that will help you to evaluate your relationship and consider the possibility of ending it.

Q: IT ISN'T FAIR TO HAVE TO WORK ALONE WHEN TWO PEOPLE ARE INVOLVED. WHY SHOULD I HAVE TO DO ALL THE WORK?

A: True, it doesn't seem fair. Two people will benefit from the work you do; both people should have to be involved in doing the work. Those who didn't help grind the wheat and knead the dough, shouldn't get to eat the bread.

But then, very little in this world is fair. Maybe it isn't important for an idea to be fair if it brings happiness and satisfaction anyway.

Besides, looked at in a different light, the situation is more than fair. Because you are not at the mercy of your partner's willingness to work! Suddenly, you don't have to wait around for your spouse anymore. You can do what you want when you want to do it!

Deciding to work alone on your relationship gives you enormous power, not power over your partner but inner power, personal strength, and an unparalleled opportunity to grow. Suddenly, instead of looking unfair, this system seems exceptionally fair, because now you do not have to wait for your partner to change before you can take your life into your own hands! What would be unfair is for you to allow your partner's lack of cooperation to hold you back.

It is rare for two separate people to be ready to change and grow at exactly the same moment. We all have individual rhythms that must be respected. If you had to wait until your partner consented to work together with you on your relationship, it might be like the old Kansas law that said, "If two trains going in opposite directions meet at an automobile crossing, they must both come to a full stop, and neither may proceed until the other is gone."

If one of you doesn't take the lead, you may remain stuck in old patterns for a very long time.

By undertaking to work on your relationship alone, you will be, in effect, giving your spouse a gift, possibly a quite powerful gift. And it is not in the nature of gifts to be fair. You don't give a gift with the idea that you will get an equal gift back. This wouldn't be a gift but some kind of a barter or bargain.

Unfairness is a minor problem when compared to the opportunities available to you when you take the initiative in your relationship. When your unilateral action leads to bilateral happiness, the unfairness of it all will fade into the background. Instead of feeling ripped off, you will feel inner strength, and the deep pleasure of having given the person you love a beautiful gift.

Q: BUT WHAT ABOUT INTIMACY, CLOSENESS, SOUL CONNECTION? DON'T BOTH PEOPLE HAVE TO BE PRESENT AND AVAILABLE FOR THAT?

A: Yes, you can't be intimate with someone who doesn't want to be intimate with you. A "soul connection" implies an experience involving two people.

In Chapter Nine, we will talk about ways for one person to entice the other into greater intimacy and to restore a feeling of mutual closeness that may be flagging.

Of course closeness is only one aspect of a long-term committed relationship. Some couples have and care about closeness and intimacy to a much greater degree than others. Some neither have nor desire a "deep soul connection." And whether you have it or not, intimacy is never enough to sustain you through the rough and tumble of day to day life with each other. You may have a soul connection and deeply love each other and still have problem areas in your relationship that can be affected by the wise actions of one party or the other.

As they begin to take effect, the suggestions in this book will "wake up" both you and your partner. The "good will" and "loving leadership" you will read about are not one route to genuine intimacy; they are the only route.

Q: TAKING CARE OF THE RELATIONSHIP HAS ALWAYS FALLEN ON WOMEN; ONE MORE TIME, AREN'T WOMEN THE ONES WHO WILL END UP DOING ALL THE WORK?

A: If we are going to engage in generalizations, don't forget that today women's dissatisfaction with men is, in general, greater than men's dissatisfaction with women. Women frequently concur with each other that men are jerks, but a similar commonly-agreed-upon epithet doesn't exist for women. (Women are demanding?) As a result, it is often the woman in a relationship who is dissatisfied and threatening to leave, and the man who comes to my workshop struggling to keep the marriage together. Men have participated in my workshops and lectures and have called in to my radio talk shows with as great or greater frequency than women.

Everything in this book works just as well for men as for women. I have taken pains to avoid the assumption that women will be my primary readers, and I refuse to perpetuate the increasingly obsolete idea that only women read relationship books. If we are ever to resolve our gender issues, we need to stay up-to-date with change as it occurs. I welcome both men and women readers as I know that, in some relationships, men are willing to "do the work."

Nevertheless, it is true that most often, women take care of the relationship. And they feel resentful when they get begrudging cooperation or none at all. One women I spoke with was feeling quite upset until she had a significant insight:

> ELIZABETH: I was complaining to my friend one more time about how I have to keep reminding Rich to listen to me when I'm talking to him, and to give me some kind of a response. Then my friend said to me, "Well, you never fix the leaky faucets either." A light bulb went off in my head! Maybe a little division of labor is okay.
>
> I did a turnaround on this whole thing. I still remind Rich to listen, but now I don't resent it or judge him; I just see it as me doing my job. Now that I view it this way, I feel fine about doing even more relationship-tending. I don't put off discussions about what I feel, the way I used to. It's like, if this is my job, I better do it well. After all, I'm good at this. Why should I mind it? Why should I be upset if Rich contributes a different set of skills to our marriage?

In my own marriage, I taught Mayer early on that he has the option of not getting defensive when I want to suggest a change. It took him a while to get the concept, but I patiently repeated it every time I needed to. Now all it takes is a quick reminder. I may even preface a sentence by saying, "Now I don't mean for you to get defensive, I just want to talk about something." I have heard Mayer tell others appreciatively that he knows he has learned a lot about communication by being with me.

Women may hold in mind an ideal partnership between men and women in which both are equally adept with relationship and communication skills and both are interested in systematically pursuing a more and more pleasurable relationship. There is nothing wrong with this ideal, but most couples are not there yet. It is a mere twenty-five years ago that the contemporary women's movement began to suggest to men that they throw over five thousand years of patriarchal conditioning (or, some would argue, several million years of biological adaptation), and become the warm, feeling, romantic, sweet men we now crave. We are still deep in the middle of this revolution. Being willing to take on the role of "emotional mentors" to the men in our lives may be appropriate for this mid-revolutionary stage. If our goal is a full partnership between the sexes with regard to relationship skills, deliberately, patiently, and cheerfully mentoring men may be an important step along the way.

Of course, mentoring men on relationship skills must be handled with extreme care; it can so easily spill over to nagging and preaching. Because women have a vested interest in the outcome, they may make poor teachers. A successful mentor/mentee relationship requires above all, mutual desire for change. Neither the man nor the woman should agree to mentoring because *she* wants *him* to change.

Although in my last book, *Eight Essential Traits of Couples Who Thrive,* I outlined specific guidelines for "emotional mentoring," most emotional mentoring is quite informal. The only explicit step you need to take is an initial agreement to a division of labor. One of her responsibilities would be to watch over the quality of communication and intimacy between you.

But you may be someone for whom this division of labor is precisely not okay. Maybe your very problem is that you resent doing all the relationship work, and that you feel you are not getting any cooperation. In that case, make this one of the problems you are looking to solve, and save it for Chapter Five, where you will discover direct problem-solving techniques.

Let me make one more comment about why the burden of relationship work falls upon women: The people who are hurting, and who realize that they are hurting, are always the ones who initiate change. The contemporary women's movement began around 1970 because women were dissatisfied. The changes we wanted then—and continue to want now—present an enormous amount of hard work. It wasn't fair for women to do all this work; but it is in the very nature of the way change works—it was women who experienced pain and wanted change.

If you are the one who now wants change in your relationship, try to regard the initiatives you take as important pioneering work. Women (and men) all over the world are working for more equal personal partnerships along with you. "Think globally, act locally." Know that with every change you are able to make in your own home, you are aiding the greater cause of moving to a true partnership society. Honor the very different contributions your spouse makes to your marriage, and try to feel generous about the ones you are making.

It may not be fair that women are more relationship-oriented than men, but at this stage of the revolution, that's usually the case. Instead of railing against the situation, take advantage of it. Go ahead and berate the patriarchy and the oppression of your gender in general. But in your own relationship, use your special female skills to work for the changes you want.

Q: ISN'T DOING THE WORK ALL ALONE BEING "CODEPENDENT," SOMETHING WE SHOULD WORK HARD TO AVOID?

A: At first glance, working on your relationship alone may seem to be codependent, but in fact it is quite the opposite. Working alone using the program in this book will help you to prevent the dreaded "codependency."

You are codependent when you try to *change your partner,* when you are tied to his or her behavior, when your own behaviors and feelings are determined by what your partner does and says. You are codependent when you are emotionally linked to someone whose behavior is dysfunctional, when you allow your partner's destructive behavior to determine how *you* will behave and feel, and when your partner is dependent upon you to maintain his or her destructive pattern. You are codependent when you are trying to do for your partner something that your partner must do alone; when you are trying to "help" your partner make a change that *you* want your partner to make but that your partner is not ready to make. Usually, in focusing on what you wish your partner would do, you also bury your own feelings in the process.

The program of working alone on your marriage that I will introduce in this book is precisely the opposite of codependency. It encourages you to do what you need to do for yourself and to stop trying to change or help your partner.

Q: WHAT WILL IT BE LIKE TO WORK ALONE? I CAN'T IMAGINE GETTING WHAT I WANT IN MY MARRIAGE WITH MY PARTNER COMPLETELY UNINVOLVED.

A: This book will invite you to take the initiative in your relationship by yourself. However, "working alone" is not a completely accurate description of what you will be doing for three reasons:

1. Whatever the struggle you are going through, or the enrichment you seek in your marriage, other couples have been there too. Periods of stress, adjustment, disappointment, even disillusionment are normal in long-term relationships. They are not a sign there is anything wrong with you as a couple. As one woman said to me, "My life with Michael right now is not bad; it is just not what I wanted or expected." Even if you feel you are on the verge of divorce, many other couples have been there too and have come back to rediscover their love for each other. Whatever your struggles, you are normal, and not alone.

2. Even though you are taking the initiative and not asking your spouse to agree to anything specific, when you begin to use this program, your spouse will not actually be uninvolved. In human behavior, just as in physical laws, for every action there is an equal and opposite reaction. When you try something new, your spouse will respond—or fail to respond, which is also a response—in some way. Based on your results, you will decide what to do next. The point of all this is to bring the two of you closer together—so that in the end, you will not be alone at all.

3. As we said in the Introduction, you are encouraged to enlist the support of a friend as you implement the ideas in this book. Ideally, you will have a support person and won't be working alone. However, we will continue to use the phrase "working alone" throughout the book to mean "taking the initiative in your relationship without consulting your partner."

Q: HOW LONG WILL IT TAKE TO GET RESULTS IF I WORK ALONE?

A: This is a good question, because the expectations with which you begin a program have a lot to do with how you end up feeling about the outcome. If you expect $5 and you get $50, you'll be delighted; but if you expect $500 and you get $50, you'll be crushed. It's the same $50; all that changed was your expectation.

The secret to success with any endeavor is to keep your hopes high and your expectations realistic.

It is possible to get very fast results from this program. The changes that take place inside you, especially, can happen almost instantly—if an idea connects with you, and you experience an internal *aha!*—or you make a shift and your partner responds in a completely unexpected way. You almost certainly will have breakthroughs like these as you do the suggested experiments.

However, most of the time change proceeds more slowly. You may become discouraged if you don't see major transformations right away. Just remember, it is perfectly normal to become discouraged when you try something and it doesn't work the first time. Let yourself feel disappointed; *just don't let your disappointment stop you from going on.*

For many couples, when they think of themselves they think of their problems. Try not to become identified with the periods of distance or tension in your relationship. Keep in mind that everything in nature, including your relationship, has seasons. It is not as though the stormy times in your relationship are the "real" you, and the sunny, happy times are not the real you. The seasons are all real; they are all part of who you are as a couple. Try not to add to your troubled times by worrying that there is something fundamentally wrong with your relationship. Chances are, you will get through this season and on to the next one.

Keep in mind two common patterns of learning and change. The first is like learning to play the piano. Progress is slow and steady, and each day's work builds on the work of the day before. Patience and tenacity are required, and big changes are hard to notice until you compare yourself with where you were six months or a year ago. Some of your learning will be like this. It is work. It requires discipline and perseverance. Be kind to yourself as you move slowly ahead. Congratulate yourself for small victories.

But you will also experience the second kind of change, like learning to ride a bicycle. You try and fall off, try and fall off, possibly many times. Then suddenly once, you get the feel—and forever thereafter, you can ride a bike! You have to endure many attempts during which no apparent progress is being made. Yet the final achievement would not be possible without all the previous apparent failures. And if you give up too soon, you will never know how wonderful it feels to succeed!

Much personal and spiritual growth is like this second model. I'm reminded of my own attempts to change my eating habits. Plagued for many years with much too high a cholesterol count, I tried many times to curb the fats in my diet. For weeks, I would be successful. But one day I would find myself eating the curly fries they served with my sandwich, or indulging in chocolate cake with butter cream frosting; and I would give up and just figure healthful eating was too impossible to achieve. But I would continue to read about the harmful effects of fat. Various well-meaning friends would clip articles for me. And it would all chip away at me. I'd try again, succeed for a little while, and then never being quite sure how it happened, find myself indulging again. For years this went on.

Then one time I went in for a checkup and my count was very high again. Something shifted inside me. I was determined to get that count down, and I became obsessive about avoiding fats. After twelve weeks of nearly perfect eating, I got tested again and had lowered my count by 58 points. I was hooked. So now, faced with a cheesy pizza or a sizzling order of onion rings or a big dish of ice cream, I just can't bring myself to eat it. And I've developed many tasty alternatives.

This change built slowly and took a long time. I had many periods of apparent regression. But I kept moving in the right direction. I was patient and not too hard on myself every time I failed. I'm certain I could never have arrived at my current eating habits without all those preliminary attempts and setbacks.

Most of life is lived in the attempt to achieve goals, not in some fairyland where the goals are already achieved. That's what makes life exciting, interesting, and full of challenge.

The overarching principles in this book will give you new ideas about how to proceed in your marriage. So in one sense, change will be immediate, because you will never again be without the fundamental idea of working alone and the model of marriage that it offers. But beyond that, let yourself change and grow at a pace that is comfortable for you, and don't let periods of discouragement deter you. Keep going. The only way you can fail is to give up.

And for how long are you supposed to go on working on your marriage by yourself?

As we go along, you will be encouraged to establish time frames and to evaluate your results. If you are getting the results you want, you will continue. If you are not, we will explore other alternatives. Don't ever feel that you are supposed to go on forever working on your marriage by yourself if you are not getting positive results. Evaluation and re-grouping are built into this program.

Q: EXACTLY HOW DO I WORK ON MY RELATIONSHIP ALL BY MYSELF?

A: Of course, we are going to become extremely specific about what you can do, but let me here present a general picture and establish a framework for the chapters to come.

I remember an incident when I was about nine years old. There was only one cookie left and my mother said to me, "Susan, you be a big girl and let your little brother have the last one." I recall feeling quite proud of myself and actually enjoying watching my little brother relish his cookie. Of course my mother was lavish with her praise for me.

Another time—I must have been three or four—we all came home from the fair with helium balloons. I thought it was fabulous the way they would go up and sit on the ceiling. Of course when we went outside, I assumed they would go up just that far and stop. When I let go—and then realized I had lost my balloon forever—I was devastated. (Wouldn't it be nice if as adults we could cry our hearts out like that when we feel heartbroken!) But my big brother, overcome with compassion for my plight, actually gave me his balloon! What a relief! What a joy for me!

He was the "big" person in this little drama.

This is the spirit I am suggesting you adopt when you undertake to work on your marriage alone. You need to be the "big" person in the relationship for the time being.

Being the "big" person in your relationship does not mean that you have to be a saint or engage in superhuman behavior. It doesn't mean you have to make all the sacrifices or that you are supposed to manipulate your partner or that you can't get angry.

What it does mean is that for the time being, as an experiment, you let go—just a little bit—of your ego. You don't worry about getting acknowledged for what you do. You give up being right, or making sure your spouse knows you are right. You become more interested in good results for the other person than in being acknowledged for what you did.

Spiritual masters are people for whom being the "big" person is a way of life. They have learned how to support and teach other people, with no concern about getting credit for teaching well. They know how to manage conflict without violence. Though you probably won't become a spiritual master by working on your relationship by yourself or by becoming the "big" person, you will be moving in that direction. The following story of a spiritual master illustrates the principle of solving a problem unobtrusively and without taking credit for it.

I once accompanied my friend Aaron to the community center in a tough, inner-city neighborhood in St. Louis where he was teaching aikido to a group of teenagers. As we approached the building, one of the young women in his class ran up and told us that a member of a rival gang wanted to join the class and that several of the boys had brought knives to class in an attempt to keep this new boy out. Aaron thanked her and then went ahead with his opening rituals. The rival gang member was indeed there: a big, very tough-looking guy named Ted. Not ten minutes into the class, one of the other big guys in the class, Jessie, pulled a knife on Ted and told him to get out. Ted pulled out his own knife.

Aaron didn't flinch. Slowly and quietly, he walked over to Jessie. The dialogue went something like this:

JESSIE: Don't mess with me.
AARON: You want Ted to leave.
JESSIE: He's going to leave.
AARON: You really want him gone.
TED: I ain't goin'.

Then Aaron made a sudden move in which he appeared to reach for Jessie's knife but instead tripped and fell, knocking Ted, the "intruder," off balance. Before anyone could see exactly what had happened, he had grabbed Ted's knife, and he was back on his feet.

AARON: Oh man, how clumsy of me. Sorry, Ted. Look, Jessie, what if we let Ted stay, and I promise I'll let the two of you fight using aikido. If he loses, then we will ask him to leave.

Jessie was feeling quite full of himself since he had just watched his teacher fall and make a fool of himself and his opponent be knocked around and stripped of his weapon. Ted was embarrassed. And since Aaron moved in so swiftly with his compromise, no one was ready to protest.

Since Aaron was a black belt in aikido, I later asked him whether he had considered using aikido moves on Jessie. "No way," he told me. "Martial arts is all about preventing violence, not escalating it. I just wanted to calm the situation."

I have a friend who is a literary agent who, twice in one week, connected authors she did not represent with editors who ended up making offers on these writers' books. My friend usually gets paid well to make connections like these; but in both these cases, the authors were represented by a different agent. When I called her to tell her how generous and selfless I thought her to be, she told me, "I once read a bumper sticker that changed my life. It said, 'You can get a lot more done in life if you don't worry about who gets the credit.' "

That's being the "big" person, not letting your ego get in the way of good results for everyone involved.

By deciding to take some initiative in your relationship, you are assuming a certain amount of power. Not power over your spouse, but inner strength that doesn't depend on recognition from others. Note that Jessie, the "troublemaker" in the story above, *appeared* to have the power, because he retained his weapon. The only power Aaron had was confidence, inner stability, inner strength. That's the type of power you need to bring harmony into your relationship.

The way Aaron used his confidence and stability was to reframe the situation: Jessie had set up a win/lose situation, a fight. Aaron's brilliance was that he did not get into Jessie's game at all; instead, he set up a different game with a different goal. Jessie's game was, "Who's going to win? Who's going to lose?" Aaron's game was, "How can I get on with my class and still save everybody's self-respect?"

In the same way, parents of small children are advised, don't "butt heads" with your child by demanding compliance when the child is fixed on one option ("I want this toy!" "I won't go now!"). Instead, introduce a new toy, move to a new spot, or in some other way, change the environment. Create a situation in which no one has to lose.

Being the big person means that you avoid getting caught up in the most immediate action and take one step back so that you can see the whole game you are a part of. Then you have the choice: simply not playing the game or maybe even inventing an entirely different game. It is the simple switch from, "We can *too* afford this. You have no right to decide we can't buy it," to "Look, here we are arguing about money again. Let's go get some ice cream and discuss this when we are in a better mood."

In the first, you are caught up in the immediate action, looking at the scene from very close up because you are right in the middle of it.

In the second, you have let go of your ego position and backed up one step. You are able to see the two of you arguing, to identify the "game" or the "drama," and to see that there are other possible scenarios.

If you try the experiments suggested in this book, you will be developing your "observer" self. This is the part of you that is able not only to engage in life, but to watch yourself engage in life. From the position of observer, you have a great deal more inner strength and power, you have more choices available to you, and you have more control than if you let yourself simply be caught up in the immediate action and act on your first impulse.

This program will show you very specifically how to be the "big" person in your relationship, how—by tapping into your own strength—you will be able to reframe the power struggles in your marriage and to put your conflicts into a larger context that will diminish their importance in your relationship.

So, in exploring the question, "How do I work alone to change my marriage?" the first part of the answer is you enter into it in a spirit of generosity, with the understanding that, by being willing to be the "big" person for a while, you will gain inner power and, at the same time, expand your own capacity for compassion.

Relationship Leadership

Another way to look at your role of working alone to improve your relationship is to view it as a leadership opportunity. You probably sometimes fantasize that if you could take over the leadership of your company or department—or your church, or the national government—you could do a better job than the current leadership. Well, here is your chance to be the relationship leader of your marriage!

Ah! But how do exemplary leaders lead?

They are not dictators. They do not come around to the rank and file with criticisms and advice all day long. They do not disregard the personal needs of the individuals they serve and then expect them to fill certain roles perfectly regardless of their individual propensities.

The best leaders lead by being *an example* of the company's values. They establish a context in which people can do quality work. They help people to feel good about themselves and their work and to stretch and grow. Good leaders respect employees and customers. They are Olympic-quality listeners. They involve everyone in problem solving and decision making. They often play the role of being the "big" person.

You have the opportunity to be an exemplary Relationship Leader in your own family. Be an example of the values and behaviors you want your family to adopt.

For example, when Dave told me how his wife taught him about commitment, I said to myself, "This was an excellent example of good Relationship Leadership on her part." This was his story:

> Whenever I came to an impasse, I would just leave, walk out. But I noticed that when my wife was furious with me, she would stay in the room and we would talk, and we would actually get somewhere. I started to try it myself. I never understood what commitment meant, but now it has taken on this concrete meaning for me: I'm committed to stay in the room and work things through. It's because I saw she was committed to me.

The following chapters present specific strategies for you to become a creative Relationship Leader, to establish a context in which family members can flourish, to listen and show respect, and to establish a cooperative atmosphere. My point here is to offer you Relationship Leadership as a metaphor. If you currently resent having to oversee the relationship, let me invite you instead to embrace your role as an opportunity. I hereby appoint you VP in charge of Relationship Quality!

This book is your job description. Be great at it!

Part Two Putting Yourself in Charge

CHAPTER TWO Give Away the Booby Prize and Go for the Gold

The booby prize of life is being right.

The first night of my groups, we award a lot of booby prizes.

BARBARA: Phil absolutely will not help around the house. I've tried everything. He'll grudgingly do something I ask—once. I've made lists for him. I've tried using reason. One time, he said he'd play Monopoly with the kids, and then as soon as I came downstairs, he said, "You take over now," and he went back to his computer. He just doesn't get it!

SAM: Jenny is doing too much, and she won't say no to anything. The kids and I never see her anymore. She has a million reasons why everything she is doing is super-important. But what she can't see is that she is totally missing being part of our family. I feel like I'm her last priority. I get her to promise to do something, and she'll even cancel out on that! I don't have that much time for the kids either, and I'm really worried.

Barbara and Sam were right: their spouses were being uncooperative and inconsiderate, and their complaints were completely legitimate.

Pause for a moment and figure out what *you* are right about in your relationship. What are your complaints about your spouse? What would you say if you were in a group to improve your marriage by yourself, and you were asked to describe the problem?

Probably, few would argue with you that you have a difficult problem, and that you have a perfect right to be upset, to feel angry, possibly even betrayed, and to be completely exasperated. Whatever your problem with your spouse is, I and probably many of your friends feel a great deal of concern and anguish right along with you. How I wish things were different for you! Why can't that blankety-blank spouse be more reasonable?

Before you give away this booby prize, it would be good for you to have the full experience of having it for your very own. So let me suggest that you do this experiment:

EXPERIMENT #3

Find Your Booby Prize

In your journal, briefly list the main problem or problems you have with your marriage. (You may want to use the list you made in Experiment #2.)

Next to each item on your list, put the initial of the person whose fault this problem is: yours, your partner's, or both.

For the purpose of this "lesson," let's focus only on the problems that are your partner's fault.

You are right. Your partner is being difficult, and you at least have the satisfaction of knowing that you are on the right side, that you are the fair one, the reasonable one of the two of you.

Let yourself experience how it feels in your body to be right about this obstacle in your relationship. There is a certain comfort in it. Of course it makes you angry too; but at least you don't have to feel guilty or in any way bad about yourself. And when you talk to your friends about this problem, you no doubt get a great deal of agreement with your position, and that makes you feel loved and supported.

Do you think you could let go of being right? Let's explore.

The problem with being right about the way you analyze your problem is that *that's all you get.* That's it. You get to be right. You don't get to solve the problem. You don't get to be closer to your spouse. You don't get to reduce the conflict in your relationship. You don't get to stop feeling angry. You don't get the changes you long for.

Being right is a dead end. Life just stops there. Nothing else happens. People all around you are actively striving for the gold medal in their relationships, while you sit clinging as if for life to the booby prize in yours, possibly for years.

There are other problems with the booby prize too. For example, being right doesn't leave room for the possibility that you *might* have the whole thing figured out wrong! I mean, this isn't likely. The facts are the facts. But look what happened to Sally in the following story when she let go of being right.

Sally and Ken were generally happy together and had much in common. But they had one big problem: money. First of all, they didn't have as much of it as they really needed, and Ken was in tight control of their finances. Even though Sally earned part of their income, Ken did all the banking and paid all the bills. Sally received a set amount each month for household expenses, and their agreement was that regarding any unusual purchases, they would make a decision together. The way it worked out in practice, however, was that whenever Ken wanted to buy a new tool or go out for dinner, Sally would say sure, go ahead, no problem. But if Sally wanted to buy a new coat or go to a workshop, Ken would give her a very hard time, try to convince her she could do without it, and insist that they could not afford it. As a result, Sally ended up feeling as if she had to "get Daddy's permission" for anything she wanted to do. "I'm a grown-up," she told me. "I managed everything just fine before I met Ken. I shouldn't have to go through this every time I want to spend some of my money."

Sally kept trying to get Ken to see the unfairness of the situation. She asked to take over the bill paying and banking; but Ken would have no part of that. When Sally talked to her mother about this, which she did often, her mother agreed that Ken was simply unreasonable and selfish about money and that he was insensitive for refusing to look at the power dynamics involved.

Then one day, Sally was discussing the situation with a new friend who said to her, "Maybe he isn't just plain selfish and unreasonable. Maybe he's scared."

The comment had a big impact on Sally. She thought more about it. She realized that she was trying to get Ken to agree that he is selfish and unreasonable. Why would he do that? Of course he was scared. His whole family was extremely anxious about money; how could he have grown up without fear about money? He could rationalize getting a new tool because he was in control of what tool he would buy and how much he would pay for it. What scared him about Sally's buying a new coat was that he had no control over which coat or how much she would spend. Maybe his argument that she didn't *need* a new coat was just his way of rationalizing?—when the truth was, he was really just anxious.

Another argument he always presented was that she should see the contribution he was making to the marriage by successfully keeping them out of debt. So Sally started to see the exact same situation with a new pair of glasses. Instead of seeing Ken as "unfair," she started seeing him as "scared."

That very week, Sally wanted money to attend an expensive fundraising event with a friend, for a cause she and Ken both supported. Usually she would approach this by trying to convince Ken that it was fair for her to have her own way. But with her new insight, she used a completely different strategy.

"Ken, honey, I know I don't tell you very often, but I do appreciate all the time and energy you put into managing our finances. You really are doing a great job. Since that first scary episode a few years ago, we have never had to borrow money or go into debt. That's pretty impressive.

"I don't want you to feel anxious about it, but I would very much like to go to the fundraising dinner with Naomi. It seems like we have a bit of a cushion right now. Do you agree? Or would you feel too uncomfortable if I went? If it would make you feel too uneasy, I'll consider not going."

Ken told me later that he was truly touched—because he felt that Sally had heard him, at last. He felt that Sally was sympathetic with his efforts and with his feelings, and he loved it. He felt supported. He never wanted Sally to feel deprived or powerless; what he wanted was for Sally to support *him!* When he felt she understood and was on his side, he didn't feel he needed to be so cautious—because now he wasn't the only one being careful. Responding from a whole different set of feelings, he felt fine about having Sally go to the event.

In her endless efforts to get Ken to hear her and to agree that the situation was unfair, Sally had been failing to listen to Ken! She may still be *right* that it was unfair for her to have to ask permission to spend money, but being right will get her nowhere! Simply by looking at it from a different angle, she expanded her view to one that was far more productive than her "right" analysis.

So one problem with insisting that you are right is that, often, there are several "right" ways to look at a situation, and your right way is only *one* of them. Being right may be keeping you from expanding your vision.

But there is an even worse problem associated with being right: It makes you helpless.

Usually, your "right" view of the situation is that the problem is your spouse's fault. See how many of the problems on your list start out, "My partner won't . . ." or "My partner is too . . ." or "My partner isn't . . ."

If the only solution to the problem is that your spouse needs to make a change, this puts you in a terribly weak position. Because if you can't induce your spouse to change, there is nothing left for you to do. Another dead end.

Besides, as you work on getting your spouse to be different, you are always giving the indirect message, "You are not okay." This will drive him or her away from you even more, when what you truly want is closeness!

Here is the bad news: Your partner won't change. *Give up on that.*

But here is the good news: There's plenty you can do to help yourself anyway.

It is extremely unlikely that your partner will change. Ken is not likely to become free and loose with money. Phil is not likely to devote eight hours a week to helping around the house. Barbara is not likely to give up all her involvements and stay home every night.

But with regard to finding a solution to your problem, *it doesn't matter.* Maybe you are right that your spouse is causing the problem. It makes no difference whose fault it is; *you* can still solve the problem.

How? By figuring out what role you play—and making a slight shift in it.

That is the gold.

You have no control over your partner. You have already discovered that. But you have enormous control over yourself, your response to your partner, and the initiatives you take with regard to your partner. Look at how Sally transformed her "problem" by a change she made all by herself. She found out what her own role in the problem was, and she changed it.

You find the gold in your relationship by figuring out what role you play in the ongoing dynamics, for it is in rewriting your own script that you will discover powerful inner strength and the ability to transform your marriage. As my friend who is a marriage counselor has told me many times, "When one person changes in a relationship, miracles can happen."

So how can you figure out what your role is so that you can begin to make these miracles happen?

I'll show you.

The following formula is easy, but it requires courage. Parts of it may make you squirm a bit. You'll get angry at some of what I suggest. (Workshop participants always do.) You'll resist looking at your situation in a new way, because you have put a lot of investment into "being right" about one particular view. If any of your friends share your view, you might find it embarrassing or even humiliating to change your story with them.

Remember two things:

- You don't have to share any of your new ideas or your change of viewpoint directly with your spouse. You certainly can if you want to, but you don't have to. Your changed behavior will almost certainly be received by your spouse as a pleasant surprise, and he or she doesn't need to know what is behind it.
- It is difficult and unpleasant to feel humiliated, embarrassed, or vulnerable, but it is part of maturity to realize you might have been walking up the wrong road and to be willing to try a new road. You are actually a stronger person when you can let yourself experience your vulnerable feelings than if you quickly push them aside or hide them.

  Pause for a minute and think of a time when you made a mistake, or apologized to your spouse for something. You probably feel a flush of heat in your face. Maybe a slight ache in your chest, or a slight nausea or churning in your stomach. It's not a great feeling, but it won't kill you. And if you can stand it for a little while, it will pass, and then you might get to feel the wonderfully pleasant, loving feelings you have been longing for. Those are the feelings that come with honesty, openness, and vulnerability.

FINDING THE GOLD IN YOUR RELATIONSHIP: YOUR HALF OF THE SCRIPT

You are already pretty clear what your partner's role is and have probably given it a lot of attention. Now we want to find out what yours is.

Got your magnifying glass out? Let's go.

EXPERIMENT #4

Find the Gold in Your Relationship

To discover your role in your relationship, follow along with me through a few easy steps. You will discover the answer "automatically," the way you end up with a picture when you connect the dots. Don't get too focused on any one of the steps; just stay with me and keep going. At the end of the trail is a gold medal.

Each of the following questions contains several suggested exercises. You may read through them and do the exercises mentally as you read. Or, for best results, get out your journal or some paper, and write down the suggested sentences.

1. If my partner were talking about me to a friend, what would s/he say about me? Can I see any validity in this point of view?

You probably know what your spouse's complaints about you are, and your usual response is most likely to defend yourself, to haul out your "right" analysis of the situation, and to explain that you have a right to behave as you do, or that you wouldn't have to behave that way if your spouse would only change.

> "I would be able to stop nagging you about taking care of the kids if you would start to *do* it!"
>
> "I do *not* talk too much and interrupt. I can't sit and be quiet just because you would like to talk more. You need to speak up. I always stop and listen when you talk."
>
> "I am *not* unreasonable about wanting sex more often. You say no to sex a lot more than you realize."

Pause now and write down (or say to yourself) what you think your partner would say about you if he or she were talking to a friend about the problems in your relationship. What are your partner's complaints about you?

What is your usual response to this complaint? Write that down too.

Now, review what you have written. Can you see any validity at all to your spouse's complaint(s) about you? Think about it.

If you can see your partner's point of view even slightly, try saying to yourself, just as an experiment, "(Partner's name), I know you are not entirely wrong. I do see that I . . . (insert what your partner's complaint about you is)."

How does that feel?

You probably wanted to add, "BUT . . ." and repeat your habitual "right" explanation.

Try saying the sentence over a few times without the "but . . ."

> "(Partner's name), I know you are not entirely wrong. I do see that I (insert what your partner's complaint about you is)."

Do you feel just a hint of humiliation? Like your partner might have a teeny tiny point? Good! Congratulations!

If you can see any truth at all in your partner's point of view—even a glimmer—you are on the path toward reclaiming yourself in this relationship and bringing the two of you together.

2. Is there any way in which I might be actually causing my partner to behave as he or she does?

In your "right" analysis, you probably believe that your spouse's behavior is causing all the problems. If he would start helping with the housework, the problem would be solved. If she would leave you alone and give you some peace, the problem would be solved. If he would talk to you and pay more attention to you, the problem would be solved.

In your journal, complete the following sentence, once or in several different ways:

> If (Partner's name) would only . . . the problem would be solved.

Now, what if you assumed, just as an exercise, that it is actually the other way around, that something you are doing might be inadvertently causing your partner's behavior?

Remember the little woven-straw finger puzzles you got at the school carnival? The more you tried to pull your fingers out, the tighter the trap closed. Your attempted solution actually made the problem worse. Could your attempted solution be making your relationship problem worse?

Paul was a "jealous type." Whenever he saw his wife, Helen, talking intently with another man at a party, or heard that she was working with another man on a project at work, he would get angry with her and then become all hurt and withdrawn and distant. These attempts to keep Helen for himself made Paul seem like a very unappealing person and simply drove Helen further from him. His attempt at solving his problem made it worse.

Similarly, when Mary tries to cheer John up, John becomes all the grouchier. When he's in a bad mood, he can't stand her sunny disposition. In our example above, when Sally tried to persuade Ken that she should be able to spend money on her own, Ken became all the more anxious.

The huge breakthrough that set "marriage and family therapy" apart from traditional psychotherapy, several decades ago, was the realization that problems within a couple or family are caused more by the *interaction among the participants* than by the pathology of any one of the family members. Family members affect each other. For example, in traditional therapy, if a parent came in for help with a troubled teenager, the focus would have been on the teenager. What about her personality or her personal neurosis is causing her to behave badly? How can we punish her for her bad behavior or induce her to behave in a positive way? How can we motivate her to be a better person? Somehow, she needs to change.

Family therapy took an entirely different approach. Family therapists asked, Could the teenager be troubled because of the way the entire family interacts? Maybe the trouble is not the teenager, but instead, the family system itself, the unspoken rules that affect everyone? Maybe the *whole family* needs to change?

Family therapists developed the term "identified patient" or IP to designate the person the family felt was causing the problems, but who, the therapists knew, might actually be the victim of a system that wasn't working well. The IP was the scapegoat, the person the family found it easiest to blame. (The family's tacit assumption that the IP was a "problem" was an example of the way the "family system" was failing, for this assumption contributed to the low self-esteem and rebellious behavior of the IP and let the rest of the family off the hook.) It was never the case, family therapists discovered, that one person in the family was "bad" and the rest of the family was "good." Instead, family therapists came to see entire families as healthy or "dysfunctional." In dysfunctional families, it was always the *interaction among the members,* and not any one individual, that caused the problems.

Of course another thing family therapists quickly discovered is that it is very hard for family members to see their own contribution to the family problems. This is simply human nature. Family members always see the fault as someone else's, just as you have probably been doing within your own relationship.

These profound insights developed in the family therapy movement are the same ones you need in your own marriage.

I asked a friend of mine who is a family therapist, "What is the first approach you take when a person comes to you alone to work on his or her relationship?" Without hesitation, she replied, "I don't make the absent partner the problem."

In other words, no matter how awful you think your spouse's behavior is, if you went to a couples therapist for help, the therapist would not buy into your story that your partner is causing your problem. Regardless of the facts, that is the most helpful stance a therapist could take. She would assume that it is the *interaction* between the two of you that is troubled and in need of a cure, not either one of you alone.

So the most helpful thing you can do for your relationship is to take that same stance yourself. Make the attempt to stop blaming your spouse. Don't make your spouse into the IP. Don't blame yourself either, of course. Look instead at how the two of you interact. You definitely have *some* role in the interactions. We are not asking you to judge your role as good or bad, helpful or destructive. We are simply asking you to identify it.

As writer Mark Gerzon says in *A House Divided,* "If you want to help the whole, don't become allied with only one part of it!"

Mike wants Susie to have sex with him more often, so he asks her for more. But his requests for more sex seem to Susie like criticism and pressure. Is Mike's pressure *causing* Susie to be more distant? Or is Susie's distancing *causing* Mike to put on more pressure? Who started it? Is the "problem" that Susie is cool and distant—or that Mike is critical and angry? A case could be made for either position, but the truth is, it doesn't matter. The fact is, Mike and Susie are both participating in perpetuating "the problem," and both of them are focusing on the other person's role, not their own.

Also, if either one of them changed, the entire drama would change.

It can be very difficult to see your role in your own relationship, because you are right smack in the middle of it. It is a bit like trying to see the whole blackboard when you are one inch from it. Don't expect perfect results right away.

For now, just try completing this sentence in five or ten different ways. I reiterate, don't judge your role as good or bad, helpful or destructive. Simply identify it.

When my partner ________________, I ________________.

As in these examples:

When my partner spaces out and ignores me, I withdraw from him because I feel hurt.

When my partner comes home late, I yell at her.

When my partner doesn't do his household job, I do it myself.

When my partner yells at the kids, I go into a slow burn and don't talk to him all evening.

When my partner nags at me, I feel distant and sad, and I leave the house.

When my partner refuses to get a job, I show him our finances and beg and plead and then finally give up.

When you have written down several versions of this formula that describe your own relationship, you are ready for the next step: Reverse each sentence. Simply write it down again in the opposite way. Using the above statements, for example:

When I withdraw and feel hurt, my partner spaces out and ignores me.

When I yell at her, my partner comes home late.

When I do it myself, my partner doesn't do his household job.

When I go into a slow burn and don't talk to him all evening, my partner yells at the kids.

When I feel distant and sad and leave the house, my partner nags at me.

When I show him our finances and beg and plead and then finally give up, my partner refuses to get a job.

The point here is that both of you engage in certain behavior. No one causes it. No one is to blame. You both do what you do. If you are beginning to get the feel of this, that is enough for now.

Patsy was a participant in one of my groups. Her husband, Jeff, was an incurable entrepreneur. He had started several small businesses, all of which had drained rather than expanded their financial resources. The situation was getting desperate, but Jeff simply refused to get a job. Patsy was working and raising their three children, and her tolerance was wearing thin. When we came to this part of the exercise, Patsy got frustrated.

"I can see that my constant begging him to get a job might make him resistant and feel unsupported. But I feel trapped. He won't get a job if I keep begging, and he certainly won't get a job if I stop begging!"

Patsy was in a classic double bind: damned if she did and damned if she didn't. You may well feel that way too; a double bind like Patsy's is very common in relationships.

But you will feel the double bind *only if you are focused on changing your partner's behavior.* You were going to give up on that for now, remember? Apparently, no matter what Patsy does, Jeff is not going to get a job. So Patsy can choose to keep begging, or she can stop begging and choose any one of dozens of other alternatives. If she stops trying to have an impact on Jeff and focuses on taking control of her own life within her relationship instead, many new options open up to her.

In this case, Patsy's role in the relationship is to try to coerce Jeff into getting a job by whatever means she can think up.

Based on the sentences you wrote above and then reversed, see if you can complete this sentence in one or more ways:

My role in our relationship is to ______________________.

Remember, we are not trying to solve any problems yet; we will get to that later. We are only trying to identify your role in the ongoing drama because that is the secret to finding the gold in your relationship.

3. How do I feel about my partner and my relationship?

Let's say your spouse and your situation make you angry.

This may be somewhat hard to swallow, but the truth is, no one else can make you angry (or disappointed or frustrated or afraid). Only you can make yourself feel a certain emotion. True, a situation or a person can cause you to make yourself angry, but no matter what happens, you actually have a *choice* about how you feel.

Let's pause to examine this concept more fully.

When I was single, I spent several weeks each year at Tassajara, a remote mountain Zen Buddhist monastery, which the monks and students operate as a resort during the summer months. The natural hot springs there have made it a tourist destination since the 1870s, and some of the gorgeous old stone buildings date from that time. One summer, I drove the rickety gravel road fourteen miles in from civilization, parked, walked toward the main buildings, and then suddenly stopped in great shock. The main stone building was gone! A mere shell of it was still standing.

"What happened?" I asked a student.

"Oh, didn't you hear? There was a fire in the kitchen that burned out the entire library and meditation room."

"Oh, how terrible!" I moaned. "How did it happen?"

The student told me some of the details, how the residents had put up a valiant fight against the flames, that in the end a precious gold Buddha figure and hundreds of valuable manuscripts had been lost, and how the buildings were being adapted until a new meditation room could be built. I couldn't help but notice the chatty way in which she related all these sad events. I kept saying, "Oh, how awful," in an anguished tone of voice and with a wrinkled forehead. Finally, I asked her, "Weren't you all terribly upset? It was such a gorgeous old building!"

I'll never forget her reply: "Well, a fire is a fire." She wished me a pleasant stay, and walked off.

As I thought about the conversation over the next several days, the contrast between this detached, calm student and my own anguished, high-pitched voice made me feel a little silly. I realized I had just experienced at first hand one of Buddhism's central teachings: All suffering is the result of inappropriate attachment. I had been attached to this beautiful building and to the idea that it would be there forever. I felt its loss deeply. But Buddhists believe that an event itself is neither good nor bad, happy nor tragic. The judgment about the event is something that we as humans add to it. Goodness or badness is not intrinsic to an event. Besides, a value judgment that we place on an event at one time may or may not be "right" when viewed from another time or another angle.

There is a famous story about a farmer whose horse ran away.

"What bad luck," said his neighbor.

"Good luck, bad luck. Nobody knows for sure," said the farmer.

The next day, the horse returned with six other beautiful horses.

"What good luck," said his neighbor.

"Good luck, bad luck. Nobody knows for sure," said the farmer.

The next day, the farmer's son broke his leg when he fell off one of the new horses trying to break it in.

"What bad luck," said the neighbor.

"Good luck, bad luck. Nobody knows for sure," said the farmer.

The following day, army recruiters arrived, ordering all the young men to leave right away for military duty. But since the farmer's son was laid up with a broken leg, the soldiers passed him by.

"What good luck," said the neighbor.

"Good luck, bad luck. Nobody knows for sure," said the farmer.

I was choosing to feel upset about the burned building. The student made a different choice. She accepted that the building had burned and went about the task of rebuilding. She chose not to add the judgment "tragic" to the event.

Of course this student had been following a spiritual practice for several years and was consciously cultivating her ability to separate events themselves from her reaction to the events. Most of us couldn't do what she did on a moment's notice, nor would we necessarily want to. For our purposes in this discussion, the point is that *you have a choice about how you react* to a given situation. Your first view of it may or may not be "right." You can either exercise your choice and play around with your options, or you can react without thinking, with the response that comes to you first like a knee-jerk reaction.

Reacting out of habit and without thinking is like living your life on automatic pilot. Instead of getting into the captain's seat and making choices and steering your life, you ride in the passenger seat and let life steer you. When something happens, you are at the mercy of that event. You simply react without realizing that you have a choice about how you react. So:

Your husband comes home late without calling; you get furious.

Your wife interrupts and dominates the conversation all evening; you feel embarrassed.

Your husband forgets your birthday entirely; you feel crushed.

Your wife spends too much money; you feel anxious.

Let us now move on to the final step in which you will receive your gold medal.

4. What do I expect, desire, and hope for from my relationship?

Usually, you feel an emotion because certain hopes, expectations, or desires you have are not met.

Why did I react with anguish about the burned building? Because I fully expected and desired that nothing would ever change at Tassajara. I was fond of the building. I didn't want it to be gone.

Why are you reacting with anger (or disappointment or fear or . . .) to the circumstances in your marriage?

Is it because you brought hopes with you into this relationship, and those hopes have not been fulfilled?

Is it because you have expectations about what marriage should be like or about how a spouse should behave, and those expectations are not being met?

Is it because everything was very different in the family you grew up in, and you assumed things would be the same in this family?

In your journal, complete this sentence in as many ways as seem appropriate. Use the same issues you have been using in the above exercises, and you may want to add some new ones:

> In our relationship, I (use either *expect, want,* or *hope for,* whichever seems more appropriate for your sentence) ______.

Here are some examples from workshops:

> In our relationship, I want John to be as affectionate and attentive and thoughtful as he was when we were courting.
>
> In our relationship, I expect Sally to bring in her share of the income.
>
> In our relationship, I want Sam to spend more time at home and take more interest in running the household and taking care of the kids.
>
> In our relationship, I want Joan to take more interest in me and my business.
>
> In our relationship, I want to have more control over our money.
>
> In our relationship, I want us to agree much more on how to treat the children.
>
> In our relationship, I want us to stop fighting so much.

Now, go back to each sentence and add to the end of it, ". . . and I feel ______ about it." Or, if you feel like taking a little bit of a leap, say instead, ". . . and I choose to feel ______ about it." (If that phrase makes you feel uncomfortable or angry or you just don't agree with it, simply say, "I feel . . .")

As, for example:

> In our relationship, I want John to be as affectionate and attentive and thoughtful as he was when we were courting, and I (choose to) feel disappointed about it.
>
> In our relationship, I expect Sally to bring in her share of the income, and I (choose to) feel angry about it.

We are close to our goal now. To complete the process of identifying your half of the script in your relationship, all you have to do is add the words "My role in our relationship is to" to the beginning of each of your sentences. Also, in the second half of the sentence, change "I" to "to." The sentences will now read as follows:

> My role in our relationship is to want John to be as affectionate and attentive and thoughtful as he was when we were courting and to feel disappointed about it.
>
> My role in our relationship is to expect Sally to bring in her share of the income and to feel angry about it.
>
> My role in our relationship is to want Joan to take more interest in me and my business and to feel sad about it.
>
> My role in our relationship is to want to have more control over our money and to feel helpless about this.
>
> My role in our relationship is to want us to agree much more on how to treat the children and to feel frustrated about it.
>
> My role in our relationship is to want us to stop fighting so much and to feel hopeless about it.

One workshop participant realized that she expected her husband to behave tyrannically as he always did and she had stopped wanting or hoping for anything else. She wrote this:

My role in this relationship is to expect Bill to be dominant and to ignore my needs and to feel angry and helpless.

If you followed the steps I've suggested, you may well have some confused or conflicting feelings right now. If you do, congratulate yourself. It means you have taken the risk of looking at some new and possibly threatening ideas. Don't expect to resolve your confusion or your mixed feelings right now. Any time you let go of the old to make room for something entirely new, you are likely to feel some fear, anger, curiosity, regret, excitement; these feelings are appropriate, so if you can, just let them be there. If you like, write about your feelings in your journal. Simply write, "Right now, I feel . . ." and let the words flow out of your pen.

Avoid the temptation to solve any problems or to make any decisions right now. In Chapters Five and Six, we will become quite specific about how to use the information you have gathered here most effectively to solve your relationship problems.

Now, let's summarize what we have said so far.

- The primary principle involved in working by yourself to change your relationship is that all the changes you make will be made *within you.* Trying to get your partner to change is both frustrating and fruitless.

  Changes you make within yourself will have a huge impact on your partner and on your relationship. You have enormous control over how your relationship will unfold from this point forward.

- We have identified one specific change you will need to make: Stop blaming your partner, and stop trying to change your partner. Your partner is not causing the problems in your relationship. The problem is not your partner; the problem is the dance that you and your partner do together. You have a part in that dance.

  No matter how terrible and wrong you feel your partner's behavior is, continuing to complain and to pester the person to change will never result in positive change. By continuing to complain and criticize, you are perpetuating the problem.

So begin trying to stop.

For many couples, that in itself would be a huge change.

Remember what we said about being patient with yourself. You may find it difficult to stop. That's understandable. Experiment. Try it in small doses at first.

EXPERIMENT #5

Work on Discontinuing Your Criticisms

Here's how to stop criticizing your spouse, an important first step in bringing the two of you together.

Make a deal with yourself that, for one evening, you will not criticize or advise your spouse in any way. You will not ask your spouse to change, you will not "nag," not suggest a better way to do something, and you will not complain about anything your spouse has or has not done.

When you get through one evening successfully, challenge yourself to try this for one day, then for three days, and when you do that, try it for a full week.

Remember, There's Always a Learning Curve

As you try to stop blaming and criticizing your spouse, you will almost certainly backslide. Don't be hard on yourself. Just notice it, and see how you feel. Smile, and say to yourself, "There I go again. I just criticized. Well, good for me for noticing it! Let's see. How did I feel when I criticized? Hmmm. I felt (angry, tense, wrought up, self-righteous . . .").

When you are trying to change a well-entrenched habit, you will probably catch yourself in each of the following stages: First, you will notice you engaged in your old behavior *after* the fact, as in the above paragraph. Next, you will catch yourself as you are doing the old behavior *during* the fact. Finally one day, you will triumphantly notice that you were about to engage in the old behavior, and you will stop yourself—*before* the fact. (Child development author Dorothy Briggs identifies these stages with regard to toilet training, which is nothing more than trying to break an old habit.)

Also, remember that this is an experiment; its purpose is to gather data. Maybe what you will discover is that you aren't able to stop criticizing and pestering your partner to change. You may feel compelled to keep asking for what you want, or letting your spouse know how unhappy you are. You may feel very tied to your "right" analysis of the problem. As long as you are paying attention to what you are doing, whatever happens is fine; it is part of the experiment. It is all a way to gather more information about yourself in this relationship.

As you do this and other experiments, you will be developing your "observer-self."

Imagine that you have two selves, your active self, and your observing self. Your active self is the one who eats breakfast, takes the kids to school, goes to work, makes decisions, goes to the movies, runs out of money, cares about politics, thinks all manner of thoughts, argues, makes love, calls a friend, reacts to events.

While your active self is busy doing all these things, your observing self is standing some distance away *watching,* much as an audience watches a play. Your active self is quite involved with whatever is occurring at the moment. Your observing self sees the present activity as one scene in a much larger drama.

Let your observer-self talk to you. "Oh, that was very good." or "Uh, uh! Be careful. That was a criticism. Now that you criticized, how do you feel?" If you like, let your observer-self make journal notations about how your experiment is going and what you are learning.

Acceptance

To reiterate, your ultimate goal is to let go of being "right" about how thick-headed your spouse is about some area of your marriage, to find your role in perpetuating whatever is going on, and to stop trying to change your spouse.

Another way to state what we are after here is this: Accept your situation exactly the way it is.

To accept a situation does not mean that you have to like it. It simply means that you recognize that it is a given, and you stop fighting against it. You give up the illusion that by doing or saying the right thing, you can change this thing you don't like. Accepting something actually has a wonderful side to it, because it means you can relax . . . give up the struggle . . . let your mate—and yourself—be exactly how you really are.

Think of a quality you don't like in your spouse. What would it be like to understand that your spouse is *always* going to be that way?

When you think about it, you have only two choices: You can accept what is, or fight it. Fighting what is, and trying to change it, takes an enormous amount of energy. And accomplishes nothing. Quite the contrary, the more you resist something, the more it persists. Fighting something that doesn't respond to efforts to change it only makes you tired and unhappy. Accepting that your partner is the way he or she is, whether you like it or not, is simply much easier.

More important, acceptance is the starting point for change.

Greg, a participant in one of my workshops, wanted his wife Louise to enjoy cooking. He bought her cookbooks. She felt criticized and pressured. He invited friends over for dinner, hoping for a delicious, graciously-served meal. She burned the meat loaf, put too much dressing on the salad, and overcooked the squash. She was humiliated; he was embarrassed and angry; the guests felt in the middle of a family scene.

Louise hates to cook. Instead of accepting this, Greg fought it. He resisted the truth. He kept trying to change it. Everybody's energy got used up. And Louise hated cooking more than ever.

When Greg began to see his role in this drama, many options opened up to him.

In the above exercises, Greg had written,

> "When Louise cooks frozen food, I criticize her and try to persuade her to cook from recipes."
>
> "When I criticize her and try to persuade her to cook from recipes, Louise cooks frozen foods."
>
> "My role in this relationship is to want Louise to love to cook and to feel disappointed and angry about it."

Over the course of our workshop, Greg began to accept that Louise hates to cook. He felt disappointed, since a cook is something he wanted in a wife, and he began to accept his disappointment too. But look at what happened when he accepted the situation as it really was rather than continually fighting against it, wishing it were otherwise, and trying to change it.

Greg discovered that he could have a lovely meal catered at home very affordably, so he invited friends over, and managed the evening himself. He had to reassure Louise that he wasn't upset with her, that he was very happy to have found a solution. Everyone enjoyed the evening enormously.

Greg tried his hand at cooking and discovered that he enjoyed it on an occasional basis. He even found that Louise enjoyed helping him if he took all the initiative. In fact, she was delighted to help him, because she was so grateful to him for letting her off the hook.

Greg even found that he could tease Louise in a lighthearted way. Since she now felt that he accepted her, she could laugh too, and they began to get some fun out of what was originally an area of conflict and hurt.

Only when you accept everything about your relationship, your partner, and your feelings—exactly as they really are—can you begin to make the changes that will bring you the peace and happiness you long for in your marriage.

So stop fighting. Stop blaming. Graciously accept your situation even if you don't like it. Accept your feelings about it too.

Remember, this is only the first step. I'll suggest specific ways to move from here.

So we've seen that you are the one who needs to make changes and that the first change you need to make is to accept your situation as it is and stop blaming your spouse for it. We have also begun to get a handle on what your specific role in your relationship is.

Are you ready to let go of the booby prize of being right and to dig for the gold of seeing your own role in your relationship problems?

As you've seen, the reason your own role is gold is that you can do something about it. Though you have no control over your partner's opinions and behaviors, you have unlimited control over your own! Instead of saying to your spouse, "You change so we can be happy," you are now able to say, "I'm going to change so we can be happy." Do you feel the power in the second statement?

Don't worry if you still feel ambivalent and skeptical about all this. It won't affect the results you can get from this idea. Accept your ambivalence, confusion, and skepticism, and keep reading.

In the next chapter, I will describe one more tool that will help you reclaim yourself in your relationship: managing the anger and resentment that are inevitable when you are going through change. Then, in Chapters Four and Five, we will explore concrete problem-solving strategies, so you can put your new knowledge of your role in your relationship—and your re-discovered inner power—to work.

CHAPTER THREE

Learn ERAP (Emergency Resentment Abatement Procedure)

For many of my workshop participants, the whole process of trying to give up their "right" analysis of their relationship made them angry. They became angry at their partners, resentful of their situation, mad at themselves, furious with me, or just plain upset. The very idea of working alone on a relationship that involves two partners made some people resentful.

Did you feel angry yourself at times while reading the last two chapters?

Anger arises in every relationship at one time or another. Whether it is frequent or infrequent, anger is upsetting and unpleasant. For many couples, it is a pivotal, defining aspect of the relationship. So we need to learn constructive ways of managing anger early on.

Your own anger is one of the best places to begin working by yourself to create a change in your relationship, because it is something over which you, potentially, have control. You may not have control at the moment you are most furious; extreme anger is a kind of temporary insanity. But as we shall see, if you choose to take it, you have a great deal more control over your own anger than you have over anything that your spouse does.

Anger is like nuclear power: It can be used to destroy or to enhance your quality of life. It is a natural emotion and an appropriate, understandable response to many situations. Like any emotion you feel, it is neither good nor bad, right nor wrong. It simply is. You are not a bad person for feeling angry; it simply means you are human.

The Emergency Resentment Abatement Procedure, or ERAP, is a four-step process, a systematic approach for making the best use of your anger. The steps are appropriate whether you are angry at the tiniest incident—your partner forgot to give you a message—or a long-term, ongoing source of frustration in your relationship—your partner doesn't seem very interested in you. ERAP incorporates the latest psychological knowledge about anger and puts it in a useable form.

After we learn the four steps, we will look at several examples of ERAP at work.

Before we become acquainted with the process itself, there is one preliminary step: It will be useful for you to identify your anger style, so you'll know how to customize ERAP for your own personal use.

WHAT IS YOUR ANGER STYLE?

There are two general anger types: On one end of the scale are people who hide their anger. They have trouble either feeling anger or expressing it, or both. These people are more likely to feel hurt, sad, or depressed than to feel angry. They may fear anger because of the damage it did when they were children, or they may have been taught that anger is "unladylike" and socially unacceptable. If this is you, you are an "anger eclipser."

At the other end are people who express their anger in outbursts or violent rages. They may insult or degrade others or even harm them physically. If this is you, you are an "anger expresser."

Most of us lie somewhere in the middle of the scale, but see if you can determine at least which end of the scale you tend to favor. If you scream and rage when you are angry, your challenge is to learn to contain your anger. If you are one who rarely exhibits anger, your challenge is to learn to feel it and to express it.

Both anger "eclipsers" and anger "expressers" engage in a range of behaviors. For example, if you are an anger eclipser, you may simply give in most of the time. You may minimize your feelings ("It doesn't matter") or give up ("I'll never get what I want"). You may strive to please and accommodate at your own expense, just to avoid confrontation ("That's fine. Let's go to your movie. I'll enjoy it"). Or, you may have strong feelings, but what you feel is tears or depression rather than anger.

If you are an anger expresser, you may become hostile, sarcastic, or cruel. You may scream and throw things. Or perhaps you become "passive-aggressive," harboring your anger within and plotting sweet revenges, like burning the toast or showing up late or being unavailable for conversation or sex. Anger expressers often get stuck in being "right." They attack, are unable to hear another point of view, and see everyone else as wrong, even though other points of view may in fact be valid. (There's the booby prize again.)

To complicate matters, most of us have different anger behavior styles for use in different situations. You may fantasize revenge on your boss, yell and scream at your children, become hurt and feel bad about yourself with your mother, and be an accommodating pleaser with your spouse. Even so, you can probably sense what your dominant style is. As you will see, you can adapt ERAP to fit your different situations and responses. You will simply need to separate them and work with one source of anger at a time. In this chapter, I will assume that you are working on issues with your intimate partner, but ERAP is easily adaptable to other relationships.

Perhaps you immediately recognize your anger style. If you're not sure, or if you want to get a clearer idea about how you express your basic style in different situations, you may want to try this experiment.

EXPERIMENT #6

Identifying Your Anger Style

1. Think of several incidents or situations with your partner that "made (or make) you mad." They can be recent or some time ago. What did you feel? How did you behave?

In your journal or with your support person, describe the incident(s) and your response.

2. Draw a line across the page in your journal. At the left end, write "anger eclipser" and the number 10. At the right end write "anger expresser" and the number 10. In the middle, place a zero. Your scale will look like this:

ANGER ECLIPSER		ANGER EXPRESSER
10	0	10

Now find a spot on the line that describes your own anger response toward your partner. Give your spot a number. (Fractions are acceptable: 5.5 or 2.75.)

Now we are ready to learn ERAP. You may want to think of an incident that made you angry or an ongoing source of anger in your relationship, so you can actually apply the steps as we go along.

As you will see at the end, ERAP is a versatile tool. You'll work your way through the stages quickly and easily in some situations. At other times, the process may be more evolutionary and may take weeks or months.

The steps of ERAP allow you to pay attention first to your body, then to your spirit, then to your mind, and finally, to your relationship.

Express (Body)
Relax (Spirit)
Assess (Mind)
Perform (Relationship)

STEP ONE—EXPRESS: LET YOUR BODY CHARGE OR DISCHARGE

All emotions, including anger, occur in the body. A thought or opinion may trigger the anger, but the anger itself is a physical response. Think of a time when another car narrowly missed you. Your face got hot, your jaws tensed, your heart raced. You may have sweated, you may have felt like screaming—all these are the body's anger responses.

Our bodies have a natural rhythm of building up and then releasing tension. We build up the tension in our stomachs when we are hungry, and then release the tension by eating. Sexual excitement is a buildup of tension which then releases in the pleasure of orgasm. When "good stress" functions adaptively in our lives, it allows us to build up excitement about something, say giving a speech, and then to release the excitement by giving the speech. This natural rhythm is echoed in music, in which tension builds to a climax (dissonance) and then releases in soothing resolution.

People who have an inappropriate balance of tension and resolution in their lives may end up with physical or psychological problems. Some people almost never build tension. They take very few risks.

They may feel bored, listless, or even depressed. Nothing excites them. These people need to find ways to build healthy tension, excitement, and anticipation in their lives. They need to "charge up" their energy.

Other people are always tense and rarely let go. They may be chronically angry, workaholic, uptight, wired, or on edge all the time. These people need to learn to release tension, to relax, and to express their feelings. They need to "discharge" their energy.

Step One of ERAP—to let your body Express feeling—is different for anger eclipsers and anger expressers, though many of us need to charge up sometimes and discharge at others. You may find it useful to do a little of each.

For Anger Eclipsers—Charge Up Your Energy

Anger is an appropriate response in certain situations. If your spouse belittles you or ignores your needs, anger is appropriate. If your partner usually gets his or her way about family decisions, anger is appropriate. If your partner agrees to do something and then offers excuses instead of results, anger is appropriate. In these situations, if you cry or pout, if you withdraw into yourself, if you become depressed, if you proceed as usual and behave as though nothing is wrong, or if you defend your partner when others criticize and become angry, then your challenge may be to find ways to feel and express your anger.

As you do these experiments, remember that your only goal is to learn something about yourself, so there is no wrong outcome. There is no way to fail. Whatever happens will be useful information for you. If you find yourself feeling frustrated or angry, let yourself feel it. It may frighten you to feel that way, but remember, no one ever died from feeling angry. Try to stay with the feeling for a little while. Anger is normal and natural. If you don't end up feeling angry, just feel what you do feel. Maybe it is fear. Maybe it is frustration. Whatever you feel is okay.

Try one or more of these experiments and see what happens.

1. In your journal, write a letter to your partner that you will *not* show to him or her. Be sure to tear it up after you write it. Begin the letter thus:

"Dear (Partner's name), I am angry with you. I feel mad at you. I feel angry because . . ."

Write at least one full page. As you write, notice how you are feeling in various parts of your body. Do you feel an ache in your chest? Is there feeling behind your eyes? Are your hands cold? Is your jaw tense?

When you become aware of any feeling, stop writing and pay attention to the feeling. Close your eyes and simply feel it. Stay with the feeling as long as you can. If it goes away, start writing again.

When you begin to feel your habitual response, tears or depression or denial, don't let those feelings happen. Say to yourself or out loud if possible, "I'm angry. I'm mad." Address your partner in an angry tone of voice, "You bum! You did this, you did that. Don't you see how unfair this is?" Don't worry about expressing your anger in the "proper" way, since your spouse isn't even there. Say or write whatever comes to you.

2. Lie on your back, if possible, or just sit straight. Take several very deep, long, slow breaths. Now begin to breathe just a bit faster, still deep breaths, but quicker, more in your chest than your abdomen. Think about the incident or situation that you think is unfair. Pay attention to any sensations in your body. If you begin to feel your habitual feelings of tears or sadness, let those pass. Don't indulge them. Rather, go back to your gentle deep breathing. If you start feeling angry, let yourself stay with that feeling, even if it is uncomfortable. Do this for ten minutes (time it), and then just lie or sit there and rest a moment. Congratulate yourself on doing the exercise, whether you feel angry now or not. Write a few sentences in your journal about how you felt during this exercise.

3. Make an appointment with a friend. Ask your friend to listen without interruption while you talk to him or her about the incident or situation with your partner. While you talk, pretend you are angry. Sound angry. Say angry-sounding things. (Prepare your friend that you plan to do this.) Sometimes, acting as if you are angry will help you to feel genuinely angry.

Next, ask your friend, "If this incident happened to you, how would you feel?" Maybe your friend will express the anger you wish you could feel. Let your friend model the anger for you. Then pretend that you feel the sensations your friend is describing.

4. You will want to do this one when no one else is in the house. Kneel at the side of your bed. With two fists and your arms extended, begin hitting the bed. This exercise works best if you pay attention to two elements: Extend your arms, reach above your head and back, and crash onto the bed with your whole arms. Bring your shoulders into the movement. Also, as you raise your arms, inhale, and as you crash down, exhale fully. If no one else is around and you can allow yourself to do it, expel a sound as you exhale. You can even say, "I'm so mad" or whatever expression of anger feels good to you. Get into it! Whether you feel your anger or not, this will get some energy moving through your body and wake you up a bit. If you like this exercise, try it standing with your knees bent. You can even use a tennis racket to hit the bed, but that takes a high ceiling and can get loud, so be sure no one else is around.

5. Get a few pillows. One at a time, hold them high above your head and throw them on the floor, hard. Bend your knees slightly as you do this. As you throw each pillow, exhale and let sound come out. It can just be "ahh," or use words, "You creep! I'm so mad." Whatever comes to you. You may even want to pretend that the pillows are your spouse.

6. If you have tried one or two of these suggestions and you still don't feel any anger, write in your journal. This time write, "I can't feel angry because if I get angry . . ." Write the sentence over and over, completing it in as many different ways as you can.

Then try this sentence, "I'm afraid to get angry because . . ." You may have quite valid reasons to fear anger. Perhaps it was never allowed in your family. Or maybe you are afraid of your partner's response if you get angry. If you feel more fear than anger, ERAP will still work for you. You might just rename it, "Emergency Fear Abatement Procedure." Resentment, anger, and fear are often closely mixed—really more a stew of emotions.

If you do feel some anger now as a result of one or more of these exercises, the next steps in ERAP will help you understand what to do with it.

For Anger Expressers—Discharge Your Energy

Feeling angry may make you want to *do* something, the way you want to eat when you feel hungry or make love when you feel sexy. If discharging your anger energy makes you feel better and calms you down, great. Releasing built-up tension is good for your body and your psyche.

However, venting your anger—screaming, raging, or kicking your car—is not a necessary step and can sometimes do more harm than good.

There is no proof that contained anger will give you a heart attack or an ulcer. Very often, expressing your anger simply keeps you angry or makes you feel even angrier. If this is true for you, then do not "vent"! Indulging feelings of self-righteousness, building an altar to your booby prize ("I'm right!"), getting out of control with your rage, and, certainly, expressing your anger passively or directly at the object of it are harmful, immature, and not at all productive. Use the following suggestions for discharging your anger energy *only* if they genuinely calm you down and make you feel better. If they make your anger more intense, don't use them. You must be the judge of this. If you aren't sure, experiment. The next time someone makes you angry, try skipping this step and move directly to Step Two on relaxation. Or, try a "venting" procedure and check to see whether you feel angrier or calmer afterward.

If your body wants to express your anger and you know you'll feel calmer afterward, try one or more (usually one is enough) of these techniques:

1. Run. Or dance a fast dance. Or stamp your feet and jump and shake your arms and legs. Let yourself get out of breath.
2. Get in your car and scream.
3. Kneel by your bed and hit it with your fists, exactly as described in #4 under "Charge Up Your Energy." This works beautifully to discharge energy.
4. Throw pillows on the floor, as described in #5 under "Charge Up Your Energy." This works to discharge energy also.
5. Write a scathing letter to the object of your anger, *one that you will never let the person see.* Be sure to tear it up right after you write it. But be careful; if this is making you angrier, abandon it. Only if it is "getting it off your chest" should you write.
6. Talk to a friend about your anger. For this exercise, ask your friend to help you to vent your anger. Your friend might say things like, "You are really angry. This is good. Get it out of your system." Again, be careful. If this is making you angrier, stop and go immediately to Step Two. As writer Carol Tavris found in her studies of anger, "Talking can freeze a hostile disposition." The point of this is for you to release your anger so you can calm down.
7. Fantasize your best revenge. In fantasy, anything and everything is possible, precisely because it is *not* reality. So get carried away. Write the letter you would like to send, or the little speech you would like to give. Devise the perfect punishment.

If possible, exaggerate this so much that you can laugh at it. Share it with a friend and laugh together.

A final caution: Try to avoid venting directly to the object of your anger. When you are getting the angry energy out of your body, letting off steam, do it when alone. I'll have more to say about "fighting" and raging at each other at the end of this chapter. But for now, since you are taking the initiative to improve your relationship, if you can avoid venting your anger directly at your spouse, you will be making a big step forward. If you catch yourself venting your anger directly at your partner, excuse yourself and immediately use one of the six suggestions above—alone. You will be setting the stage to negotiate, argue, debate, or discuss the problem in a productive way later on.

STEP TWO—RELAX: LET YOUR SPIRIT CALM DOWN

Unfortunately, in our culture, anger and violence are glorified. The media floods us with examples of rage and violence that, to many people at least, feel good. The bad guy gets his. The hero gets revenge.

In real life, though, anger and frustration do not feel good. When you are mad, you feel unappreciated, betrayed, ignored, victimized, frustrated, offended, hurt, manipulated, used, or put down. These are awful feelings. When you say, "It felt so good to let off steam," or "We had a great, blow-out fight last night and now we feel so much better," you may be right that the discharge of all that tension was a huge relief, and even that there was a sort of exhilaration in the actual battle. But now think for a moment about how you felt in the hours, or in many cases weeks or months, that led up to the battle. You probably felt miserable that whole time.

If you can find a way to stop feeling angry, you will feel better, and you are far more likely to be able to chip away at the source of your anger in a constructive way.

(This does not contradict what I said above about trying to charge up your anger if you tend to bury or deny it. Anger eclipsers are actually angry, but rather than feel this unpleasant or scary emotion, they bury it. They still have to live with the feelings of betrayal, frustration, or neglect, and they will have trouble acting to eliminate those feelings unless they can get some "charge" behind the feelings. The "charge," the emotion of anger, is a healthy human response. It is what you choose to do with the "charge," that we are discussing here.)

So, once you feel your anger and (if you choose) let your body have the release of expressing the anger in some way, of deliberately discharging the buildup of tension, the next thing you want to learn is how to calm yourself. While you are in the midst of feeling or expressing rage, you are at the mercy of your anger. You are not in control; your anger is. The point of calming down is so that you can get back in control of yourself.

When you are angry, whether over a small, one-time incident or an ongoing source of frustration, the most useful thing you can do for yourself is to become un-angry, to calm yourself down, to strive for a larger perspective. Is the thing you are angry about really all that important when measured against a lifetime relationship? Is this one matter more important than the quality of life with your partner?

Only from a place of relative control will you be able to clarify your thoughts and devise an effective plan of action (ERAP, Steps Three and Four).

So how do you relax and calm down? Try any one or a combination of the following methods; you'll find different ones useful in different situations.

1. Wait. If at all possible, let some time pass between the incident that triggered your anger and any action you may take. Hot, angry feelings virtually always diminish, given enough time. If something makes you angry in the morning, you will almost certainly feel less "charge" about it by afternoon.

If you are with your partner when you become angry, excuse yourself. Maybe you can allow yourself a quick discharge, a little angry yell, but then say something like, "I need to go calm down. I want to talk about this later," and leave the scene. A big fight when one or both of you is seething with angry emotions will almost certainly do more harm than good. You may say things you later regret, you will feel distant from each other, the energy you expend will escalate your anger and probably your partner's, and you will solve nothing.

What is the goal of fighting with your partner? To vent? You are better off doing that alone. To get your mate to change? Fighting will only get your partner more entrenched. To persuade your partner you are right? Even if you do, which is unlikely, all you will end up with is a booby prize!

Carol Tavris concluded her whole book, *Anger: The Misunderstood*

Emotion, with this advice, which she found in a fortune cookie and felt was right on target: "If you are patient in one moment of anger, you will escape a hundred days of sorrow."

One couple I interviewed who are happy and very committed to each other said,

> We used to have huge, blow-out fights and say really awful things to each other, but now we realize, just stop. Force yourself to leave. Don't fight, period. If we can get away from each other, the anger always calms way down.

So when you are angry, above all, wait. Let some time pass. Excuse yourself from the angry scene and calm yourself down (see the rest of the suggestions in this section).

If you are dealing with a long-term, ongoing frustration, you may already have waited a long time. But chances are, whenever you feel this anger, what you do about it probably escalates the anger rather than calms it. You may try talking with your partner about it, but when you always get the same old response, your anger builds. You may talk with a friend or your mother about it, and your conversation simply leaves you both all the more angry and frustrated. You may devise some strategy to "give your partner a taste of his or her own medicine." But your

EXPERIMENT #7

Looking at Your Long-term Anger

In your journal, write down one specific long-term frustration in your relationship. Now under that, in a list, jot down everything you have done in an attempt to solve this frustration, and everything you have done to express your frustration. In other words, what do you do with your anger about this?

After each item, put a little arrow, pointing UP if this activity kept you angry or made you angrier, and a little arrow pointing DOWN if this activity actually made you less angry.

If you have any down arrows, congratulations. Keep using that strategy. If not, try out some of the other calming techniques presented here.

partner doesn't get it, and you just get more angry and then resign yourself to defeat. The key issue is for you to discover and put into practice self-calming techniques that actually reduce your anger, whatever its cause.

Whether you are working on an ongoing source of anger, a current anger-producing episode, or both, the following self-calming strategies will help you to feel better and be more in control.

2. Count to ten. This age-old folk remedy has great wisdom behind it. If your partner is right there, count to yourself. Don't risk making your partner angrier.

Counting to ten occupies you while you are waiting for some time to pass. Exhale fully while you are counting; exhaling is a mini-energy-discharge. And just keep counting. Count to ten several times. Or count to fifty. Feel yourself calming down.

3. Breathe. Sit or lie down, and begin to take easy deep breaths. Think about each breath. Breathe hard if you are really angry, and be aware of slowing down your breathing a little at a time.

Envision your favorite spot in nature. Put on some soothing music.

4. Distract yourself. Become involved in whatever you were planning to do. Or, if you are too angry to do that, flip through TV channels or turn on the radio. Take a walk. You have been wounded, so let yourself have a little time off. Read a magazine or your novel, get a video or go to a movie, bake some cookies, go tinker in the basement or clean out a closet, go out for a frozen yogurt or go buy yourself a book—something that will make you feel you are getting a little treat and healing your hurt. Be your own mommy; kiss your own scraped elbow.

5. See if you can make an active choice about how you feel. Your emotions affect the quality of your life, much more than your partner's. If you are angry with your spouse, you are the one who has to go through your day crying, or feeling tight all over, or giving up what you wanted to do and instead spending all your time on the phone with your friend working out your anger.

Your partner may be affected by your emotions. But never as much as you are, and sometimes not at all, which, of course can make you all the angrier. If your husband plays golf all day while you stay home with the children and the laundry, he is probably having a wonderful day while you are spending the entire day seething. He may seem like the culprit, but you are the one who is suffering. Your anger is hurting *you,* not him.

Or suppose your wife is cool and distant, especially when you invite her to make love with you. She's the "bad guy," the one who deserves to be "punished." But you are the one who has to feel rejected, lonely, and inadequate. Your sadness is hurting *you,* not her.

Is there a way you could choose not to feel those feelings that are so unpleasant?

Take the position that you don't have to let your partner's upsetting behavior upset you. You don't have to be at the mercy of what your partner does or does not do to you. Try saying, "I'm not going to let this ruin my day!" or "I can set aside my anger and have a fine, productive day."

6. Separate your anger from your other emotions. If your partner's behavior caused damage—some friends became offended, your favorite blouse got destroyed in the laundry, the children suffered—see if you can separate your feelings of sadness from your anger at the cause of it, your spouse. You may be feeling two emotions at this time. Try to untangle these two emotions from one another. This will be hard to do, but if you can, it may help calm you down.

7. Laugh. You can't laugh and feel angry at the same time. As you calm down, there may be times when you find humor in the situation that made you angry. Very few incidents are serious enough to *make* you become a grouchy, bitter, hostile person. When you feel that way, you suffer more than anyone else.

8. Pat yourself on the back. If you find yourself calming down, praise yourself. "Good for me. I handled this without blowing up. This time I was aware of my anger, I was able to do something about it. I kept the situation from escalating. I'm feeling more in control. I'm actually feeling better."

STEP THREE—ASSESS: LET YOUR MIND CLARIFY THE SITUATION

Now that you have **E**xpressed your anger and **R**elaxed, you are ready to engage in some clear thinking about your situation. You are ready to **A**ssess.

Anger is a signal your body gives you that something is wrong and needs to be fixed. It's like a red alert siren going off in a toxic chemical plant. There's a leak! There's a crisis, yes, but there is also an opportunity to find the underlying problem that's causing the crisis and fix it so the leak won't happen again. Anger is a signal that something needs to be taken care of. Like a fever in your body, it is a symptom of a deeper problem.

First, exactly what is at issue in your dispute? Write a sentence or paragraph that pinpoints the specific problem that triggered your feeling of anger. It may be an incident or an ongoing problem.

For example:

> After promising to be home on time, Jerry was an hour late and then didn't apologize. It ruined my plans for the evening.
>
> Sarah put a big dent in my gorgeous new car.
>
> I don't have enough control over my own money and spending.
>
> Jim doesn't do his share of the housework.

If you find yourself writing half a page or more, you are probably still in the Expressing step. That's fine. Let yourself vent. Then go back to Step Two and do a calming activity, or simply let some time go by. You will have a harder time clarifying your thinking if you are still deep within your angry feelings.

When you are clear about what the problem is, the next step is to look at both sides of the issue.

Write a sentence or paragraph stating your side of this problem. Say what you want, what you deserve, what you think is fair, what you dislike, what you fear, what makes you sad, what you regret. You probably have a "stew" of feelings regarding this problem. Write about each of your feelings. If it helps, pretend you are making a statement to a judge. Or, write a letter directly to your mate.

In order for this to be useful, you must remember not to grab for the booby prize! Do not make yourself right and your partner wrong.

Your partner has a right to and a reason for his or her position. You can disagree with your partner and still honor his or her right to hold an opinion or engage in a behavior different from yours. So state your position without making your partner wrong.

For example, don't say,

> "Jim should be willing to help me get ready for this party."
>
> "Suzie is irresponsible for spending so much money."

Instead, say,

> "I'm furious that I have to do all the work for this party."
>
> "I feel anxious and angry that Suzie spent so much money."

Next, and this is the hard part, walk for a while in your partner's shoes. Try to see your partner's point of view. This doesn't mean you have to agree with it. You may strongly disagree with your partner's side of things. Still, see if you can develop some empathy for or understanding of your partner's position. As a "leader" in your relationship, you have the opportunity to see the big picture.

Just as you did for yourself, write a sentence or paragraph stating your partner's side of this problem. Say what he or she wants, deserves, thinks is fair, dislikes, fears. What makes your partner sad? What does he or she regret?

You know something about your partner's childhood. What early experiences could be influencing your spouse to behave so awfully to you? Maybe your partner is anxious or afraid or under a lot of stress. This doesn't excuse the bad behavior, but maybe it helps explain it. What is going on at work for your spouse and among his or her friends?

Try to climb inside your partner's head and heart, taking into consideration all the factors you know about, and speak from deep inside your partner. Maybe he or she wouldn't even be able to articulate all the factors you see, but be the inner voice of your partner, and tell his or her story as you see it.

For example, stating the problem:

> After promising to be home on time, Jerry was an hour late and then didn't apologize. It ruined my plans for the evening.

But, from your partner's point of view:

> Jerry feels huge financial pressure right now because we are in debt. He has enormous pressure at work until this contract is over. He's tired all the time, and he's extremely anxious that he won't finish on time. He probably honestly forgot about our plans for the evening and wasn't even aware that the time was going by. What he really wants from me is understanding and support, not more demands and requests. Right now, he just can't take any more. He probably feels like he should go live alone until this contract is over. He's not much of a companion for me right now, but he's doing the best he can.

Sarah put a big dent in my gorgeous new car.
She doesn't care as much about this car as I do. She still drives her old rattletrap. This was an accident. It could have happened to anyone. She feels terrible that this happened. She feels awful. The last thing in the world she wants to do is make me unhappy with her. She probably wants someone to comfort her, not be furious with her.

I don't have enough control over my own money and spending.
Marv doesn't think that he controls our money, he just thinks he is doing a good job of managing our finances. His family has a lot of fear and anxiety about money. They are all the way he is. He can't help it when he feels so anxious. He needs to feel in control of the money or else he'd go nuts.

Jim doesn't do his share of the housework.
Jim doesn't *want* to do any housework. He hates it. He truly sees it as women's work. His father never did any housework. The guys he works with never do any housework. He doesn't see it as hard or time-consuming. He has very little understanding of what I do. He has no picture of what it would be like for him to take over one or two tasks.

In a workshop, Kathryn did this exercise and amazed herself and all of us with the results. She was angry because her husband chose to play golf all day instead of staying with the family. She tearfully read us the following entry from her journal:

> He has been under enormous pressure at work all week. He hasn't played golf for a month. The guys he most loves to play with have asked him to play. He will truly feel like an idiot with these guys if he has to say, "Sorry, I can't play. I have to stay home and do the laundry." Since things aren't very pleasant with me right now, if he stays home he will have to face all day long how unhappy I am with him. He doesn't believe that staying home this particular day will help solve the problems with me anyway because they seem much huger than this one day. He feels I don't understand him, and he can't make me see his side of the story. He is terrified that being married to me might mean he will have to give up golf and friends forever. He is scared inside because deep down, he is truly afraid he doesn't know how to please me and will never be able to make me happy, and this makes him feel terrible because he truly loves me.

We actually saw Kathryn let go of her anger. She told us, "You know, he asked me to come play golf too. One of the other guy's wife was coming, and the idea was that the wives would play together and the guys would play. I could have done that too—and used the babysitting co-op and just forgotten the laundry."

Accepting your partner's side of the story may not happen as quickly or as thoroughly as it did with Kathryn. But give it a start. If you can see your partner's point of view and understand how he or she came to hold it, you may feel anger that has been upsetting you for a long time slowly drain away and even disappear. Remember, you are the person who will benefit from this; it feels lousy to be angry all the time.

STEP FOUR—PERFORM: DO WHAT IS BEST FOR YOUR RELATIONSHIP

You have been working on **E**xpressing the energy in your body, **R**elaxing your spirit, **A**ssessing the situation by clarifying the problem and looking at both sides of it. Now you get to **P**erform, do something about it, make a change that will make a difference.

Mini-Blow-Up

If you are angry about an isolated, recent incident, the first action you may want to consider is a Mini-Blow-Up. Especially if your mate is blissfully unaware that he or she has upset you, you may need to express your anger cleanly and clearly to your mate. With luck, your partner will at least see your point of view and may even apologize. If not, at least you have stood up for yourself and let your partner know where you stand.

For example, Yvonne and Jack planned a weekend at the beach. After they arrived, Yvonne learned that Jack had brought work along with him—with all sorts of good excuses about how he had deadlines with no notice and it was his boss's fault, etc. At first Yvonne, though very disappointed, accepted his story. But as the weekend wore on, she realized she was outraged. After she spent Saturday afternoon shopping by herself, her slow burn got hotter and hotter. She felt a need to vent (**E**xpress), so she called a friend. She reached an answering machine, but it was a close friend, so she went ahead anyway.

"Dottie, sorry to spill all this on you, but I need to talk. Jack actually brought work down here with him, and I am so furious with him. . . ." She went on for a few minutes, explaining how cheated she felt and how thoughtless Jack was—just pouring out her feelings. When she hung up, she felt better and ready to calm herself down. She sat on a park bench and let her mind roam, watching people pass by for a while (**R**elax). After a while, still feeling angry, but calmer, she carefully thought through her point of view and also Jack's (**A**ssess). Then she drove back to their cottage and said, "Jack, I need to talk with you. I am so mad that you brought work down here. We have planned this weekend for so long, and the idea was to get away from work. I realize you have deadlines, but I feel that sometimes you just need to say no. Our time together is important too! . . ." She went on in an angry tone of voice for a minute or two. Then she stopped to give Jack an opportunity to respond (**P**erform: Mini-Blow-Up).

Notice that a Mini-Blow-Up is different from venting. A Mini-Blow-Up is a way of expressing your feelings and your point of view to your partner *after* you have calmed down and assessed your anger by looking at both sides of the issue.

Usually, your spouse will sit up and take notice when you are this angry. In this case, Jack was willing to listen to Yvonne. He didn't give in completely, but he acknowledged her point and apologized that he had upset her so. He put aside his work for the rest of the weekend, and they agreed to discuss the general problem of Jack's workaholic tendencies at a later time.

If your Mini-Blow-Up leads to a fight, see my following comments on fighting.

Creative Problem Solving

Often, the source of your anger is an ongoing problem or one you have discussed many times before. Your spouse already knows what the problem is, so a Mini Blow-Up would cause a problem, and do nothing to solve it.

Instead of creating a conflict with your spouse, explore possible solutions to the problem.

Creative problem solving is the true magic of ERAP. It is your opportunity to use your anger in a constructive way, to exercise your creative abilities and your willingness to be a responsible and compassionate leader in your relationship.

To solve your problem, you have four choices: (*a*) You can make a change in yourself; (*b*) You can make a change in the situation; (*c*) You can decide not to make any changes and to accept the situation the way it is (actually, this is a form of (*a*) a shift within yourself); or (*d*) You can try to get your spouse to change.

I hope you already know better than to choose (*d*). That's probably the choice you have been making for a long time to no avail. It will never work. As we have seen, if you are trying to change your spouse, your primary message to him or her is, "You are not okay the way you are. I would love you more if you did this or that. There is something wrong with you." Yet what you most long for is closeness, intimacy, companionship, friendship. Hassling your partner will only drive the two of you apart. It will exacerbate your problem and will never solve it.

Any of the other three choices could be very productive: changing or accepting the situation, or changing yourself.

Henry James Borys wrote a lovely book called *The Way of Marriage* in which he shares portions of his journal from a period of several challenging years with his wife, Susan. Over and over, he quite beautifully shares the insights he gained by allowing himself to feel vulnerable, to learn from his mistakes and his area of weakness. He agrees that anger presents an opportunity for learning:

> When I am angry, instead of blaming Susan, why not try to see my anger as a chance to learn something about myself? The

demand for change is usually much more creative when turned one hundred and eighty degrees—inwards. For the source of my anger is never simply outside of myself. It is within me.

The best way to solve a problem is to start with a clean sheet of paper and brainstorm all the possible solutions you can think of. Take a half hour and write down everything that comes to you, even if you know it isn't possible for some reason. Even write down ideas that are absurd or funny. In brainstorming, everything counts. While you are brainstorming, don't evaluate any of your ideas; that part comes later. The process depends on associations and connections, so you have to let your brain spill over with ideas. The point is to end your brainstorming session with solutions that were not in your mind when you started the session.

To stimulate your creativity, decide on an arbitrary number of solutions, far greater than you think is reasonable, and then force yourself to create that many solutions. Often, one of the four or five you think of last is the winning solution.

Brainstorming will help you get beyond the trap of either/or thinking. Many problems seem like true dilemmas, in which you want two things that are completely incompatible. For example, we can't go to both the ball game and the party on the same afternoon. I can't both work and stay home. You either take care of the kids on Saturday, or you don't.

Either/or thinking limits your creativity. Dilemmas are rarely as black and white as they seem. If you *believe* you can create a solution that will work for both of you, you will be helping your brain to create solutions that shatter the dilemma and invent a third or fourth or fifth way out of the problem. (We'll say more about either/or thinking in Chapter Five, when we discuss power struggles.)

As you brainstorm, think up solutions that involve changing yourself, solutions that involve accepting the situation, and solutions that involve changing the situation. These categories may help stimulate your thinking. Also, after you have read the next two chapters, you will have many more ideas at your disposal for your brainstorming sessions.

What may happen as you are working on a solution for the specific problem you have chosen to focus on is that solutions for bigger, more overall problems begin to present themselves.

To see how creative problem solving works, let's use Andrea's problem as an example. Andrea was upset with her husband, Ted, because he took very little interest in their twin baby girls, their first children. When the twins were twelve weeks old, Andrea went back to her job in the training department of a large retail company, but only three days a week. Ted was a police officer with a varied schedule, but he always had Wednesdays off. Andrea had child care for the twins on two of her work days, and she thought Ted should care for them on Wednesdays. But Ted wanted no part of such a plan.

Andrea identified her immediate problem as "Ted won't help solve the day care problem and he doesn't want to spend time with the twins."

In looking at Ted's side of the story, she realized that Ted has never been around babies, he is uncomfortable around them, and has no confidence at all about taking care of them. Also, he loves his days off and often spends them with his friends playing tennis or getting things done around the house. Spending Wednesdays with the twins would give him no time to himself.

Here was Andrea's brainstorm list:

Changes in the situation:

- Get child care on Wednesdays too.
- Ask Ted to do child care for half of Wednesday.
- Ask Ted to go to a baby care class.
- Try to persuade my boss to let me work two days.
- Ask my mother to come over on Wednesdays.

Changes in me:

- Stop worrying about Ted's lack of interest in the babies.
- Stop worrying about spending the extra day-care money.

After you brainstorm, try to get away from the problem and don't even think about it for at least twenty-four hours, if you have that much time. Turn the whole thing over to your unconscious. Many creative experts report that this is an important phase of generating creative solutions. It gives your inner wisdom the time it needs to sort and muse, free of the pressure and anxiety you add when you are "working on" the problem.

Now go back to your list and evaluate each potential solution.

Be careful not to choose a solution that you in any small way resent. That's no solution, especially if your usual way of coping is simply to give in. And don't choose a solution that you think your partner would resent or that makes him or her seem like the bad guy.

Remember: You are searching not for victory, but for harmony. You do not want to win at your partner's expense. Rather, you want a solution that will make both of you feel good. You are trying to make a shift now, from being antagonistic, to working *with* your mate—insofar as you can understand his or her needs by yourself. Your goal is to solve the problem in a way that brings the two of you together.

Andrea's solution not only accomplished all of that and solved the immediate problem, it also solved one of her main, overarching problems, that she and Ted never seemed to get enough time together. While she was looking over her list of solutions, Andrea suddenly got the idea that Wednesdays could be a wonderful day for the two of them. If she could figure out a way to get Wednesdays off herself, and use child care for all three of her work days, Ted would be off the hook (she believed, as friends and family all suggested, that he would start taking more interest in the children as they got a bit older), and she could solve her biggest problem, lack of time with Ted. She ran the idea past Ted, and he loved it, even though it meant they had to pay for one more day of child care. Now, they go out for breakfast every Wednesday morning and then go shopping or play a little tennis, and still save the afternoon for time by themselves. This gives them regular time together without the children, and Andrea told me it has worked wonders in their relationship.

Before trying the ERAP process, Andrea was extremely distraught. She was devastated that Ted took so little interest in their girls, and she was extremely anxious about leaving her babies three days a week and paying for day care. Notice that by giving up her need to be right, by seeing Ted's point of view, and by being willing to do all the problem solving herself, she made a major positive change in her relationship and did it completely on her own. She didn't need Ted to "talk about it," and she didn't ask him to change.

Now let's see ERAP at work on two very different problems reported by individuals in my workshops.

Christina's main problem with Steve was that she felt he always put her needs and her feelings second. His work, his friends, his computer, his men's group, his tennis were all more important to him than she was. Christina felt neglected, misunderstood, unappreciated, and taken for granted.

One Friday evening, she and Steve had plans to go to dinner with a couple Steve had been wanting to get to know better. After a stressful week at work, Christina was exhausted and felt she could not drag herself to the dinner. Steve was adamant.

"We made these plans ages ago. They went to a lot of trouble. We can't just bag out on them. You'll feel better. You have to come."

For Christina, it was the last straw. Steve didn't even acknowledge her own needs, let alone do anything about them. She flopped on the couch and started to cry. Then she thought of ERAP. In her case, she already knew that she had a tendency to get hurt instead of angry and that she needed to charge up her anger. She looked at Steve and said, "I'm angry." Then, raising her voice, "I feel completely invisible. It doesn't matter to you one whit that I am tired. All you care about is these people we barely even know."

Steve's reply was, "I'm sorry, honey. I know you're tired. But you'll revive. I really want to go. I'd feel terrible canceling out on them at the last minute. What will they think of us? 'We were too tired' is such a flimsy excuse."

Christina was thinking to herself: Relax, Christina. She said, "Let me go to the bedroom and think about it for a few minutes."

In the bedroom, Christina cried for a few minutes. "I need this cry," she was thinking. "I'm so worn out." Then she thought, "Okay, relax and assess." She took a deep breath, stopped crying, and started to think.

Assessment: What is the problem here? I truly don't want to go to this dinner and Steve wants me to.

What's my position?: I am truly exhausted. I have had no time to myself. I have no interest in this dinner or these people whatsoever. I actually don't respect Steve's motives for having dinner with them very much; it feels sort of like a social-climb type thing. One hundred percent of me does not want to go.

Steve's position: He really wants to go and wants me to be there too. He likes showing me off to people. He will feel dreadfully embarrassed if he has to cancel.

Action: So what do I do? I feel like I'll die if I have to go to this thing. Steve can go without me. That's it. I am not willing to go. It's not that big a deal. What if I really had the flu? He can get most of his needs met by going without me, and I can certainly meet mine if I stay home.

She went back to the living room where Steve was waiting for her.

"Steve, no cell in my body wants to go to this dinner. I just can't bring myself to do it. But you can go without me and tell them I'm really sorry, I just didn't feel good. Tell them I'm on a deadline at work, which I am. I'm sorry to disappoint you. I just can't bring myself to go."

Steve just looked at her for a few minutes. He saw that she had suddenly become the Rock of Gibraltar. "Okay," he said in a resigned tone of voice, and he got up and left. On the way out the door, he said to Christina, not sarcastically but in a sincere tone of voice, "I hope you have a restful evening."

Christina used ERAP very effectively for an immediate problem. Because she was clear within herself and decisive with Steve, he was able to accept her decision. She told me she is certain that if she had not used ERAP, they would have had a big fight, the same one they had had dozens of times. She would have said, "You always ignore my needs," and he would have said, "No, I don't," over and over. In the end, she probably would have given in and gone to the dinner because Steve was almost always able to wear her down.

I spoke with Christina about a year after this incident, and she reported feeling much better about the general problem in their relationship, her feeling of being Steve's last priority. As she explained,

> By taking care of my own needs in several specific situations like this one, I feel like the whole thing is in better balance now. Steve hasn't changed, but I am taking much better care of myself. I don't expect Steve to take care of my needs for me anymore. Because I'm taking care of myself, I'm not feeling so neglected anymore. We fight less now—hardly at all. It helps me so much to know *what* I need to do—even if I don't always do it perfectly.

Another individual, Randy, used ERAP to work on a long-term problem he was having with his wife, Marsha. He felt that Marsha wouldn't accept him the way he was but was always trying to get him to be someone else. Even though she hated the term "nag," and denied that she ever nagged him, Randy honestly felt that he was being nagged all the time. One main source of conflict was his relationship with their four-year-old son, Robbie. Randy liked to tease Robbie, and Marsha felt his teasing was inappropriate. Every time they were playing together, Marsha would interfere and try to get Randy to stop. It was driving Randy crazy! Since he has a short fuse, these episodes often erupted into short yelling matches—short because they both felt reluctant to fight in front of Robbie.

One evening, Marsha was gone, and Randy and Robbie spent several lovely hours together, having dinner, playing, taking a bath, and reading bedtime stories. At the end of the evening, Randy realized how angry he was about all the times he wasn't allowed to play with his son the way he wanted to. He decided to apply ERAP. Robbie was in bed by nine, and Marsha wasn't coming home until eleven, so he had a couple of hours.

Randy felt angry and charged up, so to express his anger, he tried the bed-hitting exercise. He felt he was holding back with Robbie sleeping in the next room, so instead, he put on his Walkman and danced up a storm in the kitchen. Then, to relax himself, he sat in a chair and breathed and listened to soothing music. Then he felt ready to assess and went for his journal (which he later shared with me):

Assessment: What is the problem here? I can't play with Robbie without Marsha criticizing me about it. Marsha doesn't accept me. She's critical of me all the time. This makes me angry with her and makes me feel distant from her. I feel totally incapable of changing the way she wants me to change, and furthermore, I like the way I am. I don't want to change. . . . Marsha's mother is also very critical of her father. This is probably where Marsha gets this. . . . When we talk about it, Marsha gets defensive. She doesn't agree that she criticizes me, and she just turns the discussion back to how I ought to change and how I'm the one who is wrong.

What's my position?: I deserve to have my life around here without being criticized all the time. I want Marsha to like me the way I am. I want to feel that she adores me the way I felt when we were first together. I love many of Marsha's qualities. I know she loves me. I want the criticism to stop.

Marsha's position: I am not sensitive to Robbie, that I tease him to get my own needs met, to feel "superior" to him, and so *I* can laugh, not so *he* can laugh. (This is baloney.) Also, she feels that I don't clean the dishes well enough, that I should slice tomatoes thicker, that I put too much butter on my bread, that I should sort the laundry before I do a load, that my clothes look sloppy, that I interrupt too much and tease other people too (like my niece). She feels she has to straighten me out on these things, that she is helping me and helping other people too. She feels she has a right to ask for what she wants in the relationship.

Perform: What can I do by myself to create change?

Brainstorming:

- Plan regular evenings with me and Robbie alone.
- Try talking to Marsha again about the problem.

- Go along with everything Marsha asks me to do without a fight.
- Do the opposite of what I do now (fight back every time Marsha criticizes me) and instead thank her for her suggestion every time.
- Wear a bell around my neck and ring it every time I feel criticized.
- Make a deal with her that I will change certain things (like I could let her dress me the way she wants and could put less butter on my bread), if she will let me do the other things the way I want.
- Get a sitter and take her to movies more often—and out to dinner before.
- Plan a B&B weekend for us with Robbie at her folks, and surprise her.
- Work on letting her criticisms roll off my back. Just not let them get me so angry.
- Buy her that pair of earrings I saw on the avenue that I know she'd love.

Randy told me he had fun doing this list, that some of it made him laugh, and that he felt happy and optimistic by the time he finished.

It was easy for him to choose his actions when he went back over the list. He decided to let Marsha start telling him what to wear since he didn't have strong feelings about that and he knew it would make her happy; to try to thank her for her suggestions and try not to get angry every time; to buy the earrings, plan the B&B weekend, and get a sitter and take her to a movie the very next night. By the time Marsha came home, Randy felt buoyant and greeted her enthusiastically. She was thrilled with such a reception and happy to hear about Randy's evening with Robbie and to relate the complicated evening she had had herself.

Randy told me that his success with thanking Marsha for her suggestions and not getting angry was mixed. He was far from perfect and kept slipping up. However, when it worked, it worked really well: He felt inner strength and control because he had a choice and did not have to get angry when Marsha criticized him, and Marsha was delighted because she felt she was getting her message across. And what Randy loved even more was that he could feel inside that he was doing the right thing. He felt enormous relief that he had a plan, that even if he didn't always do it, he now had something that he *could* do when Marsha began to nag him. He found that he was able to make jokes out of the criticisms, and even that Marsha started laughing sometimes too, laughing at herself.

The problem didn't go away, but Randy had found a way to manage the problem so that its importance in their marriage faded.

Remember: Anger should always be a signal to you that something is wrong. If you have a splinter, your finger will give you a little "pain" signal. To fix the pain, pull out the splinter. Similarly, the best way to relieve anger is to "fix" the problem that is causing the anger. The Emergency Resentment Abatement Procedure gives you a formula for doing exactly that.

Notice that, in order to use ERAP effectively, you don't have to go back to your childhood and understand fully how you got to be the way you are. You don't have to analyze your family of origin, and you don't have to change your basic personality. ERAP is versatile and adaptable. Even if you come from a family in which anger was handled in destructive ways, you can learn to use anger constructively. You need only the desire and the willingness to practice. The more you use ERAP, the easier it will become for you. Of course you will experience setbacks. Don't let these deter you from trying again. Be patient with yourself while you learn.

WHEN YOUR SPOUSE IS ANGRY WITH YOU

ERAP is remarkably effective for converting your own anger into positive change in your relationship.

But what can you do when your spouse becomes angry with you?

Now I want to introduce a difficult skill. It's a key skill for you if you are to become an enlightened "leader" who promotes harmony and decreases conflict. The skill is this: Refrain from giving a knee-jerk, defensive response. For a short, easy-to-remember rule, we'll call it "ADD: Acknowledgment. Don't get Defensive."

When your partner becomes angry with you, the most natural response for you is to become defensive. For example,

"We never go out anymore."

"Yes we do! We went to the movies last night! We went out for dinner last week!"

Or,

"Hurry up! Can't you ever be on time? We're going to be late!"

"I can't help it if I got home late. I'm not always late. This is the first time in a long time I've been late!"

Defensiveness is as old as humankind. Someone throws a stone at you; you put your hands up in front of your face to protect yourself. It's the same thing we do with words: verbal assault, verbal self-protection. It is a survival instinct.

But in your marriage, you are not in a life-threatening situation. You may choose to be more concerned about the well-being of your relationship than about yourself—like the CEO of a company who declines a raise because she's more concerned about the financial well-being of the company than about herself. She knows that if the company thrives, she will thrive. Only a truly enlightened leader would behave that way. But that's the kind of leader you want to be in your relationship, isn't it?

So, when your mate verbally assaults you, instead of throwing back a defensive remark, which escalates the conflict, you can make a peace-promoting remark. In concept, it's easy; you just acknowledge your partner's concern. Like this:

"We never go out anymore."

Possible non-defensive responses would be:

"You feel like we never go out anymore?"

"It does seem like we never go out anymore."

"We do enjoy it when we go out. I love to go out too."

It's like in martial arts. When your opponent comes at you with a fist, instead of blocking the fist and hitting back, which escalates the fight, you grab the fist and pull it toward you. Using your opponent's own momentum, you pull him over onto the floor. There is very little injury, and the conflict is over.

With a non-defensive, "martial arts" response like, "Yeah, maybe you're right," your conversation can continue in a constructive way. Maybe you will never get the chance to express your point of view, that you do in fact go out a lot. But in the long run, it doesn't matter. If you did get to express your opposite opinion, all you would end up with is the booby prize—or a fight.

It doesn't matter who is right. If you take care of your partner's feelings and needs, the assaults and complaints will stop. Your partner will appreciate you. And you'll both feel good. Isn't that the result you want?

"Hurry up! Can't you ever be on time? We're going to be late!"

Possible non-defensive responses:

"I'm so sorry. I'm worried about being late too."

"It's such a drag to be late. I agree."

"I know it's frustrating. I assure you, I'm going as fast as I can."

Learning to control your automatic defensive response is a process; it won't come instantly. The first step is to catch yourself *after* you have made a defensive response. When you look back on the situation, think of a non-defensive response you might have given. Next, you may be able to notice yourself being defensive *as* it is happening.

You can't expect yourself not to *feel* defensive when your mate hurls a verbal assault or accusation at you. The idea is to feel defensive, but to avoid a verbal defense.

Memorize this sentence: "I'm feeling defensive." When you feel defensive, and you can't think of anything to say except defensive comments, say, "I feel defensive" instead.

This buys you time to think. It is a response that does not escalate the conflict; your spouse cannot argue with it. It is a substitute for all the self-protective remarks you feel the urge to say. It's an honest statement.

Let's say you forgot to pick up the dry cleaning, and this really sets your partner off. Can you be the "big" person and allow your mate a little anger discharge, even directly at you? Can you acknowledge your partner's right to be angry? Here are some additional non-defensive responses:

I don't blame you for being angry.

I can see why you are angry.

I'm sorry I blew it. I know I really messed up.

I may have used poor judgment.

I'm sorry you are so upset.

I really want to discuss this, but I don't think we should do it when we are so angry.

Acknowledge your spouse. Don't express your defensive feelings, if you can help it. Just listen to his or her side of the story and let your partner vent. Think ADD: Acknowledgment. Don't get Defensive. This requires courage and restraint.

Writing this, I vividly recall an example I personally witnessed.

Mayer and I were spending a few days with close friends of ours whom I'll call Toni and Doug. Toni had agreed to prepare their tax return early, but this was March and it still wasn't done. Doug was eager to have it completed because they were due a substantial refund which Doug had plans for. Toni had several excellent "excuses" for her delays, including extra responsibility at work and her mother's illness. Nevertheless, one evening while we were there, Doug erupted at her, explaining how important it was for her to move the taxes up on her priority list.

Toni was upset that Doug was angry with her. She knew he had a good point—that the tax return was taking longer that they had planned. At the same time, Toni knew inside herself that she was doing the best she could. So she let him "lecture" her. She told me later, "I felt he had a right to do his best to get across to me how urgent he felt this was. He was venting his anxiety." Toni didn't talk back. When Doug was finished, she said, "I know my schedule makes you very anxious. I don't blame you for being upset. I'm doing the best I can. I promise, I'll get to the taxes in the next several days."

Sometimes it makes sense to stick around and let your partner express anger at you. If you can keep your own center intact, you are giving your partner a real gift when you listen and acknowledge.

Learning to respond to anger without becoming defensive is truly an act of love.

Sometimes it takes several days to reverse your initial defensive response. Recently, a friend of mine became angry because I broke a date with her. At first, I was hurt and furious with her that she couldn't be more flexible. But after a few days as I calmed down, I saw the validity of her position and began to feel I owed her an apology. Finally, I faxed her an apologetic note, which she appreciated. It took a while for me to make the shift from defensive to non-defensive. And it was humiliating; I had to admit I was wrong. But by letting go of being defensive and insisting I was right, I mended my valuable friendship. I let go of the booby prize and went for the gold.

What About Fights?

But what about the times when what your mate says really does make you angry yourself? You are just too furious to refrain from making a defensive remark or to even think about ERAP. Your partner's anger is making you feel terrible. You feel attacked, unloved, unappreciated, unheard. As the anger is coming at you, your center begins to crumble. You want to fight back! Or something your mate does sets off your own anger.

Sometimes it is just really hard to get out of a fight. Your partner may want to fight, and you may feel like fighting too.

If you are a couple who fight rarely, your fights may be good, healthy "discharging" sessions for both of you. And since you are confident that you will make up in a few hours, it doesn't hurt to have a bit of a yelling match every now and then. If it is not destructive to either of you, it may be a way for you both to "get it off your chest."

But if you fight habitually and often and you have the same fight over and over, fighting is almost certainly doing you more harm than good. You can stop these fights by yourself—by walking away.

You have to let your partner know what you are doing. Say something like, "I don't want to fight right now. I'm going to go calm down. I promise I'll talk with you about this later."

When you are fired up and loaded with ammunition, or when you are being attacked, quitting won't be easy. But try it. Right in the moment of your fury, you won't be able to *do* the steps of ERAP, but *think* "ERAP." Just say the word to yourself, "ERAP, ERAP." It's a way of reminding yourself, "I have a choice here. I have options." The more practice you get, and the more success you have, the easier it will be simply to leave the scene. It truly does take two to fight, so if you can somehow make yourself unavailable for the fight, you won't have one.

After you leave, you can do ERAP.

USING ERAP

I have taken a lot of time to explain ERAP, but I assure you that in use it is quite uncomplicated. Like any new skill, it has a learning curve and requires practice. But this one tool incorporates much of what you need to do to enhance your relationship by yourself. The rest of the book could be viewed as possible options for Step Four, the action step.

Putting ERAP to use will increase your personal power within your relationship, help you to feel better about your mate, help your mate to feel better about you, and increase the closeness between you. All you have to remember is this:

Express (Let your body charge or discharge)
Relax (Let your spirit calm down)
Assess (Look at both sides of the issue)
Perform (Choose a potential solution and try it out)

Step One is optional; many times you can skip it. If you need to scream or go hit a pillow or run, do it. Or if you need to feel anger instead of burying it, work on that. But many times you are simply annoyed or mildly angry, and you can just **R**elax and start **A**ssessing. If you are angry about a long-term problem you are probably already calm and can even go directly to **A**ssessing, Step Three.

The beauty of ERAP is that it forces you to act. If you keep using ERAP, by definition you won't be putting up for months or years with situations you don't like.

ERAP aims at helping you to change your own *behavior* in your relationship—not your feelings, not your attitudes, and not your innate personality characteristics. You are encouraged to focus on behavior for two reasons: First, behavior is by far the easiest to change. Second, changes in behavior often lead to shifts in feelings and attitudes. If you can bring yourself to experiment with changing your behavior *even if you don't feel like it,* you may discover gentle transformations going on inside you.

ERAP does not help you to see *why* you and your partner behave as you do. You can only speculate about why anyway, and all you will end up with are theories that may or may not be correct.

This is not to say that looking behind your behavior or your spouse's might not be useful. If you see that your husband is treating you the same way he treated his mother, or your wife is assuming you will behave the way her father always does, these insights can help you to develop empathy and understanding. But if you do nothing with these insights, nothing will change. You have to experiment with changes in your behavior if you want anything to change.

Several weeks after I had completed writing this chapter, I had quite an unexpected surprise. My son, Gabe, came home for a visit. He is an instructor for a wilderness education program called Outward Bound in which they teach not only "hard skills" like backpacking, rock climbing, canoeing, kayaking, and sailing, but also, "soft skills" like cooperation, self-reliance, and problem solving. Gabe overheard me telling a friend about the Emergency Resentment Abatement Procedure, and he said, "Oh yeah. That's just like the VOMP that we use in Outward Bound."

"What's that?" I asked him.

"When our students become angry at someone, we teach them to VOMP: Vent, Own Up, Moccasins, Plan. Vent your feelings, own up to your own part in what happened, walk in the other person's moccasins to see his or her point of view, and make a plan about what to do that will work for both of you."

Imagine my surprise! I was quite amazed at the parallels. Just as VOMP works for Outward Bounders, so ERAP works for couples! My son and I had been teaching the same thing in very different settings, without realizing the coincidence.

You are already accumulating some powerful tools to use in transforming your relationship all by yourself. We are only getting started, but let's take a quick inventory of the tool chest so far:

1. Take the position that you are going to be the "big" person in your relationship, that your goal is to make both you and your partner feel good, and that you are not worried about getting "credit" from your partner. You are going to learn some good leadership skills and put them to use in your relationship.

2. Give up your ideas about who is to blame for any particular problem. Don't blame your spouse or yourself. Focus only on the dynamics between you, the "dance" you do together. Accept your partner and your partner's behavior. Above all, don't make yourself right and your partner wrong. No matter how awful you think your partner's behavior is, you are part of the dance. Since you have powerful control over your half of the action, focus on what *you* can do. Stop trying to solve your problems by getting your partner to change.

3. When you feel angry or resentful, think, "This is a signal to me to do something constructive." Work on managing your anger so that it helps you and your partner move forward, rather than continuing to pile up negative experiences. Think ERAP. Think ADD.

In the next chapter, you will learn specific actions you can try on your own to get more of what you want from your relationship.

Part Three

Short-term Strategies for Creating a Thriving Relationship by Yourself

CHAPTER FOUR

Create Harmony in Your Home

Most couples think that in order to be happy together, they have to solve their problems. "If we can just get over certain hurdles, we can be happy," they think. Or, "If only my partner would . . . , then we'd be one of those happy couples."

The thriving couples I interviewed for my last book operate from the opposite philosophy: "When we are happy together, we can much more easily manage our problems."

Problems are not the *cause* of unhappiness in marriage; they are the *symptoms* of unhappy marriage.

Put another way, you may think, "We have problems; therefore we don't feel good." But what is far more likely is, "We don't feel good; therefore we have problems." If you can find a way to feel better about yourself and your partner, your problems may disappear, or certainly, your feeling of powerlessness to work them through.

If the cause of your headache is bad glasses and all you do for the problem is take aspirin, the headaches will continue to recur. You need to get new glasses. In the same way, maybe what your marriage needs is not more aspirin (better communication, solutions to problems), but new glasses (a whole new idea about what you need to feel close).

The new idea is this: You can be happy together, even if you don't solve all your problems. Focus on your desire for a close relationship. Pay far more attention to the parts of your relationship that you like, and to the positive qualities in your partner, than to your areas of dissatisfaction.

If you focus on problems, your life will be filled with problems. The weakest, most dissatisfying parts of your relationship will be receiving all your attention. Of course you will view your marriage as problematic because that is what you are choosing to emphasize. As psychologist George Pransky says in his book *Divorce Is Not the Answer,* problems are like goldfish: the more you feed them, the bigger they get.

If you can't "solve" your problems, you will become discouraged; and you will believe that, since you can't solve your problems, you can't be happy. A better plan is to focus on what you want from your marriage, paying most attention to the strong parts of it, putting your efforts into creating happiness rather than diminishing unhappiness. The truth is, the happy get happier because they know how to be happy; the troubled get more troubled because they pour all their life energy into their troubles.

To begin to reverse this cycle, you need to *believe* that you can be happy—even if you can't solve your problems.

Behavioral science has shown that you will always behave in a manner consistent with what you believe. Remember the teacher who was told her children were "slow learners," even though they tested average or above average? They performed poorly only because they and their teacher *believed* they were slow. Breaking the four-minute mile was considered impossible until one runner accomplished this feat. Then, many runners were able to do it. Beliefs are powerful. They determine virtually everything about our lives. Whatever you believe, you will manifest, because you are viewing the world through the filter of your beliefs. Those beliefs determine how you experience the world, how you feel, and what you do.

If you believe you have to solve all your problems before you can be happy, that will be true for you. But if you can make an inner shift, adopt a different "mind-set"—believing that first you can learn to be happy together and later you can work on certain problems—transforming your marriage becomes a whole lot easier. You don't have to convince your partner to believe something different. All you have to do is change your own belief about your marriage.

This chapter will help you do exactly that.

The difference between couples who thrive and couples who don't is not that the couples who thrive don't have problems. They have incompatibilities, conflicts, annoying habits, personal weaknesses just like all the rest of us. The difference is, thriving couples begin with a desire to be happy together, a belief that they *will* be happy together, and a commitment to staying close through adversities. They begin with a picture of themselves as a happy couple, and they actively nurture that picture. You can do the same.

Let's use a metaphor. Jane wants to go to Hawaii, but she has been unable to save up the money to do it. One friend suggests that she design a strict budget, pay all her bills on time to save interest payments, and start a fixed savings plan so that next year she can have her trip. Jane goes away discouraged and angry at her circumstances. She tries to save but feels so discouraged that she has little success.

Then she solicits a second opinion. This friend suggests that she borrow the money to go on the trip and shows her how to manage when she comes home so that she can pay off the debt in a timely way with little pain. Jane feels excited and energized, and goes home and starts to pack. She has a fabulous time in Hawaii, and when she returns, is highly motivated to pay off the debt.

Whatever your financial philosophy is, I recommend the second approach for your relationship. Focus directly on creating good feelings between you. After you create some happiness and fun, you will view your problems in a whole new light, you will have more energy and motivation to solve them, and you will have created a safe, loving environment in which to work on them. You may even find that some of them simply disappear.

After all, your goal in your relationship is not to get more help with housework, to spend your money the way you want to, to be on time to dinner parties, to be able to watch TV without being pestered, or whatever you feel your problem is. Your goal is to feel close, to enjoy each other's company, to experience pleasure, and to feel mutually supportive. It makes sense to focus on your true goals, and not forever on your lesser ones.

Before we look more specifically at how you can create happiness, let me assure you, I am going to provide you with very specific solutions to problems. In both this chapter, on how to create a happy atmosphere in your marriage even before you have solved all your problems, and in the next chapter, which contains solutions to specific problems, I will offer you, as promised, direct actions you can take after you have charged or discharged angry feelings, relaxed your anger, and looked at both sides of your situation, the first three steps of ERAP.

These actions are different from the ones we usually associate with "improving your relationship." They do not involve sitting down with your partner and "communicating." They do not involve agreements or contracts or exercises you do together. These are all actions you can take by yourself without even telling your spouse.

Writer Stephen Covey observed that most of us spend time on the activities in our lives that seem urgent—even if they are not important—and that the things that are truly important often get neglected because they don't seem urgent. It is never urgent to spend relaxing time with your spouse, to fix a meal together, or to take a walk. But these activities are far more important than certain phone calls or meetings, or many of the "urgent" activities that fill our calendars.

Here, then, are several "important" actions designed specifically to help you create a pleasant atmosphere in your marriage, to help you change your belief from "First we have to solve our problems; then we can be happy," to "First we need to feel happy; then we can solve our problems."

As George Pransky says in *Divorce Is Not the Answer,*

> If you have a sore on your arm, the last thing you should do is poke at it. Your doctor would treat the wound gently, creating the best possible healing environment. So-called relationship problems should be treated the same way.

This chapter will help you create the healing environment.

You may wish to read through all of the suggestions in this chapter first and then choose your favorite to start with. If you enjoy one, then try another. As you will see, the ideas reinforce each other. If you are using one action, the others will follow more easily.

1. "ACT AS IF" YOU ARE A LOVING SPOUSE

Remember the song from *The King and I?*

> *Whenever I feel afraid,*
> *I hold my head up high,*
> *And whistle a happy tune,*
> *And no one ever knows I'm afraid.*

The significant lyrics come later:

> *The result of this deception*
> *Is very strange to tell;*
> *For when I fool the people I fear,*
> ***I fool myself as well!***

That songwriter was decades ahead of his time! The strategy of changing your feelings by *acting the way you want to feel* is a fundamental principle of the new science called Neuro Linguistic Programming. To change your feelings or your "state," change your physiology. It's the same principle that is involved when you are feeling blue and you go for a run or take a bike ride, and afterward your mood has changed.

If you can "act as if" you love and adore your spouse and you are happy in your relationship, even if only for five minutes a day or two hours a week, you may be doing more to "solve your problems" than if you spent five hours "working things out" with your spouse. You can create the atmosphere and the feelings you want with your mate directly, rather than assuming that these feelings are the light at the end of a long tunnel of "hard work." If you start to behave as you would if you were happy, and make your body behave as you would if you were happy, your feelings will actually follow suit.

Let's look for a moment at the old model, the one most people assume they have to use—because they assume it is the only one.

When you aren't happy with your spouse, you may become engaged in a downward spiral. Your partner is not doing what you want or is behaving badly. Therefore you feel angry, resentful, and distant and behave accordingly. Since you are not feeling very loving, your partner picks this up and also becomes angry, resentful, and distant. The more distant your spouse becomes, the more justified you feel in remaining distant yourself.

But the thing about a spiral is, it's a circle. So it can start anywhere. You may feel this circle started with your spouse's behaving in certain ways you don't like. But it could just as easily have started at the point where you respond to these behaviors. And besides, no matter where it started, any place that you interrupt it and change the pattern, the downward spiral will end.

The way to interrupt a downward spiral is with new behavior. As we have said, you can't will your *feelings* to change, so experiment with changing your *behavior* even if you don't feel like it. That is the only way you can assure that something will change.

"Acting as if" is a critical skill for a happy marriage. You act as if, not as a deception, but as an experiment, a deliberate effort to change, and a gesture of good will. "Acting as if" is a simple, direct way to set change in motion. If you want to feel close, act as if you feel close, even if it is just for a moment. If you wish you were looking forward to seeing your partner at the end of the day, act as if you are happy to see him or her.

"Acting as if" opens up several possibilities. When you act as if you feel close, you may actually feel closer. In addition, when you behave in a loving way toward you spouse, your spouse may begin to feel different too, and to respond positively toward some of your new behaviors.

The thriving couples I interviewed used the "act as if" strategy without knowing it. For example, one man had a blow-up with his wife and stormed out of the house to go off to a meeting. Five minutes later, he pulled over to a public phone and called her. He said, "I'm still angry, but I love you and we will work this out." He "acted as if" he felt loving when he was actually feeling angry.

When John and Barbara left for a two-week vacation in Mexico, they had been spending almost no time together and weren't feeling very close. Barbara told me,

> At first I thought I should talk about it with John, see if he felt the same way I did, if anything in particular was bothering him. But it never seemed like the right moment, and I kept putting it off. Then I remembered "act as if." Right away, it was a huge relief. I started to relax and focus on having a good time. Over dinner, instead of bringing up my cool feelings, I talked about our plans for the next day and how beautiful the shore birds were. I was amazed at how well this worked. I gradually started enjoying his company and feeling very loving toward him. By the second week, we were feeling as close as ever and having a wonderful time. There was nothing to "discuss." The distance was gone.

Another workshop participant, Charlene, told me this:

> "Acting as if" works well for me with sex. Often when Michael wants to make love, I don't feel in the mood. I used to say no a lot, and he'd be upset and it would become a big deal. Now, I "act as if" I'm in the mood, and it doesn't take long for me to be in the mood. I "act as if" in a spirit of good will toward Michael, because I really do want to give him what he wants. Now that I know it works, it's not hard to do. Michael is so happy about the change—and so am I!

Jerry also had a revelation about his sex life when he began to "act as if":

> After Sue and I had been married a couple of years, it began to sink in that she is not the super-sexy lover I first thought she was. I felt disappointed, but talking with her about it only made her feel bad. I was skeptical, but as an experiment I tried to act as I would if she were the sexy lover I imagined. It was actually quite amazing. She loved the change in me and responded accordingly. Now, I love our sex life. It's right for who we really are, and not some fantasy I had in my head. I really see now that doing an experiment is a lot different from thinking about doing one. I was genuinely surprised by these results.

"Acting as if" can work very well applied to your own moods, too. June told me this:

> When I'm having a down day or feeling out of sorts with Dan, I just go ahead behaving as though I feel fine. I don't give in to the blue mood, and very often, I find myself feeling just fine again after a few hours.
>
> It's funny. I feel like I spent the last two decades learning the opposite: Be honest about how you feel. Go deep into your feelings. What I see now is, that may be appropriate for therapy, but not for everyday life. "Acting as if" isn't being dishonest with myself; it's just making a different choice about what to do with what I feel. I like it much better.

Try directly creating the feeling you wish you had in your relationship. What a novel concept! Ask yourself, "How would I behave if I were a loving spouse?" You might do favors for your partner. You might greet him or her enthusiastically when you come together at the end of the work day. Maybe you'd fix your partner a drink and suggest a little cocktail hour. You could bring home a book you know he would enjoy, or graciously give her the quiet time you know she craves.

Here are some ideas to get you started with "acting as if" you already feel the way you truly want to feel. Let them stimulate your own creativity.

Try giving to your mate the very things you would most like to be receiving back. The strategy works because, at some level, you will be creating what you want. Also, it could happen that your partner will eventually pick up on the behavior you are modeling.

As one workshop participant told us after two weeks of experimenting with "acting as if," "It's so easy to get affection; just give it."

Another woman, Emily, told me she loves to receive flowers or other little gifts spontaneously, not just at Christmas and her birthday. She mentioned this to her partner, but nothing happened. Meantime, she brought home thoughtful little items and funny gifts from time to time herself. One day she came home to discover a beautiful pair of skis with a bow on them in her living room. She was thrilled. Her partner got the picture!

What do you wish you could do with your partner? Don't wait. Do it now. Do you wish she would tease you in a loving way? Tease her. Do you wish he would demonstrate his love for you in concrete ways? You demonstrate yours in concrete ways. Do you wish he would be considerate of your needs? Be considerate of his, even if they are very different from your own.

Build on your partner's particular strength. For example, Andrea's husband, Ted, is a wonderful storyteller. He is a police officer, and whenever they get together with friends or family, everyone greatly enjoys his stories about everything from the politics in the department to the incidents he has been a part of. So when Andrea wanted to "act like a loving wife," she asked what had gone on at the station that week. Ted loved that his wife appreciated his stories.

Keep track of the nice things your partner does for you and mention them later. When I ask workshop participants to write down everything their spouse does for them in a day, they are often quite surprised at how long the list is.

"And don't kiss it off because it isn't perfect," one woman told us. "He brought home milk but it wasn't skim, and I got mad. I could have been appreciative that he brought home milk!"

How long have you been waiting for your feelings toward your spouse to change, hoping that something would happen to make a difference?

Don't wait anymore. You can *help* your feelings to change, and start an upward spiral that can keep going up and up—just by acting as you would act if you were a totally adoring, loving spouse. Give it a try.

Do not be discouraged if your feelings or your mate's responses don't change quickly and dramatically. Patiently proceed with acting like a loving spouse on a regular basis. If you find this difficult because you are full of negative feelings toward your spouse, begin on a very small basis. Act like a loving spouse for just five minutes each day. Or for just a half day a week. Increase the amount of time as you feel comfortable with it.

Inner voices will try to sabotage you. Expect this: "My partner doesn't deserve this loving behavior. This is too one-sided. I shouldn't have to bring her flowers. She should know I love her. I shouldn't have to iron his shirts. He should iron his own." Try to let these inner voices pass in and out of your head, and "act as if" anyway. As Dan Millman observes in *The Way of the Peaceful Warrior,* "Old urges will continue to arise, perhaps for years. Urges do not matter, actions do."

Actions matter. When you are trying to create a happy, safe, comfortable atmosphere in your marriage, actions are what will make this happen. Create the atmosphere you want first. Only then will trust and respect have a chance to grow. Problems will be far easier to handle later on.

EXPERIMENT #8

"Act As If" You Are a Loving Spouse

1. In your journal, write a fantasy of how your partner would behave if he or she fulfilled your every fantasy.
2. If your spouse were that way, how would you behave? See if you can get into feeling grateful, appreciative, even lucky to be with this person. Close your eyes and get into this fantasy for a time. See if you can actually feel some of these warm feelings in your body.
3. Continue your fantasy by imagining some actions or behaviors you would take if you felt this way. How would you demonstrate your appreciation to your spouse? How would you support him or her? Don't go to Hollywood movies or romance novels for your actions. What would *you* do if you felt truly loving toward your spouse? Write down several actions you might take.
4. Now choose one action and carry it out. It might just be an attitude you will have when you next see your spouse. Choose a specific time and a specific length of time. It could be five minutes, half a day, or a full week. Whatever suits you.

In order to learn from an experiment, you have to observe the results carefully. So pay close attention as you do the experiment to how it is making you feel. You may resist carrying out your planned experiment. Your spouse may start behaving differently. You may start to feel different yourself. As you notice changes in yourself and your spouse, make notes in your journal. Maybe you feel resentment, maybe delight. Or anything in between. Remember, with an experiment, you can never fail, only learn.

2. THINK "GOOD WILL"

In interviewing couples for *Eight Essential Traits of Couples Who Thrive,* I discovered one major trait that separated couples who thrive from couples who don't. It wasn't communication. The best communication skills in the world won't help you if you have nothing wonderful or special to communicate. It wasn't the absence of problems and challenges in their marriage.

It was good will.

Couples who thrive exhibit a fundamental good will toward each other. They want the best for each other. Even in conflicts, they don't feel like adversaries but like allies, striving to maintain trust and safety within the bounds of their twosome.

Their good will toward each other underlies and supports everything they do. Good will means paying attention to the positive aspects of each other and minimizing the qualities they care less for. Couples who thrive tolerate and accept what they wish were different, rather than focusing on it. They fundamentally trust and respect each other. They are grateful for their relationship, and treat each other with a spirit of generosity and openness.

Good will means making your love active, not passive. It means taking the initiative to act on your loving feelings, not just to feel them. Henry Borys discusses active love in *The Way of Marriage,* excerpts from his own journal:

> Looking back over the years together, I can see that my love for Susan has been far too passive. How many times have I felt a moment of appreciation or love and let it pass by unnoticed? . . .
>
> What good is my love if it stays in my heart, hidden from the

world and from Susan? Love can be an action as simple as doing the vacuuming, surprising Susan with flowers, making dinner for her, or giving her an unexpected hug. Love can even be as simple as giving Susan more attention than I give to the TV. Yet if I fail to make these simple gestures, if I fail to act on my love, then no matter how much love I feel, my relationship with Susan will not be one of love, but one of neglect.

Love means action, because when we fail to act on our love, our love soon fades into familiarity.

"But what if I'm the only one with good will?" you may ask. "What if I develop it, but I don't feel any coming from my partner?"

Good will begets good will, but someone has to start. If you begin exhibiting good will toward your partner and moving directly toward happiness, following the suggestions in this chapter, and you get no response at all from your partner, this will be useful information for you when we evaluate your relationship in the last chapter of this book. But no response at all is extremely unlikely. Good will is highly contagious.

Because good will is such a predominant distinguishing characteristic of thriving couples, I believe the cultivation of good will is the most direct route to turning a lagging relationship around. If you just begin *thinking* good will, positive actions will occur to you; but without good will, even the best of intentions are likely to fall flat.

In addition to appointing you VP of Relationship Quality, I hereby appoint you the Ambassador of Good Will.

EXPERIMENT #9

Think "Good Will"

Complete this sentence in as many different ways as occur to you: "If I had good will toward my spouse, I would ______."

See if you actually want to carry out any of the suggestions that occur to you.

3. FOCUS ON POSITIVE QUALITIES

What do you like about your partner? What do you like about your relationship? What do you like about yourself in this relationship?

What would happen if you forgot all about the things you have been trying to change or to put up with, the things you wish were different, and you focused all your attention on what you love about your partner? What would happen if you started to look for evidence that your mate loves you, instead of always focusing on any evidence that your mate doesn't love you?

What will most likely happen is that you will start an upward spiral.

When you pay attention to what makes you happy, you will enjoy yourself more and feel better. When you enjoy yourself more, you will be more attractive and more fun to be with. When you are more fun to be with, your spouse will find you more appealing and will start to feel good also. When your spouse starts to feel good, you'll feel better.

This is so much better than focusing on your problems, getting nowhere with them, and feeling worse and worse.

Focusing on the positive qualities in yourself, your partner, and your relationship means that you will need to put your negative thoughts and feelings on the shelf for a while. Don't talk about them. Talking about them often only escalates them anyway. When you find yourself thinking about problems, gently encourage yourself to think about something positive instead. It is difficult to make yourself stop thinking about something; what is far more successful is to replace a negative thought with a positive one.

To illustrate the effectiveness of moving past your problems and focusing directly on good will and the positive qualities in your relationship, I want to tell you the story of a man who was already very happy with his marriage when he tried this, and the story of a woman who was on the verge of divorce when she tried it.

Doug and Elaine met and married in a whirlwind of bliss when Doug was forty-three and Elaine, thirty-four. In his earlier years, Doug had inherited a business from his father and always had plenty of money, so he had spent many years dating glamorous women whom he would fly to Mazatlán in his private plane. He had fancy cars and memberships in all the right international social clubs. Around age forty, he began having a serious crisis of spirit. Over a period of months, he saw the meaninglessness of his lifestyle and determined to change it. Over the next several years, he sold his business, which catered only to the rich and glamorous, and started a socially responsible business. He unloaded his fancy trimmings, bought a modest home, and joined a spiritual group that nurtured his new beliefs.

Now he knew that he wanted to be a part of a long-term relationship with a woman who shared his new values. It didn't take him long to meet Elaine, a therapist who was passionate about her work and deeply engaged with her clients. She was so used to independence, Doug had to be patient while she decided it was okay for her to marry at all. But his patience was rewarded and they were married in a lovely, large wedding with all their friends and family greatly relieved that they had found each other.

Now, six years into the marriage, Doug was still in love, but he was annoyed by certain qualities in Elaine. For example, he liked to talk and socialize. But Elaine was very happy in her own little world, and could go for hours—even driving somewhere in the car together—without saying a word. Also, she wasn't especially affectionate and didn't fawn over him the way his women had for years before. He began to feel he was missing something important. When he tried to talk with Elaine about these things, she felt criticized and threatened, for she knew she could not transform herself into something she wasn't. So the tension between them had begun to escalate.

When Doug came to me, he told me all he had tried in his attempt to persuade Elaine to come his way fifty percent. The more he tried, the more discouraged he became. As he spoke, I got the vision of someone watching a spectacular sunset with an ugly telephone pole marring one corner of it. But instead of taking in the beauty of the sunset, this person was looking at the telephone pole and thinking, "If only that ugly telephone pole weren't there!"

Doug was making it hard for Elaine to be loving to him, because he was criticizing her all the time and implying that she wasn't good enough the way she was.

I suggested to Doug that for two weeks he say nothing to Elaine except positive, loving comments. I asked him to make a list of all the qualities he liked in her, and to mention all of them over the course of two weeks. "Every time you have a negative thought, replace it with a positive one," I told him.

At the end of two weeks, I saw him again, and this is what he told me.

> I'm relieved. I now see that I was creating the problems. I am married to a remarkable woman, and I love the life we have created together. I feel like a fool for being so negative with her, for

> looking only at the little things I wasn't getting instead of the big things I was getting. All we needed was a happier atmosphere around the house. Elaine has the brightest, happiest disposition of anyone I ever met. And I was dampening her spirits! Maybe there are a few things I wish were a little different about her. But if I were married to someone who was affectionate, she'd probably be moody or something—which Elaine is not. At the beginning of every day now, I count my blessings. It's a great exercise. It affects my whole day.

Margaret and Mitch were at a low point in their relationship. For three years, Mitch had been extremely unhappy in his work situation but, for a variety of reasons, had been unable to make any changes. An old friend wanted to start a new business with him. Margaret thought this would be a fine idea, but Mitch couldn't bring himself to do it. He was feeling awful about himself, and this made him very hard to live with. Margaret felt the confident man she had married was now possessed by an alien spirit. She had tried commiserating with him, cheering him up, ignoring him—nothing brought him back to his old self. The house was a glum place. Margaret and Mitch were barely talking to each other anymore, and Margaret was seriously thinking that she couldn't go on living this way. She wanted out.

One evening, they were lying in bed reading, when one of their two daughters came in crying, saying she had had a bad dream. They took her into their bed and she snuggled up to Mitch and fell asleep. Suddenly Margaret turned to him and said, "You are such a wonderful father. The girls are lucky to have you." Then, she was stunned to realize it was probably the first positive words she had said to her husband in at least a month. He turned to her and smiled. As she was going to sleep, her realization sank in deeper, and she determined to build on it. The next morning, she fixed Mitch breakfast (which she had stopped doing), and told him how grateful she was for all the gardening he did and how lovely their yard looked. He kissed her good-bye before leaving!

Now, Margaret doubled her efforts. She found lots of ways to thank Mitch, to praise and compliment him, and to show her love. She began to feel hopeful and positive herself, and she was amazed at the transformation in Mitch. He seemed to be waking up. Margaret didn't comment on the changes; she felt they were too fragile. But she was feeling buoyant.

Exactly one week after the bad dream incident, Mitch came home and announced that he had called his old friend and that they were meeting to discuss the idea of the new business.

This was over three years ago. Mitch and his friend have gone into business together and are doing well. And Margaret and Mitch are back to their old selves and feeling very lucky to be together.

EXPERIMENT #10

Focusing on Positive Qualities

1. Make an agreement with yourself that for two full weeks, you will not mention anything negative, anything that you see as a problem within your relationship. Especially directly to your spouse, you will make only bright, positive comments. For two weeks, put all your problems on a shelf, out of the way. You can always come back to them later.

2. In your journal, make a list of all the qualities you like in your spouse and in your relationship. If you find it helpful, at the top of the list, write, "I feel lucky because . . ."

3. Deliberately mention at least one of these qualities to your spouse every day for the next two weeks in the form of thanks, praise, a compliment. Or you could begin a sentence with, "Isn't it nice that . . ." Or, "I feel lucky that . . ."

4. Every time a negative thought or a problem comes into your head, deliberately start thinking about a positive quality in your relationship instead. Don't be hard on yourself if the negative thoughts persist. Just keep gently replacing them with positive thoughts.

4. CHANGE "INCOMPATIBLE" TO "COMPLEMENTARY"

For over twelve years, I conducted workshops for single men and women who were looking for love, and for twelve years, I saw them all make the same mistake. I was amused to see a different form of the same mistake turn up in couples workshops.

In singles workshops, I asked singles to list the qualities they were looking for in a mate. Inevitably, they would write good listener, sense of humor, considerate, generous, attractive, and so on. Men wrote "slender." Women wrote "financially secure."

Then I asked them to distinguish between essential and desirable qualities, and to choose their top five essentials.

Almost never did I hear on these essentials lists the primary quality I think these singles should be seeking, namely, "I want to be with someone who is wildly enthusiastic about me and wants to be with me." For if you find a person who is perfection itself with regard to all the "checklist" qualities, but that person doesn't want to be with you, you just end up with a bigger heartache.

I see couples focusing their attention on the same irrelevant checklists. "If only my wife were more interested in my business." "If only my husband danced or played tennis." "We don't have very much in common," I hear people observe, as though this were a death knell.

My father used to joke with people that he wanted only two things in a wife: a bridge master and a pianist. My mother plays passable bridge and never went near a piano. My dad's comment was never taken as belittling my mother or complaining, because it is obvious to all how much he adores her. His tone conveyed his meaning. He was saying, "I got so much more in my wonderful wife that these two deficits pale into insignificance. How could I ever have thought they would be important?"

Like father, like daughter. I had only two criteria when *I* was looking for a mate. I wanted a great dancer and someone with a fine singing voice. Mayer dances passably when he has to, and almost never sings. But I wouldn't trade Mayer for a hundred Arthur Murrays or a thousand Kris Kristoffersons.

"Not having things in common" or "being incompatible" is a *symptom* of a lack of closeness, not a cause of it.

What most people really want in their relationship is to feel close, to be friends, to be allies. If you focus on your closeness, you will be able to manage your differences. If you focus on your differences, you will lose your closeness—and then wonder where it went.

When you pay attention to and nurture your closeness, differences become something you appreciate and manage. For example, when you are feeling close, if one of you likes to save money and the other spend, you will be able to see the balance this brings to your family and be grateful that you have complementary attributes. If you experience tension over whether to spend money or not, your little "fight" will remind you of how peaceful your relationship is in general; and when you resolve the tension, you will be all the more grateful for each other and the closeness you share. When you have good will toward each other, it supersedes your differences.

Think of an "incompatibility" in your relationship. What happens if you suddenly relabel it as an area in which you are "complementary"? The word "complementary" comes from the word "complete." Is there a way in which your mate and you, because of your differences, make a complete unit?

My mother got to hear about my father's duplicate bridge tournaments and celebrate with him when he won. It was a whole world she wouldn't have known otherwise. When I go folk dancing, Mayer finds something else to do, because he knows how important dancing is to me. We manage our difference. One of you is a stay-at-home, the other likes to travel. Fabulous. You can broaden and enrich each other. One of you can travel more than you would have on your own. The other can learn the simple pleasures of nesting and quiet evenings at home. If you want to be together and you already feel close, you will find ways to make these adaptations for each other.

What is the difference between being incompatible and being complementary?

Good will.

The difference is the attitude you start with. If you begin with positive feelings and a desire to have a warm relationship, you will accommodate your differences and joke about them. If you don't have good will and a spirit of cooperation, differences can become enormous "problems" for you.

Another positive approach you can take to the "incompatibilities" or "nothing in common" issue is to work on actively creating something you do have in common. Maybe there is something you did together when you first met that you could revive, like dancing, playing tennis, or going out for breakfast. Or think of something your mate *might* get behind, and try it once. One woman had an old cribbage board that had been collecting dust for years. She got a book from the library on how to play cribbage and invited her hubby to try it one night. Now they play every chance they get, and even have a little two-person tournament going.

Another woman bought a bird book just so she could start identifying the birds in her own back yard. Gradually, her husband became interested also, and they decided to go on a bird walk. Now, they are enthusiastic bird watchers.

Developing a hobby or interest together might take a while, and you may have to try several ideas, but at least realize that "having little in common" may be a phase, and that maybe you can move beyond it—especially if you take some initiative on your own!

According to psychologist George Pransky, "It is the thought of incompatibility that creates the feeling of incompatibility." He points out that the same trait can be viewed as positive or negative, depending upon the "predisposition" from which it is viewed. For example, a person who readily offers comments might be viewed as "opinionated" by a spouse with a negative predisposition, or as "articulate, outspoken, and passionate" by a spouse with good will. Or a person who tends to notice the positive side of life might be viewed as "unrealistic" by an unsupportive spouse or as "optimistic" by a spouse who starts out with love and good will.

EXPERIMENT #11

Change "Incompatible" to "Complementary"

1. In your journal, make a list of what you have thought were incompatibilities between you and your mate. If "we don't have much in common" is something you say about yourselves, list your interests and your mate's separately.

2. Even if you don't feel a lot of good will at the moment, "act as if" you do for a few minutes. First write, "If I felt close and loving, . . ." Then go back over your lists and write down what you would do about this difference if you felt close (or how you do manage it if you do feel close). For example, if you wrote, "______ likes bowling and I don't," you might write, "If I felt close and loving, I would go watch the bowling occasionally." If you wrote, "______ likes rock music and I like classical," you might write, "If I felt close and loving, I would surprise ______ with tickets to a rock concert."

3. Start a list in your journal of activities or interests that you would enjoy and that you think your partner *might* enjoy. When you get a chance, invite your mate to join you in doing one of them. If it doesn't work out, try another idea on your list. Give this project some time to work itself out.

"Yesterday's refreshing differences become today's incompatibilities," Pransky says. It's all in your attitude. Think good will!

5. CREATE RELAXING TIME TOGETHER

If the most outstanding common thread among the thriving couples I interviewed was that they all operated out of a fundamental good will toward each other, the second significant theme among them was that they spent relaxing time together as often as they could.

It is virtually impossible to build and sustain a close, intimate relationship if you never spend quality time together. On the other hand, when you are feeling your love for each other and enjoying each other's company, the more time you spend together, the better it gets.

For many couples, planning good time together is an enormous challenge because of scheduling alone. If you have two jobs and children, you may barely see each other all week as it is.

Spending relaxing fun time together may not feel urgent, but it is probably more important for yourselves and your children than virtually anything else you do. If you can chalk up hours of good time together when you are not preoccupied with problems, your problems will be easier to deal with when they do emerge.

During the year I was so occupied with the presidency of my professional association, Mayer keenly felt the diminished amount of time we had together. He missed me, and, though he knew it wasn't rational, he slowly began to worry that I was going to disappear, that I valued my obligations more than I valued him. Gradually, he began to protect himself by distancing himself even more from me. This was subtle, and he didn't realize what he had done until after the year was over and we were back to a more normal routine. But it was an interesting lesson for us. I would have thought that when we had less time together, the quality of the time we did have would be all the better because we would be so happy to have it. But the opposite turned out to be the case: The less time we spent together, the harder it was for us to reconnect.

See if you can find a way for the two of you to get a little cozy time every day. It might be a phone call in the late afternoon. It might be a little snack before bed. One man told me he goes past a farmers market on the way home from work and keeps excellent fresh fruits on hand. Every night before they go upstairs, he cuts up a delicious apple, or an orange or melon. His wife enjoys this, and it gives them a relaxed moment together every evening.

If you can't get "cozy time" every day, find a time every week when you can settle in with each other a bit. As the Ambassador of Good Will, consider this your job. Your spouse may not even notice that you are creating special time, but this will almost certainly begin to create—at least in little spurts—the kind of atmosphere you long for.

An Ambassador of Good Will in one of my workshops arranged for a baby-sitter and, unbeknown to him, switched her husband's work schedule around so that she could take him to a fancy hotel for an overnight. He loved the surprise, and she accomplished what she had been waiting and hoping for: a time when they could relax and just have fun.

Ken realized that one of the things he and Shelley enjoyed about vacations was endless hours to play Scrabble. So he initiated a weekly Scrabble date on Thursday evenings that has now become sacred for them. All week they look forward to their "date" on Thursdays.

EXPERIMENT #12

Creating Time Together

1. Think of a time in your day or week when you can unobtrusively create a little "cozy time" for the two of you. You don't have to announce what you are doing; just do it.

2. In your journal, create a section entitled "Ideas for Time Together." List ideas for weekend outings; vacations; evening activities; dates; daily, weekly, or monthly rituals; ideas for holiday celebrations; or anything else that you would like to do sometime to have a pleasurable time with your mate. Whenever you think up a new idea, now you have a place to record it. You can view the list as goals you have for the two of you, as the VP in charge of Relationship Quality.

6. SEVEN STEPS TO BRING THE TWO OF YOU TOGETHER

Now let's get even more specific.

What we have discussed so far are principles or attitudes:

- "act as if" you are a loving spouse
- think good will
- focus on positive qualities
- change "incompatible" to "complementary"
- make "cozy time" a priority

If you understand and believe in these ideas, you can put them all to work in the following Seven Steps to Bring the Two of You Together. These seven steps are adapted from the program, "Seven Steps to a More Passionate Relationship" developed by Barbara and Michael Jonas, who have been married for over thirty-two years, are creators of romantic games (including *An Enchanting Evening®* and *Romantic Sensations®*), and are authors of *The Book of Love, Laughter, and Romance.*

I recommend that you view this as a systematic "program" to bring the two of you closer. Make a deliberate plan to do all the steps, in order, over a period of two weeks or so.

Do not wait until you have resolved all your conflicts or solved all your problems. This program will create the atmosphere you want in your marriage so that you can then work on your problems if you still want to.

Step One: Find an imaginative way to say "I love you."

Dena told me that her husband is a writer who works at home and drinks lots of coffee. One morning before she trundled off to work, she left a little "I love you" note on his coffeepot.

Several days later, he was to pick up a new bike for her on his way home from work. They live on the fifth floor, and he would be unable to leave the bike unattended while he came up to get her, so he told her to watch for him out the window. At the appointed time, he drove up with a huge bike-sized cardboard box strapped to the top of his car. Painted on the box in huge red letters were the words, "Dena, I love you!"

No one can help but be touched by finding an "I love you" note in an unexpected place. I've been known to leave them for Mayer under his covers if I'm going to be away overnight. You can leave one on your partner's voice mail or at work, on the dashboard of the car, on the toothpaste tube, in her purse or his briefcase, or even send one through the mail.

A simple little "I love you" note in an unexpected place can say so very much, no matter what kind of a mood you are in with each other at the time.

Step Two: Mail your partner a love letter.

Do whatever you need to get yourself in the mood to write a love letter. Pretend you and your partner have been separated for a month, and that you miss him or her terribly. Pretend it is your anniversary. Or pretend you are not yet married and you are trying to woo him or her.

Put yourself in a romantic environment. Maybe take a bubble bath first, or light a candle and put fresh flowers on the table or desk where you will write. Play romantic music.

Then sit down and write a love letter.

It doesn't have to be mushy or corny. And it doesn't have to be long, although it certainly can be if you get into it. Maybe it will be funny. Write it in your own style. Be sincere. Be yourself. Write from your heart.

This is not the time to dredge up all the rough spots you have been through. This letter is not about *all* your feelings, only your love and appreciation.

If a "formula" would be helpful, use this one (borrowed from an old boyfriend of mine who actually did this for me): Write "I love you because you are ______." Keep writing the sentence over and over, filling in with all the different qualities you appreciate. If you like, write each line in a different color. (That's what my boyfriend did.)

Do you have a favorite poet who expresses your sentiments? Include a sonnet from Shakespeare or a poem by Browning or Gibran. Or use the words from a favorite romantic song.

Here's a little outline for a love letter. Use it if it helps:

Why I love you.

Things I love about you.

Why I love our relationship.

How you make me feel.

What I want for you.

What I want for us.

What I want to give you.

Now, mail your letter. Would it be more fun for your mate to receive it at home or at work? If you like, you can arrange to have your love letter mailed from a romantic-sounding city or town. Just put your stamped, addressed envelope inside a second envelope addressed to the Postmaster of the town you choose. Attach a note requesting that your letter be hand-stamped and mailed.

Loveland, Colorado 80537

Loving, New Mexico 88256

Romance, West Virginia 25175

(My thanks for this tip go to Gregory Godek who wrote *1001 Ways to Be Romantic*.)

Here are some comments from workshop participants after writing and mailing their love letters.

I didn't even know that I loved my wife that much. I'm so grateful that I found out now.

I resisted this. But I'm so happy I did it. It tapped into feelings I didn't know I had.

My husband was so moved, he teared up. I've never seen him do that.

Now that I think about it, I just can't believe that I don't say all this stuff more often. What's the difference between love that never gets expressed and no love at all? I mean, I do show my love, but why not express it like this. We both loved it.

I wasn't sure before, but now I know there are more things I love about my wife than things I don't love.

I cried all the way through writing this. It was really hard for me, and I was afraid my husband would laugh at it. He was a little blown away when he got it. He kept asking me questions like, "Why did you do this?" But that night he gave me a huge hug—like he really meant it, and he thanked me.

Step Three: Give your partner a simple, unexpected gift.

Charley came to my workshop primarily because his wife was depressed and he was feeling helpless about it. She had enjoyed house plants before they met, but they had moved around so much, she had let them go. One day out of a clear blue sky, he brought her a large, full grape ivy plant. She was delighted by his thoughtfulness and genuinely appreciative. A week later, she asked if he would mind if she got a few more plants. When she went to the local nursery, she saw a help-wanted sign and ended up with a job there. It was the beginning of the end of her depression.

Your gift might be a book about your mate's hobby, a CD, a favorite food, tickets to a play or movie. Maybe it will be something funny. One woman whose husband is an antique dealer gave him a box of assorted junk from garage sales. Each piece was wrapped and accompanied by a certificate she had done up on her computer certifying the authenticity and explaining the use of each piece. She told me they laughed about it for weeks.

One woman who collects miniatures received a "miniature of the month" subscription from her husband. He had twelve miniatures all wrapped ahead of time, and the first of each month, she received an addition to her collection.

It doesn't matter so much what your little gift is. The unexpectedness of it and the thoughtfulness will work its magic. It is a great pleasure to give the perfect little gift, and a great pleasure to receive gifts. The only wonder is that we don't all do it more often!

Step Four: Do your partner a favor.

Take over one of your mate's household chores unexpectedly. Or pitch in and help him or her with a project. Actually give up some of your own time to make a loving gesture. It can be as simple as emptying the dishwasher or vacuuming. Wash his car, water her garden, offer to drive the children somewhere, or to spend the afternoon with them.

Anne and her husband, Roger, couldn't seem to stop bickering.

Every time they tried to talk about their bickering they would get to bickering about bickering! In the workshop, Anne kept telling us that she was sure their problem was minor and stress-related.

First, we told Anne to stop focusing on the problem. Then she started doing these Seven Steps to Bring the Two of You Together.

Roger was the secretary of his local political group and had to get a small newsletter out every two months. He loved designing it on his computer, but loathed the folding, labeling, and stamping. One Monday night he arrived home from work with the newsletters and announced he would get the mailing out Tuesday evening. But Tuesday afternoon, Anne commandeered a friend and completed the whole job. Roger was so elated—and *moved*—when he arrived home and saw the whole project done, that he took Anne to her favorite restaurant for dinner. The next morning, they were still in a romantic mood, so Roger decided to take the day off. They had a romantic, leisurely morning and then went to a museum show in the afternoon. Now, what they have come to call "mini-vacations," days off in the middle of the week when they just play, have become a habit for them. They do it six or eight times a year.

And they aren't bickering anymore.

Step Five: Plan an outing for just the two of you.

If you already drive a lot, go for a walk. If you already walk a lot, go for a drive or a bike ride. If you have time to make it a full day, take a picnic lunch. Make this a relaxing time with nothing particular scheduled. If the weather permits, plan your outing outdoors in a beautiful setting.

One woman told me that she and her husband had friends over for the evening, and they all decided to take a walk after dinner. It was so pleasant, she said to her husband, "Evenings are such a lovely time to be outdoors, and we so rarely come out after dinner. We could take a walk any evening. We don't have to wait until people come over." The next night, they took their twosome walk, and now they take a walk almost every evening after dinner. Sometimes, they even drive to different neighborhoods to walk. She told me, "The best part of it is that we talk casually, and subjects come up that we might otherwise never have talked about. I feel like I'm getting a lot more details about what goes on in his office, for example. It is a wonderful time for us."

Plan a casual outing, and invite your spouse to join you. If he or she doesn't want to or develops conflicting plans, let that be fine. Just plan another one and keep trying until you are successful.

Step Six: Plan a surprise "date."

Figure out something you know your partner would love to do and plan a whole evening as a surprise. Tell him or her ahead of time to save the date, but that the rest is a surprise. You can even deliver a written invitation to the surprise event.

Plan anything you think the two of you would enjoy. It could be a movie, play, or concert. It could be an evening with friends, a sports event, your partner's favorite game like bridge or bowling. This surprise should not be related to a birthday or holiday, just an out-of-the-blue surprise.

Many, many couples have had fun adventures with this activity. One woman planned a reunion for her husband with a college friend he had not seen for fifteen years. A man took his wife for a ride in a hot air balloon. I've heard about couples who have gone sailing, sky-diving, snorkeling, and skating. One woman took her husband to New York to visit Ellis Island where his grandmother had arrived in 1902. One man told me, "My wife made it easy for me. She's always saying, 'I've lived in New York for seventeen years, and I've still never been to the top of the Empire State Building!' " Guess where he took her!

Step Seven: Plan a full-blown romantic evening and surprise your partner with it.

Think about the good times you have had together, and try to recreate the feeling you had. Maybe you can't go to the Caribbean for a week just now, but you can conjure up the feeling you had there—even if you haven't yet resolved your dissatisfactions with each other.

Barbara Jonas (her real name) did exactly this with extraordinary results.

She and her husband, Michael, had a major argument over something they now feel was quite trivial, but they blew it way out of proportion. Michael left for a week-long business trip when both of them were still furious and hurt.

During the week (fortunately, she had a built-in "relaxing" period), Barbara said to herself, "This is stupid. I love Michael. I don't even want to get into this dumb fight when he comes home. I'm going to do something really special for him."

She sat down with a pen and a set of index cards and made up a game—sort of on the order of Monopoly, but all the cards and instructions were imaginative, funny, sensual, affectionate, or erotic activities for them to do with each other.

When Michael arrived home, he found a note on the door: "Please shower, shave, put on comfortable clothes, and meet me in the den at 7:30."

When Michael arrived in the den, he found romance itself: candles, flowers, champagne, finger foods like strawberries and chocolates, and a new CD of his favorite jazz group playing in the background. Barbara invited him to play her game. They completely forgot the fight—it never came up again—and had a delicious, funny, and romantic evening. By the end of it, they felt extremely close.

There is an epilogue to this story. Barbara put her game away, but several months later a friend asked if she could borrow it. Gradually other friends borrowed her index cards, and they all were excessively grateful. When one friend told Barbara, "We spent the most romantic night we have had in fifty-two years of marriage," Barbara and Michael decided they were on to something! They began to market the game, which they call "An Enchanting Evening," and have now sold more than 700,000 games. (Look for it in a game, gift, or lingerie store or department near you, or call 800/776-7662.)

Don't be timid about copying Barbara's idea! Remember, she didn't wait to solve her problem before she "acted like a loving spouse." Plan a romantic evening for your partner! Create whatever *your* version of a romantic evening would be, and surprise your spouse with it.

Remember, everything you try is an experiment. You want to have a good time, and you hope your activity will bring the two of you closer.

No matter how an experiment turns out, you can learn from it. Maybe some of these activities won't go well. Maybe you will feel worse after doing them. Your partner's response may not be what you hoped for or imagined. This is all valuable information for you. Whatever the outcome, you are still moving forward, because you are taking action, moving off dead center, expanding beyond the stalemate you have fallen into.

Especially if your experiments do not produce the results you hoped for, make notes in your journal. These notes will be useful when we evaluate everything at the end of the book.

Now that, all by yourself, you have created or begun to create a happy atmosphere in your home, we will discuss ways that you can make a direct assault on the problems in your relationship—all by yourself.

CHAPTER FIVE

Resolve Your Most Upsetting Problems —by Yourself

Now that you have taken your focus *off* of your problems and put it onto the pleasant, enjoyable aspects of your relationship, you have created an atmosphere that is conducive to effective problem solving.

Take a moment and imagine the worst problem in your relationship—*gone!* . . . What would your lives be like? Would you be happier?

Of course you would! That's the miracle of working on your relationship alone; you can feel better about yourself and your partner right away.

Note that none of the approaches in this new chapter has anything to do with "discussing" or expressing feelings. One of the most common traditional methods couples have used to solve problems is to discuss them. As often as not, these "discussions" turn into fights and cause both partners to become more entrenched and angry. The solutions in this chapter bypass all that frustration.

I need to warn you about one thing: To illustrate these strategies, I have selected stories of couples for whom the strategies *worked.* These are all true stories, but I don't intend to imply that each strategy *always* works like a dream. Of course I have also worked with individuals who didn't have spectacular results, but telling their stories wouldn't demonstrate these principles.

Sometimes these solutions will work beautifully for you. Sometimes the results will be a bit sloppy. Sometimes the whole thing will bomb. Remember to treat everything you do as an experiment. What you may learn from an experiment is that it doesn't work for you. So you have learned something valuable, and you are far better off than if you had never tried the experiment at all. But I'm willing to bet you will find ideas here that you haven't tried. If you *believe* that they have the possibility of working, and you have the courage and good will to implement them, you could see wonderful changes in the quality of your relationship.

There are eight specific approaches I present in this chapter. These are concrete actions you can take to solve the problems in your relationship:

1. Act On Your Own
2. Reverse Direction: Do the Opposite of What You Have Been Doing
3. Reframe the Power Struggle
4. Enlist Your Partner's Help in Solving *Your* Problem
5. Express Empathy for Your Partner's Position
6. Gracefully Accept What You Can't Change
7. Ask for What You Want
8A. For Men Only: Space In
8B. For Women Only: Stop Coaching

SOLVING RELATIONSHIP PROBLEMS BY YOURSELF: APPROACH #1

Act On Your Own

Marlene told me that buying a couch was a big turning point in her marriage.

"Carlos's sister had given us a couch for our family room when we moved. It was generous of her, but I hated the thing, and besides, it had a big hole in it. I kept telling Carlos we should buy a new one, but he said it was pointless and this couch was fine. I was feeling angry and powerless. A couch just wasn't a priority for him.

"One day it dawned on me that a new couch *was* a priority for me, so I went out and bought one. Carlos was always buying fishing and boat equipment without consulting me, so I didn't need his permission to do this!

"He was quite happy with the new couch, and he felt freer too, that I took charge of this situation. The incident was very enlightening for me."

Another example from my own marriage: Shortly after I married

Mayer, my high school reunion was taking place 2,000 miles away. Mayer insisted that we couldn't afford to fly me back there and went into elaborate rationalizations about now that we were married we had to make certain sacrifices. But I was crystal clear that missing this reunion was simply not an option for me. I told Mayer I was sorry he wasn't comfortable with it, bought my ticket, and went.

I wasn't oblivious to Mayer's concerns, but I weighed his discomfort against my disappointment if I missed my high school reunion, and the answer was clear. Mayer didn't like it, but when he saw he had no alternative, he was gracious.

In my workshops and interviews, I heard numerous examples of people solving problems by taking matters into their own hands.

Jill told me she was planning to attend a fancy craft fair. The entire week before, her husband kept telling her, "Now don't spend any money." Jill didn't argue with this, but she didn't agree to it either.

At the fair, she found an absolutely stunning handwoven coat that was perfect for her wardrobe. It was $510. Jill wasn't a frivolous spender, but she felt certain that this coat was a lifetime item, an entirely sensible purchase, and one that would give her a great deal of pleasure. She paid a third out of the checking account, a third on the credit card, and borrowed a third from her friend. She spared her husband the pain of having to swallow the idea of a $510 purchase, and she felt wonderful about her beautiful coat.

You Balance the Scales

Marriage is a process of negotiating over and over when to meet *your* needs at your partner's expense and when to meet *your partner's needs* at your expense. The giving and taking must be kept in approximate balance over a period of time.

Most people make the mistake of assuming that both partners have to cooperate to keep the scales balanced, that both partners have to do their share: "If I give a certain percentage of the time, my partner should give about the same amount." This is a huge mistake in any relationship, but especially when you have undertaken to work on the relationship by yourself since you have no control over how much your partner gives.

The secret to success is to be willing to take the responsibility yourself of keeping the giving and taking in balance. You make certain—not that you give a certain amount and your partner gives a certain amount—but that *you give* a certain amount and *you take* a certain amount.

If you are like most people, you imagine an invisible balance scale between you and your partner, and begin to feel cheated if you think you are giving more than you are receiving. Erase that picture. The balance scales that matter are not positioned between you and your partner; they are positioned entirely within you. The balance scale you should be watching is not how much am I giving and how much am I receiving from my partner: A far healthier balance to keep an eye on is how much am I giving and *how much am I taking care of my own needs.* You can balance the scales all by yourself—by acting on your own when you are certain you are doing the right thing for yourself, and then giving to your spouse when you know it will not be too great a sacrifice for you.

This shift—from hoping your partner will take care of your needs to being willing to take care of yourself—is at the very heart of working on your relationship by yourself. You can be the "big" person and be generous and giving often—*if* you have taken care of your own needs on issues of the greatest importance to you.

Acting on your own is deeply empowering, because it puts you completely in charge. You are not dependent on your partner to make you feel good about your life. Now, everything you receive from your partner is a delicious treat.

Don't expect your partner to take care of your needs. Instead, be certain that you meet your partner's needs often, so that when you feel a deep inner certainty about something you need for yourself, you can feel fine about doing it even if it makes your partner uncomfortable or unhappy.

A couple of guidelines for acting on your own:

1. Try to hold out for items that are truly "non-negotiable" for you when you act on your own. Don't act on your own when you feel ambivalence within yourself. If your partner is quite upset about what you did, he or she will be able to slay you with your own doubts.

When you feel uncertain yourself, that is the time to give in to your partner's clearer desires. Try not to feel resentful, because if you give often, you will find it easier to act on your own on the issues that are truly important to you.

2. A second guideline for balancing your own scales is this: When you decide to act on your own over the objection of your partner, always use both of these steps: First, express understanding of your mate's position; second, be clear that you will not be dissuaded from your own. In other words, be empathic and decisive. When you are empathic, you take care of your spouse to the best of your ability. When you are decisive, you take care of yourself.

For example, Jane's husband, Warren, wanted her to miss her women's group one week to attend a business dinner with him. It was a hard decision for Jane, but after weighing all the factors, she decided to go to her women's group. She told Warren, "I know this dinner means a lot to you and that you'd love to have me there. I agree it is important (Empathy). But because this is Laura's last time in the group, and also because I feel a big need to talk about something this week, I truly don't want to miss my women's group this time. I'm really sorry I won't be able to be at the dinner (Decisiveness)."

You can solve many of your relationship problems by acting on your own, by meeting your own needs and not waiting for your partner to meet them for you.

- If your husband hasn't gotten around to putting the screens up, hire someone to do it.
- When you want to invite friends over for dinner and your partner doesn't want to cook for them, bring the food yourself from a local restaurant.
- If your wife doesn't like to talk about movies after seeing them, invite a couple to join you when you see a movie.
- If your husband is withdrawn and preoccupied when he comes home at the end of the day, use that time to call a friend and share your day with her.
- If your partner doesn't like to go to the opera, get season tickets with a friend.
- If your wife is consistently late after promising to be ready on time, leave without her one time. See if she is ready the next time.
- If your husband won't do his share of the housework, stop doing his laundry and fixing his dinner.
- I once heard about a man who couldn't get his wife to stop picking lint off his suits. So he put a little thread on his lapel—that was attached to a spool of thread in his pocket. Everyone got a huge laugh when she tried to take that piece of lint off!

One woman I interviewed, Sydney, acted on her own on her anniversary, with delightful results.

Sydney and her husband, Larry, had recently moved. Since Larry had been out of town on a business trip all week, Sydney had done most of the unpacking, but there were still many boxes to go. To celebrate their anniversary, they had made reservations at a fancy restaurant, but by the end of the day, Sydney was exhausted. Also, she realized that a far greater gift to her than dinner out would be several hours of help with the unpacking.

She got out some paper and markers and made herself an anniversary card as though it were from Larry. Inside she wrote a loving note from Larry to her, which said in part, "Since I know that you would so much rather have help with the unpacking than go out to dinner, I have canceled our reservations and want to give you a whole evening of helping to set up our new home. Happy Anniversary!" Larry thought the card was very clever. He got the message, and he even felt off the hook for getting her a card or gift. He was grateful that Sydney had creatively acted on her own.

I heard about another woman who kept showing her husband a pin she adored in a jewelry store window. After Christmas and Valentine's Day both went by with no results, for her birthday, she bought the pin herself and put his name on the card. He paid the bill without a murmur.

Your Partner's Response

Of course, as you have already realized while reading this, when you act on your own, your partner will respond.

Amazingly often, your partner's response will be positive. Most people want to be married to a capable, independent, fully-functioning adult, and they will like the person they see taking charge. Your partner may be angry at first, but later may be grateful that you found a way to get your message across. You may be solving a problem that has been plaguing both of you and that your partner no longer has to worry about.

But sometimes, your partner will have difficulty with your newfound independence. Your solo actions signal a change in you that may make him or her uncomfortable or anxious. If your partner is used to having all the power in your relationship and to controlling everything, he or she could feel threatened.

Remember, you do not need to persuade your partner that you are right. If your partner gets angry or argues with you, don't argue back. Instead, be empathic and decisive. "I don't blame you for being upset. I can understand why you feel the way you do. But this is very, very important to me, and I am going to do it. I'm really sorry you don't like it, but I need to do it this way."

If you have a long-standing habit of acquiescing to your partner, and are upsetting a well-established pattern in your relationship by acting on your own, you may both feel confused and uneasy for a while. That's okay. Try very hard not to argue with your partner about this. You will help both of you move through this period of transition if you acknowledge the validity of your partner's point of view—but remain firm in your conviction and decisive in your actions. The secret to success in dealing with any negative reactions by your mate is always to be *both* empathic and decisive.

EXPERIMENT #13

Act On Your Own

Again look at your "master list" of problems in your marriage.

With regard to each one, list a few actions you could take that would solve this problem without the consent of your partner. How could you act on your own to solve each of your problems? Come up with as many solutions as possible.

One way to help yourself discover actions you might take on your own is to ask yourself what you would be doing if you were not married. The experiment on page 122 will stimulate your imagination.

As a result of that experiment, workshop participants have made changes in their lives ranging all the way from minor to major. One woman joined her church choir. Another formed a women's group. Yet another started having dinner with a friend one night a week. One man realized that if his wife were gone, he would have to have much more involvement with his children, and he took over some of the car pool responsibilities, including watching his daughter's ballet lesson every week.

One man I worked with, Gil, made an important breakthrough when he tried the experiment.

EXPERIMENT #14

What If You Were Alone?

Imagine it was suddenly necessary for your spouse to go overseas for two years. How would your life change? Assume you still will have the money your partner contributes, but that for some reason, you will be doing your whole life by yourself.

Write a paragraph or make a list of everything you would do differently.

Now go back over the list and see whether you could make any of the changes you have listed, but right away.

Gil's mother was a self-involved person who paid little attention to him, so he had learned to bury his needs rather than ask to have them fulfilled, and he believed that he could never get a woman's approval. Gil was married to a woman he could never please. He fixed the roof, and she complained that he didn't build the shelves she needed. He brought her flowers, and she complained he wouldn't spend more money on her. Gil felt frustrated, but could never quite experience that he had a right to his own feelings and behavior. He felt like a victim of her lack of approval.

Gil had a lot of work to do on himself to learn at a deep level that it was okay for him to have his own needs, but this experiment provided an important step. He realized that if he were not married, he would be able to live his life the way he wanted to live it, and he wouldn't have to worry about trying to please his wife. This insight gave him independence from her. He realized he would never be able to please her, and he *gave up trying!* Suddenly, his backbone became stronger. It was an important step for him in his journey to reach the feelings and needs that he had buried for so long.

Acting on your own is a powerful solution to a wide variety of problems. It allows you to balance the giving and taking in your relationship all by yourself.

SOLVING RELATIONSHIP PROBLEMS BY YOURSELF: APPROACH #2

Reverse Direction: Do the Opposite of What You Have Been Doing

The primary principle behind working on your relationship by yourself is that any given problem is not the fault of you or your spouse but of the interaction between you. So if you can figure out your role in the "dance" and change it, you can have a great impact on the problem. One way for you to change your role is to do the exact opposite of whatever you have been doing.

Sally was writing a novel. She and Ken agreed that they could live on his salary for a year while she explored her passion. But one year stretched into two. Ken was getting angry and anxious, but Sally just couldn't bring herself to go back to work, even part-time.

When Ken came to me, he felt completely "right" about his view of the problem. This problem was clearly Sally's fault. She had gone back on her agreement. She was refusing to do what she had promised and what the family needed her to do.

I first encouraged Ken to do the exercises in Chapter Three to discover what his role in the problem was. At the end of the exercise, he wrote this:

> My role in our relationship is to expect Sally to bring in her share of the income and to feel angry that she isn't.

I asked Ken, if you were going to do the exact opposite of this, what would it be? After some discussion, we agreed the opposite would be *not* to expect Sally to bring in her share of the income and *not* to feel angry about it.

Of course this was a hard shift for Ken to make in one minute. But he had to admit that if he could do it, the problem would completely disappear. Sally would certainly be happy, and if he could let go of his expectation, so would he. The "problem" wasn't Sally's decision; the problem was Ken's feeling about Sally's decision.

Since he couldn't adopt the opposite attitude instantly, I asked Ken instead to "act as if" he had made the shift. I asked him to act as he would if he were entirely happy with the situation as it was. For example, he might say to Sally, "Honey, I'm so happy I can give you this opportunity to fulfill your passion of writing. Isn't it wonderful that we can manage on my salary for a while? I really hope you are enjoying your writing and that you are successful with it soon."

I asked Ken to "act as if" for one full week, without telling Sally that he was doing an experiment. He agreed to try it.

The next time I saw him, this is what he told me:

> I ended up doing it for two weeks, because it took me a while to get into it, but once I did, I could see I was feeling different, so I decided to try it a while longer.
>
> One instant change is that Sally was so appreciative. She couldn't get over it. The tension between us started to melt, and we had a nice week. She cooked my favorite meal, which she hadn't for a while. I still thought the whole thing wasn't fair, but I was absolutely resolute not to talk about it and to try to pretend I didn't feel that way. But the pretend started to have an impact on me. I got his huge realization: we have a good friend who is putting her husband through law school, and this was no different.
>
> Then an amazing thing happened. One night at dinner, Sally brought up the subject of money all by herself. She told me she was tired of living with financial strain and saying no to everything we want. She said she felt like the end was in sight and that she was eager to go back to work and get more money in our lives. I was truly amazed. You could have pushed me over with a feather.

To be sure, this experiment doesn't always work so magically. Ken had lots of good will toward Sally, and felt ready to take a risk. These are prerequisites not all couples have. Still, this strategy of doing the opposite often does have a huge impact, even under less ideal circumstances.

Doing the opposite works because it shifts the roles the two of you have been automatically playing. When you do the opposite, you give your partner a chance to do the opposite too. Ken was so worried about money, Sally unconsciously figured that worrying-about-money was being handled in their family and she didn't need to feel her own worry-about-money. Only when Ken stopped playing that role did her own money worries have a chance to surface.

Watch how doing the opposite worked for another couple:

Brenda and Art had been living together for two years. Brenda felt the relationship was stalemating, that Art was losing interest in her. I asked her what she was doing about the problem.

"I've tried everything," she told me. "I've tried to get him to talk about it, but he's never in the mood to do that. What's hardest is times when we are both around the house. He just wants to busy himself, and it's like I'm not even there."

"What do you do at those times?" I asked her.

"I try to talk to him, start conversations. I put his favorite music on. I make him lunch. But it's hard, because I'm just not feeling good. I feel sad and—I guess rejected. I think, 'Why are we doing this?' Part of me wants to go back to living apart and just seeing each other for dates. Then I think I'd get his undivided attention when I am with him."

"What would be the opposite of what you do when you are around the house together?"

Brenda thought about it. "I suppose it would be to stop making any moves toward him at all, to go off and do my own thing."

I pressed her for more. "You said you feel bad when you are both around the house. What would the opposite of that be?"

"To feel good."

"Can you imagine that?"

Brenda thought some more. "Well, I do crave time alone for myself. I suppose if I thought of it as alone time for me, I could actually enjoy that."

"What do you do with your alone time whenever you do get it?"

"I write in my journal, play the piano, read, clean up the house, talk on the phone, bake—it doesn't matter, I just love times when I am alone in the house with no agenda."

We agreed that the opposite of trying to make contact with Art when they are home together would be to pretend Art isn't there, and to enjoy the time as though she had it to herself. Brenda agreed to try it. When she didn't feel good, she was supposed to "act as if" she did feel good. It was her behavior we were seeking to change in this experiment, not her feelings.

Brenda received support and encouragement every week from our workshop group. After a month, this was her report.

> I could do it sometimes and not others. I still found myself privately crying. But then I'd get my resolve up and try again. I decided to read a novel, and I really did enjoy having time to read that. If I fixed lunch, I'd just fix it for myself. Art was perfectly fine with that. He grazed in the kitchen too when he felt like it. Some of the time, I found I really was enjoying myself. Art was happy. The tension did seem to be less between us. And

we had some good times. We'd fix dinner together. We had friends over.

The hardest part was playing the piano with him there. Usually I do that only when I am alone, but then I decided, what the heck, that's what I want to do now so I'm going to do it.

That night at dinner, he told me that he loved hearing me play the piano. He said, "I feel you are sharing something very private with me." Then he said—now mind you, we hadn't discussed my "problem" with our being at home together for over a month—"I love being around the house with you here. It feels good to know you are around. This is so great. I love having you in my life." And he reached over and kissed me! It was an absolutely wonderful moment for me.

Brenda had been playing the role of making sure they felt together in the house. But her efforts were backfiring, making Art feel inadequate to meet her needs. When she stopped taking care of togetherness, it gave Art the opportunity to meet those needs in his own way.

Doing the opposite of whatever you have been doing with your spouse almost always feels like it will make the problem worse. Ken was afraid that if he stopped harping at Sally about making money, she would think she could go on writing forever. Brenda was afraid if she stopped pressuring Art to pay attention to her, he would lose interest altogether and move out. It always takes courage and a leap of faith to try the opposite.

Here are some of the "opposite strategies" that have amazed workshop participants.

- Gail became upset and angry with her husband when he was away from home and didn't call her. The next time, he was away four days before he called. But instead of being angry with him, she thanked him for calling. He called her the next two days in a row and, on his next trip, he called her three times in five days.
- Bob always created a scene when his wife came home from shopping for clothes. He felt she lost her rational mind when she went shopping and was completely unreasonable. The next time she came home from shopping, he asked to see her clothes, admired them, and told her he appreciates that she is such a fine dresser. After showing him all her purchases, she decided she had overdone it, and she returned an expensive suit.

- Joyce's husband was unemployed and appeared to be doing nothing about it. Every day Joyce gave him pep talks, suggested interviews for him, offered to help with his résumé. He kept thanking her for her help and concern but did nothing. Joyce abruptly stopped all her encouragement and coaching. Instead, she expressed hope that he was able to enjoy this unexpected period of relaxation and suggested that he might even be able to get in a bit more tennis. Within a couple of weeks, he had seven interviews lined up, and in six weeks he was employed.

EXPERIMENT #15

Try the Opposite of What You Usually Do

Think about how you respond when your partner does something you don't like. Then figure out what the opposite of that response would be.

This part of the exercise will require some careful thinking and planning. It is probably best to discuss it with your support person or a trusted friend who understands what you are trying to accomplish with this experiment.

It is important to commit your experiment to writing. In your journal, write down the problem you want to address and your usual behavior with regard to this problem. Now write down exactly what the opposite behavior would be. You may find it helpful to go through the exercises in Chapter Two to find out exactly what your role is and then see what the reverse would be. Remember, you are not expected to change your feelings in this experiment, only your behavior.

Now give yourself a time frame for this experiment. Usually two weeks to one month is enough time to see some changes in yourself or your partner.

As you do the experiment with your spouse, at the end of each day, or at least every few days, make notes in your journal about how you are doing and what you see happening.

Remember, you will almost certainly feel afraid of the consequences before you try this. Go ahead and try it anyway.

SOLVING RELATIONSHIP PROBLEMS BY YOURSELF: APPROACH #3

Reframe the Power Struggle

Many marital rough spots feel like a power struggle. That is, the real problem is not where we go on vacation or which school we choose for Susie, but rather, who is going to win. Who has the power? The way decisions get made in the family doesn't feel fair.

One way of reframing the power struggle for yourself we have already discussed: Don't focus on balancing the scales *between* you (When are you going to win and when is your partner going to win?); rather, focus on balancing the scales *within* you (When am I going to stand up for my own needs and when am I going to stand up for my partner's?). This strategy keeps your own inner power intact and still meets many of your partner's needs.

But let's look more closely at the "power struggle" in order to make the job of balancing your inner scales easier and to learn some additional tools.

When you get into a tug-of-war with your partner over something, that awful feeling of powerlessness and frustration may emerge: You feel as though you are in an arm wrestle, struggling to survive but being pushed almost beyond tolerance. The anger rises, and you find yourselves in opposite corners. The more you talk, or shout, the more you polarize your problem.

A black-and-white, either/or view of any problem is virtually always inaccurate, and always limits the possibilities for solutions and for personal growth. The secret to getting out of the trap is to depolarize, to find the third way out.

I remember a time years ago when I had come to the unhappy conclusion that I would either be thin and feel deprived and resentful all the time, or I would be overweight but enjoy eating. Both paths made me very unhappy, but I saw no alternatives. I felt doomed.

A friend recommended a book, and I remember thinking after I read it, "Never in my life have I spent a more life-changing two hours." Magically, amazingly, this book shattered my tidy polarization by presenting a *third* choice: I could eat whatever I wanted, as long as I was eating because I truly wanted that food, and not because I was tired or lonely, or because everyone else was eating too, or because it was time to eat. The foods had to "hum" like a tune I couldn't get out of my head, and not "beckon" like a bakery window or the smell of pizza, deliberately tempting me. I remember experiencing this insight as a true epiphany, dramatic and liberating.

But how do you get the liberating insight, the third alternative, if someone doesn't hand you a book at the right moment? How do you depolarize a relationship problem that seems to have only *two mutually exclusive* solutions?

Here's how: First, you create the conditions that will allow a third alternative to present itself. Then, you wait and listen.

Creating the conditions that will allow a third alternative to present itself involves two steps: (1) Develop empathy for the other point of view (as you have already been encouraged to do as a part of ERAP), and (2) relax the urgency about your own.

Taking the initiative to depolarize a conflict is not easy. But commensurate with its difficulty is its potential to expand and deepen you. Here you are, doing all the work again. But here you are reaping all the personal rewards too. Let's look at a few of them.

As you learn to move out of either/or thinking, your world will actually expand. As you see that more options present themselves, you will feel more confident, less at the mercy of the world and its restrictions.

You will be going a long way to build trust between you and your partner. For if you support your partner, your partner will trust you more and be more open to your view. Trust builds trust, but someone has to trust first. If you can take that risk, you will be creating a safe environment in which the two of you can come together more easily.

Let's now look more closely at the three steps to depolarize a conflict: Develop empathy, relax your urgency, and wait.

1. Develop Empathy for the Other Point of View

To develop empathy, answer these questions by either talking with a friend or writing in your journal:

a. What is your partner's position in this conflict?

State it as objectively as you can. Summarize your partner's arguments accurately and completely.

b. What in your partner's background or present life might have led him or her to this opinion?

Think of all you know about your partner's childhood and growing up, or about previous experiences that might be relevant to this conflict. Suppose your struggle is that you want to get new carpeting and your partner feels that would be an outrageous expense. Maybe his (let's say) childhood home didn't have carpeting. His family always worried about money and spent very little on their home. Or, your friends just got carpeting and it cost them almost twice what they anticipated.

List everything you can think of that is affecting your partner's position.

c. In what ways do you respect your partner for holding this opinion?

You are glad your partner stands up for himself as opposed to letting you make all the decisions and then being resentful. You are happy he keeps a close eye on money in general. Part of you finds his simple, unpretentious taste appealing.

d. Can you accept your partner's opinion even though you may not agree with it?

Think about this: In addition to wanting your own way in this conflict, you want your partner to accept you and your opinion. You want to be with someone who sees the world your way, someone to whom you don't have to explain your opinions and values. With the carpet example, you want him to accept you, even if you have this "harebrained" idea about the carpet. You want him to understand your point of view, and not to condemn you for having it. You don't want to be in conflict; you want to feel together. Underneath everything, you want to feel loved.

Always remember that the same thing is true for your partner. Can you see some validity in the opposite opinion, and accept that your partner is okay, even though he or she holds this other point of view?

2. Relax the Urgency About Your Own Position

Notice, you are not being asked to give up or to relax your *position,* not at all. Relaxing or letting go does not mean that you give up what you want; instead, it means you give up your *anxiety* about what you want.

In *The Seven Spiritual Laws of Success,* spiritual writer Deepak Chopra introduces The Law of Intention. Intention, Chopra says, is desire with no attachment to the outcome. You still have your intention, which is a powerful force, and you still have your desire. But you also trust that the best outcome will emerge on its own; it doesn't require you to force or manipulate it. Keep your strong intention, and relax.

The more you become attached to one outcome, the more you fear what will happen if you do not get it. Fear closes you down. When you are afraid, you become protective. You are less able to be open, to be flexible, to be creative. You help bring about a power struggle when you become certain that your own point of view is the *only* right one and you zealously cling to it.

To help you relax the urgency about your own point of view, again, talk with a friend or write in your journal. Ask yourself these questions:

With regard to the argument we are having, do I have my own inner conflict as well? Is there any part of my partner's position that I would like for myself?

Let me explain this question.

Usually a power struggle between two people reflects an inner struggle in one or both of the individuals. The conflict forces the ambivalent person to take an extreme position and to cover up the inner ambivalence.

For example, if you are always late and your partner is always on time, there is a part of you that would like to be more organized, less frenzied about time. But when your partner accuses you of being late, your natural reaction is to defend yourself. Your partner's accusations will be painful for you because they highlight areas of weakness you know you have. But when your partner is yelling at you, you don't feel at all like sharing this vulnerability. So you appear strong and clear—and may fool yourself in the process.

The more ambivalence you have within yourself, the more painful a power struggle will be for you, because it will highlight your own inner struggle.

Here's an issue that crops up periodically for Mayer and me. He loves relaxed evenings around home with the two of us and our sweet dog. So do I, but I also adore evenings with my women friends, lectures and bookstore readings, committee meetings, plays, concerts, and a million or so other critical events that I will die if I have to miss. When I book up every night of the week, Mayer feels abandoned and starts to complain. Then we have this emotion-filled dialogue in which I accuse him of trying to cut me off from the world and he accuses me of ignoring him. These quarrels are always painful for me because I am deeply divided within myself. Part of me longs for a quieter, more relaxed life, and loves how much he enjoys being home with me. But the other half is terrified of missing anything and has extreme difficulty saying no. I don't talk about these doubts when I am arguing with Mayer. Instead, I passionately defend my territory. "I want to do all these things. You don't appreciate how much I give up. I already miss almost everything. All these engagements are extremely important to me! I can't just stay home all the time."

That is why this question can be extremely enlightening, "Is there any part of my partner's position that I would like for myself?" I start to depolarize when I realize there is much about what Mayer wants that I also want for myself but have a much harder time achieving.

A second, very similar question may help you uncover your own struggle in a slightly different way:

On what parts of this conflict are we in agreement?

With regard to any power struggle, there will always be areas of agreement. Usually, you agree on the goal but disagree on the way to achieve the goal. You both want to have a fun vacation, but one of you wants to go to New England and the other, Florida. You both want your son to be healthy, but one of you thinks he should be forced to eat his vegetables and the other thinks he should be allowed to eat as he pleases. Mayer and I both want me to feel satisfied and us to have good times together. We only differ on how to achieve this.

Look for the parts of your conflict upon which you can agree.

3. Wait

Now you have done all you can, and you need to let nature take its course. Finding alternatives to your either/or conflict isn't automatic. You have to let them emerge. While you are waiting, you have to be willing to live temporarily in the realm of uncertainty, what Gestalt therapist Fritz Perls called, the "fertile void." Your confusion and lack of resolution may be disturbing and difficult, but you have to be willing to live with this uneasy feeling for a while. Some people fear the unknown so much that they cling to religions, groups, or even cults that provide them with absolute answers about everything. Since these people are already certain about all there is to know, they will never expand or find new solutions. Learning to tolerate the discomfort of the unresolved is the only way to move to new levels of knowledge and awareness.

Don't push the universe for an answer to your polarized problem, your power struggle. Relax, and let the answer come to you in its own time. Even if you are in a hurry for an answer, assume this attitude. Don't worry, the answer will arrive by the time you need it.

Let's use an example now to describe these three steps toward depolarizing a power struggle: (1) Develop empathy for the other point of view, (2) Relax the urgency about your own, and (3) Wait.

Deborah's and Hank's daughter, Kara, wanted to attend a private high school. Hank was firmly opposed to the idea. He was a strong supporter of public education and had even written letters to the editor of the local paper defending it. Their public high school had a good reputation, and Hank felt they could not justify the expense of the private school.

Deborah supported Kara. Several of her friends were attending the private school, it had a better music program, and Deborah was ready to make financial sacrifices for her daughter.

Deborah and Hank had already blown up at each other several times and were getting nowhere. Deborah decided to try depolarizing their conflict by developing empathy for Hank's point of view and softening her urgency about her own. She wrote several pages in her journal, answering all the questions suggested above. She knew Hank was someone who took pride in "walking his talk," and that it would be unbearably humiliating for him to act in opposition to his public statements about public education. She realized that she respected Hank's integrity, and the motivation behind his position. She did indeed have empathy for his point of view.

She still felt strongly that she wanted the best for Kara, and that the best was the private school. But when she came to the part about her own inner conflict, she realized that she, too, was worried about the financial strain of tuition payments, though she had not admitted this to Hank. Money anxiety was harder on their family tranquility than almost anything else. Also, she believed in the principle of public education herself. In the ideal world, there wouldn't be two separate education systems, one for the rich and one for the poor. She wasn't helping to move toward the ideal world by withdrawing her support from public education. She began to feel that her upset was more about the conflict this situation created for her, and that it was Hank's certainty that she found so unsettling. But she was also clear that she didn't want to sacrifice her daughter's welfare for a long-range social goal.

Now that Deborah had made the effort to develop empathy for Hank and soften her own urgency, she felt confused. But she knew that her next step was to sit back and wait. She had created the opening for a third alternative to present itself. Now she knew she couldn't force the process.

Over the next several days, Hank and Kara got into it a few times about the school issue, but Deborah stayed out of the discussions. As she listened, an idea occurred to her. Part of what was motivating Kara concerned her two best friends. One of them was definitely going to the private school; the other was apparently still undecided. So Deborah suggested that all three families get together for a discussion.

The discussion was useful because many pros and cons emerged on both sides. One of the strongest pulls of the private school, it turned out, was the choral music program, since all three of the girls were in the senior ensemble at their present school. One of the parents had the idea that the girls could try out for the citywide girls chorus which was under the leadership of the University choral conductor. Membership included voice lessons. The chorus was already scheduled to appear with the symphony orchestra, and was hoping to tour several other cities in the spring. It was expensive, but not nearly the cost of tuition at the private school.

Kara agreed that if she were accepted into the chorus, she would be okay with the public school. Fortunately, she was.

Deborah told me that if she had not completed the depolarizing exercise and stepped back from the conflict, she probably would not have thought of getting the other families together, and it was they who knew about the citywide chorus—a third alternative Hank and Deborah never would have imagined if they had stayed locked into their either/or conflict.

Do not worry that if you are the one who develops empathy and softens your urgency, you are the one who will "lose." When you soften your position, you open up a space for your partner to soften also, and you may be amazed to see your partner coming in your direction. That's what happened for Carl when he insisted that he and Stephanie use movers to make their move. Stephanie felt they could make the move themselves, using their friend's pick-up truck and her nephews to help. When Carl softened, he realized he was most worried about his back and that he could be extremely careful and let others lift the heavy items. But when he waited and said nothing for a few days, Stephanie told him she, too, was worried about his back, that she had done more checking and had found some inexpensive movers, and that she felt they should go ahead and use professionals after all.

When you can find a way to relax your urgency, often the universe is able to support you in ways you could never have anticipated while you were still trying to control everything. The more you polarize and defend your position, the less likely you are to see alternatives that may be very close at hand. The solution that emerges will meet everyone's needs; otherwise it won't be a solution. It could end up being your original solution, your partner's, some combination, or a completely new idea. You will never know as long as you remain locked into your single answer and your polarized "power struggle."

EXPERIMENT #16

Reframe the Power Struggle

Think of a conflict you are having with your partner. Do you feel polarized into two rigid positions?

First, write down the two positions.

Now, using the questions above (either talking with a friend or writing in your journal), develop empathy for the other point of view and relax the urgency about your own.

Now wait. During the waiting time, do not discuss the problem with your partner.

After the conflict has been resolved—whether it is that evening, or a week, or a month later, make an entry in your journal about how the problem resolved itself.

SOLVING RELATIONSHIP PROBLEMS BY YOURSELF: APPROACH #4

Enlist Your Partner's Help in Solving Your Problem

Sometimes it is possible to reframe what seems to be a problem between the two of you so that it becomes *your* problem, and you can persuade your partner to help you out of your distress.

Early in their marriage, Doris and Conrad had financial strains. As the situation improved, Doris felt that Conrad was not updating his attitude. Whenever she bought clothes, or a gift for someone or an item for the children or the house, he became anxious and gave her lectures on "we can't afford that."

Doris was exasperated. When she tried to discuss the dynamics of how financial decisions get made, Conrad would talk only about the value of one particular purchase or another.

I encouraged Doris to frame the problem as hers and ask Conrad for help with it. This is approximately how the conversation went:

"Honey," she said. "I have a sticky problem that won't go away. Would you see if you have any suggestions for me?"

"Sure, Sweetheart. What's the problem?"

"When I was single, I had complete financial independence, and I did a pretty good job of managing my money. As you know, I even managed to save quite a bit. Now, I have no independence at all. We have enough money for the lifestyle I want, but I can never make a purchase on my own and just make up my own mind about what to buy. Of course I want to respect the family finances, but I'd like not to feel so frustrated."

Doris actually had some solutions in mind, like going into her own savings account, increasing her hours at work to have some money that would be just hers, or increasing her grocery allowance. But since the idea of this strategy is to get your partner to come up with original solutions, she didn't mention hers right away.

Conrad did understand Doris's frustration, and he did go to work on the problem. Not right then, but the next morning, he suggested that together they set up a separate checking account for Doris, one that he would never see, and that they put a certain amount in every month. That way, her expenditures would not only be budgeted, they would be private. It solved the problem for him too, because he still felt he would have control over the amount in her checking account.

Here are other examples from my workshops of problems that were reframed to elicit the support and help of the other partner:

- You are always late.

  became

  I like to be places on time, and it drives me nuts to wait while you are getting ready, when I know it is going to make us late. Do you have any suggestions for how I could better handle my stress?

- I hate that you invite your parents every Sunday.

  became

  I need more time for myself on weekends. Do you have any ideas for me?

- You go out every night of the week. You are never around!

  became

  On nights when I'm alone around the house, I start feeling sad and I can't figure out what to do. Could you help me figure out what I could do to feel better about those nights?

You must be very careful to avoid an implied accusation when you reframe the question. For example, the last problem would not have worked if the questioner said, "On nights when you're not here, I feel lonely. Can you help me figure out what to do when you are not around?"

Write down exactly what you want help with before you ask. See if you can isolate the genuine problem you are having.

EXPERIMENT #17

Enlist Your Partner's Help

Go to your Master List of Problems. Select one, and see whether you can rephrase it so that it becomes a problem that your partner might be willing to help you solve.

Choose a time when you and your spouse are both feeling relaxed, and bring up your problem in a casual way. Say something like, "I've been dealing with a problem. I wonder if you have any suggestions that might help me solve it."

Afterward, make a note in your journal about how the conversation went. If it didn't "work," what might you do differently to make it more successful the next time?

SOLVING RELATIONSHIP PROBLEMS BY YOURSELF: APPROACH #5

Express Empathy for Your Partner's Position

We have already discussed empathy as a part of several other solutions. Focusing on your partner's position is a step of ERAP and a part of the depolarizing process.

But a powerful problem-solving strategy in and of itself is to go beyond discovering empathy within yourself to actually expressing empathy to your partner out loud. This simple act can work wonders to reduce conflict and to restore warm feelings between you.

Expressing empathy out loud is usually not difficult. Most often we fail to do it only because it doesn't occur to us. The secret to success is just to remember to do it.

First, figure out what your partner's position is. Then, sometime when the subject arises naturally, or when you feel comfortable bringing it up, casually affirm your partner for what he or she is doing or what he or she believes. You must be very careful not to let any sarcasm or cynicism creep into your message. Don't say anything until you can say it sincerely. This doesn't mean you have completely overcome your anger or upset about this issue, and it doesn't mean you are agreeing with or that you understand your partner; it only means that you can express your partner's point of view.

After you make your empathic statement, add the phrase, "Is that right?"

Michael's daughter, Kim, had the lead in her class play. Months before, Michael had arranged a rock-climbing expedition with several friends. He was scheduled to arrive back the afternoon of the play. Michael's wife, Sharon, begged him either not to go or at least to return early so as not to risk missing the play. But Michael assured her that all would be fine.

As it turned out, Michael's companion injured himself, there was a lot of confusion and delay, and Michael was not able to return until twenty-four hours after the play was over. Kim was crushed, and Sharon was furious.

I spoke with Michael and Sharon two months after this incident, and they were still experiencing a great deal of tension over it. "I told him not to go! He always puts the family second," Sharon was saying, over and over in different ways.

"No, I don't. I never planned on missing the play. How could I know my plans would get all screwed up? This climb meant a lot to me."

I suggested the empathy strategy to Sharon privately, and she agreed to try it when she got a chance.

Here is what she told me:

> We were watching TV, and during a commercial, I hit the mute button and just turned to him and said, "I'll bet you were disappointed to miss Kim's play, weren't you? But you did have a fabulous climb, too. You probably wouldn't have missed it for anything. I can see how excruciating these choices are for you. I'm sure I wouldn't have wanted to miss the climb if I had been you, either. Is that right?"
>
> Michael didn't have a huge reaction. He just said, "Yeah, honey, that's right. It was a really hard choice. I feel terrible that I missed the play."
>
> That was it, but Michael wanted to make love that night, and the next day I felt a lot lighter about it. I still think he made the wrong decision, but I don't feel like I need to drag it around anymore.

Here's another example:

Marv started his own business selling a particular type of farm equipment. After two years, the business was growing slowly but still not paying its own way. Even though he had allowed himself three years for it to become profitable, he was discouraged and was becoming depressed and irritable. Karen kept trying to encourage him, both to make him feel better and because she was tired of living with this grouch.

"You know it's all going well. Your business is on schedule! Besides it does no good to worry. Anxiety is a choice! Just relax and let go of the worry. You'll feel better, and everything will go along fine, just as it has been."

She would point out to him all his successes and upward trends. But Marv became all the grouchier and depressed. "It could go well, or it could just die," he would say. "Most small businesses fail. I just hate not having enough money. I don't know if I can take this any longer."

I suggested the idea of expressing empathy to Karen. That night, when Marv started in, she said, "I know, it must be so difficult to have worked so hard for two years and still not be breaking even. You have put in so much time, and you are brilliant at what you do. I'm sorry it's tough—you know, maybe the second year of a new business is like the "transition" stage of labor, just before the final push. That's when women always say something like, 'I can't go on with this. I just can't do it.' It really feels awful."

"Yeah, it does!" responded Marv. "But, you know, I believe the end is in sight. I know if I can persevere, this business will be a huge success. I like that labor metaphor. I'm sure I'm not going to have a stillbirth." And he went on to count up his successes and envision a rosy future. Both of them felt their spirits lifting right away.

When you listen to another person and then express empathy with what you have heard—even if you don't agree with it, you will be giving that person one of the most important gifts there is: validation. Expressing empathy is the very least we can do for each other as intimate partners.

Besides, when your partner says something and you *don't* express empathy, or even worse, you argue against the position, he or she will feel unheard and invalidated and will continue to repeat the position over and over.

I know of no other skill that is so talked about and taught, and so little practiced. I hear people abuse the principle of empathic listening several times every day. I go into the nearby fabric store to pick up some Velcro for a quick project. "We're out of it," says the salesperson.

"Oh nuts!" I respond in frustration. "You don't have any in the back or anywhere? I just need a little."

"We didn't get our shipment this week," she replies. No empathy. No expression of understanding that this is a bummer for me. I just go away fuming, realizing I'll have to figure out something else to wear now that I can't make this quickie repair. How different I would have felt if she had said, "How frustrating for you. I'm so sorry. I'm sure it's very annoying. I wish I could help you. Could you use a snap?" I would have calmed right down and lightened up. The less I feel heard, the more I feel I have to keep expressing my feeling and the more it escalates. Just like with Marv and Karen. When she expressed empathy, he felt heard and understood, and he could back off.

Empathy is a miracle in a tiny, simple package. Sometimes it can be one or two words, like "Oh, how awful!" or "Oh, no!" or "Gee, I'm sorry," or "That's really sad."

Three of the kindest words you can ever say to anyone are, "Tell me more." That says, "Not only do I understand, but if it would help you to talk about this, I'm here for you, I'm interested."

Expressing empathy is especially effective when you are in a disagreement with your partner. As we have seen, in a dispute we tend to polarize. Expressing empathy for your partner's point of view will automatically relax the hostilities, give you both more breathing space, and, coincidentally, bring the two of you closer together.

"But," I always hear in workshops, "I express empathy for my partner, but I never get it expressed back!"

That can feel frustrating and unfair, indeed. It is unfair. There are several solutions.

First, you can gently coach your spouse to express empathy for your position. For example, "I'm not saying I want any changes or that we need to solve anything here. I just want you to appreciate what a challenge it is for me to interrupt my day at 3:00 every day to pick up Jenny. I realize I have to do it, but it is a big sacrifice for me. I just want some appreciation." Or, "I completely see that you want to be left alone for a little while when you come home in the evening, and I'm willing to do that. But can you see my point of view, that I am eager for some time to connect with you, too? I'm not asking you to change anything. I just would like to know that you hear my side of the story."

Sometimes this sort of coaching works well. Basically, you express the empathy you want, and get your partner to agree with it. But sometimes it is a big flop. If that is the case, then I suggest the second approach: Be the "big" person. Let go of your hope that you will get empathy from your partner, and look elsewhere for it. Make an agreement with your support person that you will listen to and express empathy for each other. Talk with a friend who you think will understand and feel empathy for you.

But don't stop expressing empathy for your spouse. Expressing empathy could be the single most powerful suggestion in this book. It can de-escalate hostilities, calm tension, create a safer atmosphere to talk. It will feel loving for both the giver and the receiver. It is the simplest action you can take to bring the two of you closer.

Remember, expressing empathy for your partner's position does not mean that you are agreeing with it, or that you are giving in to it in any way. Not at all. Expressing empathy for your partner's position will make it easier for you to express your own, and will make your conversation far more effective. When you develop the habit of expressing empathy, you will find that you use it several times every day—in a whole variety of situations, from happy to excited to disappointing or frustrating.

Paula and Sergei couldn't agree on where to go on vacation. She wanted to go to the beach because she thought the children would be able to occupy themselves better, and it would be more restful for her. He wanted to go to the mountains because he wanted to start teaching his older son to rock climb. They both felt convinced, and kept repeating their own position more and more vigorously. Sergei had been coming to my workshop, and he suddenly remembered about expressing empathy.

"Okay," he said. "You really want to go to the beach. You want to swim. You know the younger kids can play in the sand and water all day. You've really got your heart set on this. Is that right?"

"I do!" she replied. "That's it."

"Well, I can understand that. I do want you to feel good about this vacation."

"Oh thank you, Honey," Paula said. "I'm glad you see my point."

"Let's talk about it later," Sergei said.

"That's fine," she said.

They ultimately found a compromise that met both of their needs, but Sergei told me, "We had a great evening that night instead of an escalating fight. I felt right then that your course had a perfect title, because one of us actually did bring the two of us closer together."

Expressing empathy is actually a shortened version of depolarizing. So one more hint that will help you express empathy is that whatever your partner's need is, you have some form of that need in yourself, too.

When Sharon was furious with Michael for planning his climb right before the class play, she knew that if she possibly could, she would love to go away with her friends on a weekend excursion, and that if it conflicted with something else, she would have a hard choice. Sergei could fully understand Paula's need for a vacation that would thrill the children and let her relax too. That is exactly what he wanted also. Or again, when Michael was complaining about his slow-growing business, Karen also had a need to feel that Michael was succeeding, and she also had a need for financial security.

Expressing empathy is a wonderful way to express your love and to put it into action. It is a powerful way for one of you to bring the two of you together.

EXPERIMENT #18

Express Empathy

1. For a week, put the word "empathy" in the front of your brain. Make it a priority and use it as often as you can. Let your partner know that you hear and understand whatever he or she is saying or feeling. At the end of the day, make a few notes about each of the times you expressed empathy that day.

2. Look over your Master List of relationship problems. For each problem, write a paragraph expressing your partner's position on this issue. Choose one, and try expressing empathy to your partner just out of a clear blue sky, the way Sharon did with Michael about missing the class play.

Keep experimenting with expressing empathy and see if you notice subtle shifts in yourself or your spouse. Try to develop the habit of expressing empathy—not only with your spouse, but with your children, friends, and co-workers as well.

SOLVING RELATIONSHIP PROBLEMS BY YOURSELF: APPROACH #6

Gracefully Accept What You Can't Change

One of the most empowering inner shifts you can make is to stop fighting the quality or situation you don't like, and to accept it. Simply stop labeling whatever you don't like a "problem," and start labeling it a "fact of life." As psychologist Susan Campbell says, "It is not your differences but your resistance to differences that causes pain."

Connie and Ron had been married for thirty-two years when I was with them at a dinner party. Another guest was telling a story about her family, and Ron kept interrupting with puns and one-liners, some of which were quite funny. But Connie thought he was being rude, and she finally blew up at him right in front of all of us. "Ron, please. She's trying to tell a story! Just keep your smart comments to yourself. When it's your turn, you can have the stage."

All of us were a bit embarrassed by the outburst, which was far more disruptive than the little puns had been. I had seen Connie criticize Ron in front of others on numerous previous occasions.

Shortly after this incident, I was talking with Connie and gently brought the subject up. I suggested that, since she had been trying to stop this behavior for thirty-two years, with little or no success, maybe she could just give up on the idea. I also mentioned that her public scourging of her husband was embarrassing to the rest of us.

Connie was grateful for my comment. She realized I was right about ever getting Ron to change, and she was surprised to hear that the rest of us were embarrassed. She always thought that she was speaking for the group when she tried to silence Ron and doing a favor to the person trying to tell the story.

A few months later, Connie thanked me again for my comment. She told me she had had numerous occasions to bite her tongue and that she was pleased with the results. When she relaxed and gave up the responsibility of monitoring her husband's behavior, she actually began to enjoy some of his humor and to appreciate how clever he is sometimes. One time, after a couple of puns, Ron, apparently surprised at her silence, winked at her—and then stopped interrupting. She was stunned to see that he was capable of monitoring his own behavior. Another time, the person who was being interrupted turned to Ron and said, slightly annoyed, but with a smile, "Come on, Ron! Enough already. Let me tell my story." Connie was amazed! She realized that, left to their own devices, people take care of themselves.

All that changed in this situation is that Connie switched to accepting that her husband's puns were a fact of life. She made a small change all by herself without even discussing it with her husband. She simply stopped fighting her "problem," and accepted it.

When one partner is trying to change the other, the conflict is usually caused by the partner who is not willing to be accepting, not the partner who is not willing to change. If you are experiencing a conflict with your spouse, ask yourself, Is it your demands, your opinions, your judgments that are causing the problem, or the circumstances themselves?

Diane is the person I mentioned in Chapter One who said she made a small adjustment that made a big difference, just like the minor modification that makes a plane from Los Angeles end up in Miami instead of New York. I want to tell the entire story Diane shared with me, for it sheds a great deal of light on the power of acceptance.

Diane's and Peter's children were two and three years old, ages that require constant supervision, and Diane's teenage daughter also lived with them. Circumstances had forced them to move twice in one year. They used a baby-sitter in the mornings so that Diane could work at home as a freelance copywriter. And on top of all this, Peter started a brand new job with a one-hour commute each way, and a great deal of pressure to perform.

"When he started the new job," Diane told me, "he instantly turned from a fun companion and a sweet, thoughtful guy into a boring, cold zombie who passed through our household only to eat and sleep. I really panicked. I felt I had lost my husband. When I tried to talk to him about it, he always got defensive and annoyed and his only comment was couldn't I please get off his case."

Diane went on:

> Meantime, I was trying to get all our boxes unpacked from our move, manage all the things that needed to be fixed around the house, be a mother to these two toddlers and a guide and chauffeur for a confused teenager, do my own work, and maintain a lifeline to a few badly needed friends. I could have managed all the overwhelm, but what was putting me over the edge was my broken heart.
>
> Of course I could understand Peter's stress too. But I didn't feel his was any greater than mine. I envied him his commute because it was mostly through gorgeous countryside, and he always listened to books on tape. I hadn't read a novel in three years! Let's just say I was building up a lot of hurt and resentment.
>
> One day, eight months after Peter's new job started, I was reading a magazine in the backyard while the kids were playing in the sandbox. It was a gorgeous day, and I was feeling very happy. I happened to think about how stressed I had been eight months earlier, and I asked myself what had shifted. "Acceptance!" I said to myself. "I have accepted Peter's job."
>
> In order for you to understand what this word meant to me, I have to tell you another story.
>
> When I was nineteen, my sister was killed in an auto accident, so I had become very familiar with the stages of grief. I was definitely in denial for a long time. I just couldn't let it in that she had died. Then gradually, I became more and more filled with rage. I became so angry, I had to drop out of school.

Then I got really depressed and was in complete despair. That is when I finally began to see a therapist, about four years after she died.

Then a fairly amazing thing happened. I became obsessed with the idea of becoming a nun. I was very clear that I wanted to become quiet and contemplative, to study theology and try to explain death in a way no one had so far, and to write the story of my sister's life as it would be if she had not died—since we were all sure that my sister's life was going to be a great adventure.

I began talking to my priest and to various convents and orders. I was really serious.

Just at that time, my family took a vacation together to Washington, D.C. We were extremely busy. We saw everything and had a wonderful time together.

The next time I saw my therapist, I told her I hadn't thought about the convent the entire week in Washington, and I wasn't so sure about it anymore. She said to me, "I think you were in the bargaining stage of grief."

She explained that people who are dying or facing the death of a loved one often go through a stage in which they try to bargain with God. It is as though I was saying, "I will do anything to get my sister back. I will give up my life, my plans, my friends, my love life—I will sacrifice everything if only I can somehow make it that my sister isn't really dead."

Something in me truly shifted after that therapy session. I had assumed that pain would be my constant companion my entire life, that I would always go around with a terrible ache in my heart, and would simply need to learn to live with it. But somehow, after that therapy session, the ache was gone. It was as though I was able to let my sister go. I felt like I could talk to her, like now I could have her with me in a new form. She was four years older now. She had grown up with me. I felt a lightness I thought I would never again feel. I had accepted her death. It was a very strong experience.

My counselor helped me see that I had had the courage to feel all the feelings that were tumbling around in me during the years after her death, and that I had gone through a fairly classic experience of grief.

Well, on that sunny afternoon, I began to realize that perhaps I had gone through a mini-grief experience with regard to the

> change in my husband. I could remember that I had been in denial about it at first: "Oh this is temporary. This will change in a few weeks." Then I became very angry about it all, and then depressed and discouraged. When I went through a brief period of thinking about leaving Peter, that was bargaining. And now, I was accepting my situation and even counting my blessings. Of course, in my panic at first, I had exaggerated the changes in Peter too. We still had lots of the good qualities between us that we started out with.

You may be able to make the decision to accept your partner exactly the way he or she is in the blink of an eye, as Connie did with Ron's puns. She made a decision to accept Ron's behavior, or at least to "act as if" she were accepting it. After she behaved in an accepting way, and saw that the results were good, her inner shift to true acceptance followed close behind.

But acceptance may also take time and effort. You may need to let go of expectations you had for your relationship, to experience a loss of some dream or picture of what life with your spouse would be like. This isn't easy.

However, it is both easier and less painful than *not* accepting something that isn't going to change.

Every couple, without exception, fails to meet each other's expectations in some ways. The primary difference between couples who thrive and couples who don't is that couples who thrive gracefully take what they get, even when it turns out to be different from what they thought they were getting. They adapt. They focus on what they love and graciously accept what they don't love but can't change.

Of course, figuring out what you can change and what you can't is a big part of the challenge. Sometimes, if you just think about it, you'll know what you can't change. Sometimes you won't know until you experiment with trying to change it, and nothing happens. But even if you are hoping to change something about your partner, acceptance is the starting point. When you are spending your energy fighting against reality, you will have no energy left for creative solutions.

You probably won't be able to order yourself suddenly to begin accepting something you don't like. "Self, just start accepting this awful thing about your spouse! Right now!"

Instead, the best way to begin is to start behaving as though you accept it.

Accepting your partner and your situation is a powerful change

EXPERIMENT #19

Gracefully Accept What You Can't Change

Go back to the Master List of problems you created in Experiment #2. Select one of the major ones.

Write this sentence in your journal:

"I accept ______________________________________."

Fill in the blank with the problem you have selected. For example, "I accept that John seems more interested in work than in me." Or "I accept that Mary isn't very warm and outgoing with guests."

Now write, "Ways I Can Demonstrate My Acceptance of This Issue," and under it, list behaviors you could try to "act as if" you accept this thing you don't like. For example,

Ask John about his work more often and act very interested.

Stop complaining about the small amount of time he spends with me.

Make my own plans several evenings a week.

OR

Stop apologizing for Mary's behavior with company.

Stop trying to bring Mary into the conversation.

Talk as much as I want and let Mary take care of herself.

Realize I am not responsible for how others feel about Mary.

you can make all by yourself. It may not be easy, and it may take time, but it will almost always produce positive change in your relationship.

SOLVING RELATIONSHIP PROBLEMS BY YOURSELF: APPROACH #7

Ask for What You Want

Asking for what you want seems like the most direct, natural way to get what you want. In fact, this is the strategy that most people instinctively use first when they want something.

> Would you please take the garbage out.
>
> Honey, stop interrupting me!
>
> I wish you wanted to go to the movies more often!
>
> Would you please vacuum while I run a few errands?
>
> Please don't shop at that expensive produce store anymore!
>
> Don't nag me!
>
> I wish you'd give me little spontaneous kisses more often.
>
> I wish you'd take more responsibility around the house. Maybe you'd consider cleaning up the kitchen every evening.

Ironically, asking for what you want is usually the *least* effective method of getting what you want.

As we have seen, you will get the results you long for more quickly and surely by modeling what you want, exhibiting love and understanding toward your spouse, expressing empathy, graciously accepting what you can't change, taking responsibility for balancing your own give-and-take scales, and "thinking good will,"—in short, by being a good spouse instead of always focusing on having a good spouse.

Asking for what you want usually doesn't work. It won't work when

- you are asking in an atmosphere of negativity and your request adds to the negativity.
- you aren't really asking for what you want; you are expressing an opinion or feeling.
- you ask for things all the time without expecting results; your requests aren't taken seriously.
- your requests imply a criticism—whether or not you intend this.
- you ask for something that is very difficult for your partner to give, given who he or she is.

- your request makes your partner feel unsafe or threatened, even though you do not intend this.
- you convey that you think you are entitled to what you are asking for, that your request is fair, that you are "right."
- you imply that "no" is not an acceptable answer.

Nevertheless, there certainly is a place in every loving relationship to ask for what you want. But it is absolutely critical that you do it in the right way. Critical, that is, if you care about getting a positive response to your request.

Here is how to make asking for what you want work for you. This method will greatly increase your chances for excellent results.

1. STOP ASKING FOR THINGS FREQUENTLY OR FRIVOLOUSLY. For a week or so, try to avoid asking for anything at all. At the very least, this experiment will give you some sense of how often you make requests of your mate. You don't have to be rigid if you have a simple little need. But definitely tuck your "biggies" away out of sight for a while and don't mention them.

2. ESTABLISH A LOVING ATMOSPHERE IN YOUR HOME. Don't even attempt to ask for what you want until you have experimented with several of the suggestions in Chapters Four and Five. When your spouse feels supported and understood and feels a spirit of good will from you, he or she will be far more receptive to a request.

People do change, but only when they feel change to be in their own best interest and when they believe that changing will make them feel good. People are not motivated to change when they think, "I'm bad. I have to change so I can be good." They are far more likely to change if they think, "I'm good! If I change, I can show that I'm good, and I can experience that goodness!"

So the more you can contribute to your spouse's feeling good about him or herself, the more likely you are to get the changes you want.

3. CAREFULLY SELECT ONE REQUEST YOU WOULD LIKE TO MAKE. First, list in your journal everything you can think of that you would like to ask for. Make two lists, side by side. Label one "Big Things" and the other, "Little Things." Now you can write down everything from "throw away your own teabag" and "take the mail into the den instead of dumping it on the dining room table" to "be more affectionate with

me," "be more interested in my work," "express your feelings more," "don't pester and nag me so much," to "be more slow and playful when we are going to make love."

Now, select one item. It is probably best not to begin with your most important request. Practice first with something you care about—from either the "big things" or the "little things" list—but not your deepest heart's desire.

4. **Clarify for yourself exactly what you want, and be highly specific.** Under your lists in your journal, write out your request, just the way you might say it to your mate. Be as specific as you possibly can.

For example, do not say, "I would like you to remember my birthday." Say, "What would make me really happy is, I'd like you to go shopping ahead of time and pick out a little gift, wrap it up or have it wrapped, and give it to me, with a card, on my birthday."

Do not say, "I'd like you to be more affectionate." Say, "I'd like a big, warm hug every evening when I come home from work (after I have put down my stuff), and I'd like you to come out to the kitchen after dinner and give me a kiss, a nice, long, warm one, minimum thirty seconds."

Do not say, "I'd like you to be a better conversationalist." Say, "Once a week, I'd like you to tell me about something interesting you have read or seen on TV that week. And whenever we go on a drive anywhere, I would like you to have in mind one topic you would like to discuss."

Let your partner know exactly what would make you happy.

5. **Prepare yourself that your partner may say "no."** The essence of asking for what you want effectively is to do so with respect. You must convey to your spouse when you ask that you understand he or she has a right to turn you down. Otherwise your spouse will feel backed into a corner, or will feel manipulated and without options.

Be clear, before you ask, that "no" may be the answer, and convey this in the way you ask. The phrasing suggestions below will help.

6. Carefully choose your phrasing. For "Little Things," the following two phrases are magic. Memorize them and use them often.

"Would you consider . . ."

or

"Would you be willing to . . ."

These words convey that you are willing to discuss the subject, and that you understand that the answer may be "no." They are respectful and courteous.

Those two phrases are useful for even the most minor, spur-of-the-moment requests. Mayer and I use them all the time, and over the years, I have passed them along to many grateful friends.

For requests that are a bit more major in nature, these are the magic phrases:

"How would you feel if . . ."

or

"There is something I would really like. May I tell you what it is?"

With these phrases, you aren't simply asking for a "yes" or "no" answer; you are starting a conversation.

Two additional suggestions about how to phrase your request:

a. Do not explain why you want this thing or justify it in any way. This will weaken your request and divert your focus. You have a right to want what you want for whatever reasons. You will come across with far more confidence if you just ask.

For example, don't say, "Birthdays were always really important in my family, and when I don't get anything from you, it taps into all my old feelings, and I know it isn't rational but it makes me think you don't love me, and blah, blah, blah." Don't say, "I do so much more work around here than you, and I have to leave earlier in the morning and I already take Susie to child care, so I think it would be fair if you emptied the dishwasher in the morning."

Just state your request, graciously and confidently.

b. Sometimes it is useful to add the sentence, before you make your request, "Please understand, I am not being critical in any way. I just want to tell you something I'd like." Here's why that sentence can make a critical difference in your success:

With regard to many requests, it is difficult to avoid making the request sound like a criticism. That is one of the reasons "asking for what you want" is often unsuccessful. It *sounds* critical, even when it isn't. "Would you be willing to give me a big hug every evening when I come home?" implies, "You aren't affectionate enough with me." "I would like you to buy me a gift for my birthday" implies, "You're not thoughtful or generous enough."

Mayer and I have a useful in-joke that helps us out of these situations. When I met him, he was house-sharing with a man whom we considered to be somewhat quaint. He believed himself to be an expert at human relationships. But in fact, he was quite controlling, and relied heavily on psychobabble, to which we were subjected in great quantities every day. A phrase he used frequently was, "I'm not placing blame." Now, when either of us is making a request that could sound critical, we simply quote our old friend, "I'm not placing blame."

Sometimes, I feel a need to move beyond the in-joke and make a more serious statement, and I will say to Mayer, "I truly don't mean to be critical here. I just want to let you know that . . ." Or, if I have not made my preliminary statements that I don't intend to be critical, and Mayer's response is defensive, I say, "I don't mean to put you on the defensive at all. I don't mean to be critical." This gives him the opportunity to shift, and to listen to my comments more openly. I have taught these words to many other couples with excellent results also.

Choose from the above phrases the one you want to use with the request you are working on now.

7. **Choose a propitious moment.** Select a time when both of you are fairly relaxed, not in the middle of some other unresolved issue, and not likely to be interrupted. Of course, given most people's chaotic lives, this is often the most challenging part of the assignment. Don't put your request off forever, but don't make it when your spouse is feeling harried or hurried.

8. **Go for it.** Make your request.

9. **If your partner says "yes" . . .** express appreciation. And don't discount what you are getting because you had to ask for it. Some people never ask for what they want because they think if it didn't come

spontaneously, it's worthless. That kind of withholding is no favor to either of you. Your mate probably wants to make you happy and give you what you want but may genuinely not know what that is. Gifts or favors you requested are not inferior to the unprompted kind; they are just different.

10. IF YOUR PARTNER SAYS "NO" . . . graciously accept the decline. Then, give yourself time to re-group and decide what to do next.

If your partner's "no" or the conversation that results from it makes you angry, it may be hard for you to hide your annoyance, but it is best if you can avoid a full-blown expression of anger. For no matter what response you get this time, you are paving the way for future requests at the same time. If your spouse can see that you are flexible and open to not getting your way with this thing, you will be creating a safer setting for future conversations.

If you have taken care to make your request in a careful and deliberate way, and your partner still says no, there may be a valid reason, valid for your partner, that is. What might that reason be? See if you can understand why your partner said "no." Try to move toward empathy instead of anger.

You do have several recourses when your partner says "no." One is, you can wait a respectable period of time and then ask again. This time, do say more about your reasons for the request, and see whether your partner is willing to discuss the matter. Perhaps suggest some kind of compromise. Give your partner a chance to explain his or her position.

Sometimes, your partner will agree to what you have asked, but then not do it. Or you'll get compliance for a short while, and then a quick reversion to the old pattern.

In this case, you can try the strategy of patient persistence. Gently and with respect, keep asking for what you want again and again over a period of months or years. The secret to success is, don't give up! Eventually, you may see a shift.

You must reserve patient persistence for one or maybe two requests that are of great importance to you. If you use it all the time for everything, it will completely lose its effectiveness.

For example, one woman told me she likes to move slowly during sex with plenty of teasing early on. She would explain this to her husband and get a kind of dutiful compliance for the next several times they'd make love. But then he would revert to his old ways.

Finally one morning, after they had made love, she said to him, "I've talked about this so much before, and you still don't do it. I feel like either you don't believe me, because it isn't that way for you, or you just don't care what I want. Is either one of those true?" They had a discussion that, she told me, has finally made a real difference for her. "I said it in many different ways many times over the years. I don't think it was what I said that made the difference this time; it was the fact that it was the 100th time I'd said it. For some reason, this time he really paid attention."

This woman made another comment during our conversation that I loved. It is a perfect example of how to start with acceptance but still be able to ask for change:

> At some point along the way I made the important realization that I was not asking my husband to change who he is and suddenly become this super Don Juan type. Instead, I was just asking him to give me one thing that I want. This shift made me feel much lighter about the whole thing. It seemed like a lot less I was asking for, and shifted the focus from him [You change!] to me [This is what I like].

Asking for what you want can work wonders for you if you use it selectively, and you do it right!

SOLVING RELATIONSHIP PROBLEMS BY YOURSELF: APPROACH #8A

For Men Only: Space In

If you are a man, working on your relationship by yourself, I will give you a few generic strategies that will almost certainly help bring you and your wife closer together, regardless of what your particular "problem" is.

Women's primary complaint about men is that they don't participate in the relationship enough. This objection takes many forms, but they boil down to the same root complaint: men are spaced out, preoccupied, not available. For example, though it may not be especially pleasant, look at these extremely common accusations:

- He doesn't talk to me.
- He won't do his share of the housework.

- I tell him what I like in sex, but he keeps doing the same thing anyway.
- He's not home enough.
- He never tells me he loves me.
- He forgets birthdays and anniversaries.
- He's always buried in the paper.
- He doesn't consider my needs.
- He won't talk to me about feelings.
- He cares more about his work than about me.

If you are working on your relationship by yourself, chances are you feel your wife is unhappy with you, and you are overwhelmed with what she is asking you for. You feel she wants you to become a completely different person. You may feel inadequate to meet her demands.

Here is a big secret: To most women, little things make a huge difference. You may be able to please your wife and even turn her complaints completely around by making a few minor changes. For example, try this one:

Give Your Wife Five Minutes Every Day

Create a time every day when you pay exclusive attention to your wife for five minutes. Make this a new part of your daily routines. Only you know what time will work best for you. Maybe it's as you climb into bed at night, just before you start reading the paper in the morning, right after dinner while one of you is cleaning up, during dinner, during the first couple commercial breaks while you are watching TV (using the mute button of course), or right after you put the children to bed. It could even be a phone call during your lunch break or late in the afternoon as you get ready to leave work. You pick a time that fits into your routine every day.

It doesn't matter what you do during this "space-in" time, as long as you are focused fully and exclusively on your wife. Here is a little kitbag of possible ways to spend your five minutes that will work wonders when used with some frequency:

A. ASK HER ABOUT HER DAY. "How was your day, honey? What went on for you today?" Those are magic words for any woman. Then you need to listen to her—just for five minutes. If she doesn't have much to tell, that's okay. Try one of the other items in the kitbag. Tomorrow she'll have more to tell. When she does, she will be thrilled to have your undivided attention. She will read into your attentive listening that you care about her, that you are genuinely interested in her, that you are enjoying her company—all of the highest importance to women.

B. SAY SOMETHING POSITIVE ABOUT HER OR ABOUT YOUR RELATIONSHIP. This can be a feeling, a compliment, an observation, anything positive. For example:

- You look so pretty.
- I love what a great mother you are.
- I'm lucky you are such a great cook.
- I so enjoy our evenings together.
- I love you.
- I appreciate how tidy you keep the house.
- You're the greatest.
- I'm glad you enjoy your work so much.
- You sure did a great job on that PTA fund-raiser.

C. TOUCH HER AFFECTIONATELY. Give your wife a spontaneous hug or a kiss on the back of her neck or on her forehead. Put your arm around her. Hold her face in your hands and smile at her. Put your hand on her back, or your hands around her waist. Rub her shoulders for a few seconds. Women *love* non-sexual touching. It is a way of saying, "I love you, and I am thinking about that and enjoying you right now."

Vary your touch. If you usually hug her firmly, hug her very tenderly and gently. If you usually kiss her on the lips, kiss her eyes or her cheek.

I have heard so many woman lament, "He touches me only when he wants to make love." You can score *big* with a woman with a few gentle squeezes or affectionate kisses.

D. Ask her about something specific going on in her life. When you remember that her sister is ill, or she is working on a difficult report at work, or her boss spoke angrily to her, or that she went to the doctor today, and you ask her about that specifically, you show her that you are tuned in to her, that you are paying attention, that you care—which is what your wife wants from you more than anything else.

Whatever you do with it, take five minutes every day to give undivided attention to your wife, to "space in," as a daily routine, just like brushing your teeth. Many men in my workshops have reported outstanding results from this experiment.

EXPERIMENT #20A (MEN ONLY)

Space In

Figure out the time in your own day most convenient for your five-minute "space-in."

For the first week, try each of the four suggestions above: Ask your partner about her day, give her a compliment or positive comment about your relationship, touch her affectionately, or ask her about something specific in her life. The next day, when you get to your five-minute time slot, see what comes naturally for you to do to pay special attention to your partner.

Don't be hard on yourself if you forget, or you can't fit the five minutes in on some days that are hurried and hectic. But make a concerted effort to "space-in" every day for at least two weeks.

At the end of two weeks, in your journal or with your support person, answer these questions:

Do you like the space-in exercise? Why or why not?

Have you seen any change in your wife? Did she mention that she saw any change in you?

Do you want to continue to "space-in" for five minutes every day? Why or why not?

GIL: My wife has been asking me for years to "love her more," and I could never imagine what she meant—because she was never specific about what she wanted. This exercise was so interesting to me. I thought the activities were dumb, but I did them anyway. My wife couldn't believe the change in me, and she kept asking me *what had happened.* I loved seeing the change in *her.* This little "space-in" thing made a huge difference in our lives.

ROY: It was super hard for me to do this. I wanted to, but I kept forgetting it. A friend and I were trying this experiment together, and one day he said, "You are so spaced out, you can't even remember to space in, let alone actually space in!" He was kidding with me, but somehow it hit me that he was right. I really wasn't paying attention. So then I started to think I should put out the effort. . . . When I hugged my wife, she hugged me back, and we had these great hugs. When I asked her about her day, she had lots to tell me. I started to see why these little gestures were not so little. . . . I'd say the main value of the experiment for me was to help me understand what women want. I just figured our life together—and making love—was enough. It was for me, but women are different.

In *The Way of Marriage,* Henry Borys shares this anecdote from his journal (his wife's name is Susan):

> [I realized] maybe I had slipped some in my giving to Susan lately. So I made a secret resolution to give at least two things each day to make her life easier.
>
> It has been almost three weeks now, and so far I have stuck to my resolution. Each night at dinner I mentally check to make sure I have given at least two things to help her in some way; if I haven't given two things, then I get them done before bed. Giving two things a day may not seem like much, but it is doing wonders for our relationship. I do not know how many times in the past week Susan has said, with a look of awe on her face, "I can't believe how much you're changing."

SOLVING RELATIONSHIP PROBLEMS BY YOURSELF: APPROACH #8B

For Women Only: Stop Coaching

"I have one question," a man said to me after a talk I gave. "Why do women always want to change men?"

He was voicing men's most common complaint about women. Men often feel criticized, unappreciated, pestered, reprimanded, and blamed by the women who allegedly love them.

- She nags me too much.
- I never feel I have pleased her.
- She wants me to be someone else.
- She'd like to control me—when I watch TV, when I read the paper, exactly how I play with the kids. Everything.
- She's always telling me a better way to do something.
- She won't let me alone. Even on my own projects, she has advice.

Pause for a moment and think about the behaviors you still want the man in your life to change. What do you keep "reminding" him about? His table manners? His driving? His behavior with the children? He doesn't get the dishes clean enough? His office is too messy? (You list your pet peeves.)

Now, exactly what are you accomplishing with your persistent coaching? You are certainly not causing the behavior to change; otherwise, you wouldn't still be harping on it.

Instead, your subliminal message to the man you love is, "You aren't quite good enough the way you are."

If your husband is lucky, his natural instincts will rush to protect him against such assaults. Especially if he was criticized as a child, he has learned to fend off these verbal arrows with his own inner message, "I am fine the way I am. I am good enough. I like myself, even if you don't." The "defensive" response you don't like is a healthy, protective response for him. Do not read his unwillingness to change as deliberate stubbornness or lack of cooperation. The truth is, he is doing what he needs to do to feel good about himself in the face of your criticisms. (No matter how you phrase them, that is how he hears

EXPERIMENT #20B (WOMEN ONLY)

Stop Coaching

1. During the next several days, pay close attention to everything you say to your husband and notice every time you coach, suggest, correct, or advise him. If you can keep pencil and paper in your pocket, jot down the subject of your criticism or suggestion. OR, if you are already well aware of what annoys you the most, list those offending behaviors or habits in your journal.

2. For a specific period of time that is comfortable for you (it could be one hour or one weekend or one full week or two weeks) make a solemn vow with yourself that every time you are tempted to correct, advise, coach, or suggest anything to your husband, you will hold your tongue. Some of those times, pay your husband a little compliment instead. It may be related to the behavior you were about to correct, or something entirely different.

3. When you slip up and are unable to stop yourself, just smile at yourself. "Oops. There I go." Give yourself credit for noticing that you slipped up, and pay attention to how you feel now that you have "coached," and to how things feel between the two of you.

4. At the end of your trial period, write a short evaluation in your journal. Answer these questions:

a. How successful were you in stopping your coaching behavior cold turkey? Give yourself a grade: A, B, C, D, or F.

b. How do you feel about the experiment? Did you love it, hate it, or somewhere in between? Explain your feelings as best you can.

c. Have you noticed any specific changes in your husband? What are they? How do they make you feel?

d. How do things feel between the two of you right now? Is any of this related to your experiment?

e. Would you like to continue this experiment for another period of time? Why or why not? (If yes, set your next period of time and go for it!)

them.) Your husband is taking care of himself. But in order to do this, he has to keep a certain distance from you.

If your partner isn't so lucky, he will internalize your messages, believe you that he is not okay, and feel bad about himself. While you think you are helping him, you are causing the steady erosion of his self-esteem. That response also drives him further from you.

No matter what he is doing that upsets you, *your relationship is more important than any particular behavior or habit you don't like.* When you coach and advise, you aren't succeeding in changing your husband's behavior; you are only making it hard for your husband to feel close to you—the one thing you most want.

Just stop. Your husband does not need your advise, your suggestions, your reminders, or your corrections. Give it all up, right now, cold turkey. You don't get to call all the shots in this marriage. You don't get to control your husband's behavior. That wasn't in the marriage vows. Both you and your husband will start feeling better right away when you go on total abstinence from your coaching and advising.

Here is another entry from Henry Borys journal, *The Way of Marriage:*

> . . . Love is preferable to criticism. Love nurtures and softens, it creates trust, it paves the way for helping each other to grow. Criticism, however, sparks defenses into action. It polarizes. It undermines trust. It is never selfless. Behind every personal criticism lies a negative reaction, an ego in some degree invulnerable and out of balance; this makes criticism hard to accept, even when it is accurate.
>
> Criticism speaks to the fault within the person; love speaks to the person behind the fault.

We have now learned six immediately useable ideas for brightening and easing the atmosphere in your home and eight ways to resolve or diminish specific problems in your marriage. The natural result of these strategies will be to bring you and your partner closer together so you will be experiencing more mutual enjoyment and support.

In the next chapter, we will look at how you can directly address the quality of closeness you have and even close any "intimacy gap" you may be experiencing.

CHAPTER SIX

Discover How One of You Can Bring the Two of You *Very* Close Together: Intimacy and Companionship

They say love is a verb, that to love is to behave with love. Maybe so. But love is a feeling too! One of the qualities that sustains a loving relationship over the years is a rich array of emotions between the two of you. Of course the feelings come and go, but most couples long for the experience of closeness with each other, passionate moments, feelings of special connection, warm rushes of affection and adoration, and the deep comfort of each other's presence. In addition to being intimate, most couples want their relationship to feel intimate.

A couple can have low levels of conflict and a lot of general compatibility. But if they do nothing to nurture the *feelings* of love between them, the relationship will go flat. They will begin to sense that something is missing, that they are being cheated, that the flame has died out.

In just the last thirty years, the sexual revolution, the contemporary Women's Movement, and the rise of humanistic therapies have created more focus on intimacy than was true in previous generations. Whereas people used to marry for security, a family, and a place in the community, now we have come to expect far more: We want deep friendship, passion, great sex, radical self-disclosure, spiritual bonding, a heart connection. We are satisfied with nothing less than a soulmate. This is appropriate. If science and technology can progress, why not also human relationships?

But our new, positive visions of love are not without unwanted side effects. As with any major shift, the transition period is a time of confusion, differing expectations, laborious communications, and experimentation. In particular, our rising expectations about what is possible between two people have accented the differences between men and women, and between those who desire more intimacy and those who are quite content with less of it.

To see how one of you can bring the two of you *very* close together, we need to examine those differences.

THE INTIMACY GAP

It is widely accepted that women are more interested in intimacy than men. Men are famous for saying things like, "I told you I love you when we got married, and that stands unless I tell you something has changed." Women talk endlessly with each other about how men don't express their affection unless they want sex, about how they always seem distracted, they don't notice when we dress up specially, or serve their favorite dessert. They seem to love without being aware of their love. They never *talk* about it.

This "intimacy gap" seems like a cruel cosmic joke. Women long for romance and affection from the very creatures who lack both the interest and the skills to provide this, and who are genetically designed to view virtually everything else as more important.

Women are in a double bind: If we ask for more affection and verbal expressions of love, men feel criticized and pressured, and may become even more distant. But if we don't ask for it, the whole subject of closeness will be forgotten. What's a woman to do?

There is a solution to the intimacy gap based on the principles in this book. It's not just theoretical, it works. It can end your frustration. Let's go on a little journey of discovery.

First, let's approach the Intimacy Gap as a classic power struggle and apply the method for reframing a power struggle that we learned in Chapter Five. As we said there, setting a problem up as a polarization with only two equally undesirable solutions is a trap. What we must do then, is set up the conditions that will allow a third alternative to emerge.

Throughout interviews about intimacy with thoughtful men and women, I tried setting up those conditions. I took the position that I needed to soften the urgency of my own position, and develop empathy for the other side. I invite you to try the same thing as you read through what follows.

From women, I heard exactly what I expected to hear. Women

want *verbal* expressions of love. We are baffled at why it is such a big deal for a man to say, "You are so special! I feel very lucky to be with you," or "Gee, honey, you look absolutely gorgeous!" or "I love you," or a thousand other simple verbal affirmations.

We want physical affection from men, not only when it is designed to lead to sex. We want romantic gestures like flowers or thoughtful favors, on special occasions, but even better, on just any day.

We want moments of being together with our focus only on each other and nothing else. We want that feeling of being in a sacred space together, a space that only the two of us have ever shared. We want moments when we are basking in the pleasure of being together and so absorbed with each other that, for the moment, nothing else exists.

In short, we want men not only to love us, but to realize that they love us, to pay attention to how it feels to love us, and to express those feelings. We don't want men to take us or our love for granted.

When men talk about intimacy and about what they crave in a relationship, it sounds quite different. All the men I interviewed sounded the same themes:

> "I want the comfort of being with the person I love every day. I enjoy the pleasure of her company."
>
> "I love curling up together in bed at night. I love doing the fun things we do together—laughing, gardening, taking little trips on weekends, relating to the children, decorating the house, making dinner, going to movies. Just everyday together. I like the ease that comes to a relationship from knowing someone very well, not having to be on guard all the time."
>
> "I like that my partner allows me to be imperfect, like I got short with my wife for something and she just dropped it and let it go. She didn't take it personally."
>
> "I like talking about our work, mine or hers, sharing our excitement and our problems."
>
> "I like special occasions like dining out, going dancing."

One man stated in a more startling way what I felt I was hearing from the other men:

> MICHAEL: I don't stop and reflect on our relationship. I take it for granted. I believe that "taking the relationship for granted" should *not* have a negative connotation! For me, taking the re-

lationship for granted is a good thing. It's what I long for. I'm confident and secure. The relationship is easy. I know we love each other deeply. I have real joy in having found my soulmate and in being at ease with that. I don't have to worry about it. And I don't have to do anything to make it happen—or to keep it that way.

If a relationship is going badly, I can't take it for granted. I was in a marriage like that for years, and it was awful. I was always on edge; I couldn't relax.

You have to go through a lot to get to a place where you can take your relationship for granted. At the beginning, I idealized my wife. I was so vulnerable and open and trusting. But then things happened that caused me to become more cautious with my feelings of openness. It was nothing malicious or anything. But like when my wife made a bad business decision, or when she became depressed as I never expected she would, that was painful. Now I find the relationship transcends all that. There's nothing scary about it. I know my wife. There won't be any more big surprises. I have come to a place that is more rational and balanced than when I was infatuated with her. It's a wonderful, comfortable place to be. I can trust her completely because I know her so well.

This quality I'm talking about is kind of like a meditation, where you try to remove everything extraneous to achieve enlightenment. It's like being so immersed in a piece of work that it just flows and you lose track of time. It's mindless and joyful, like the Zen of relationship. You reach a point where it happens without your having to make it happen. There is so much pleasure in being in that space, to know that we love each other and not have to affirm each other all the time. I think it is the best place in the world to be with someone. I see it as total bliss. There is no insecurity. You don't have to nurse it.

One reason I don't express my love verbally so much is that this feeling I'm describing is very hard to convey in words. I feel like I have used up all the words I have, and they really aren't adequate. But I would not say that I am not conscious of feeling happy and in love. Quite the contrary, I'm conscious all the time of how happy my wife makes me. And look! When you ask me, I can talk about it.

But I also want to say, I know my wife wants to hear me say I love her, that she means everything to me, and that she wants

> flowers and hugs, and I don't ignore that. I'm sure I don't do it as much as she would like, but I certainly do it! One reason I don't verbalize my love more is that she does it so much. I like that she talks about our relationship, and it makes me feel like I don't have to worry about it. Certainty that we love each other is "handled." I can take it for granted! What a deeply satisfying pleasure!

As I listened to these men, all of a sudden I began to see that *men are just as deprived of what they want as women are.* A man can't experience this flowing, secure, comforting love if his partner is constantly criticizing him for not being romantic enough, and badgering him to be more expressive. Just as women can't have their precious moments of heightened closeness if men are so enjoying the pleasure of being able to take the relationship for granted.

I felt empathy for men that I had never felt before.

Let's listen to men some more.

Though Michael used the phrase "taking the relationship for granted" to refer to a positive feeling of security and effortless flow, most other men and women I tried it out on were not comfortable with those words. As Bruce put it,

> "Taking our love for granted" means to me a lack of respect, a lack of caring. It means the relationship doesn't matter very much. It means there is no appreciation there, that you are not thankful for what you have, that you don't even notice what you have.
>
> I think what Michael means is "trust," a deep security, no need to do extraordinary things to keep the relationship safe.

> DAVID: My wife says I don't talk about how I love her enough. But I feel that I *show* her my love all the time. I always have her breakfast ready for her when she comes downstairs. I pay the bills. I get us theater tickets. I remind her to bring her rain hat if it might rain. I make love with her very passionately. I bring home a good paycheck. It goes on and on! Maybe I feel an "intimacy gap" too! I feel she doesn't appreciate what I do for her and for us. Because I forget to tell her she looks lovely, all I do for her is forgotten, wiped off the slate, totally minimized!
>
> I admit I think nice thoughts about her a lot that never get verbalized. She'll cook a delicious meal, or she'll look especially

pretty, which she does most of the time, and I don't say anything. I can't tell you why this is. It's not deliberate. It's just I don't think of saying it, or I never get around to it, or something. It doesn't mean I don't appreciate and love her though. And she knows this! Of course she knows I love her. My whole life is about loving her.

JEFFREY: What frustrates me is that I feel really good about who I am and what I do. I'm competent and successful. And I know my girlfriend loves that about me. She wouldn't want to be with some wimp. But all I hear is that she wants me to "be vulnerable." I'm not some macho type. I admit when I'm wrong. I listen to her talk about what's going on with her, and I carefully refrain from offering solutions right away! I just feel she wants something from me that I'm not, and that this creates a barrier that wouldn't need to be there.

ADAM: When Donna says "Let's talk," for her this is a great, wonderful thing. She just can't wait. That's her idea of a perfect afternoon—whether we are going to talk about how great we are together or some area she thinks we need to work on. But for me when she says, "Let's talk," I have the opposite reaction. Not that I won't do it with her, but what happens to me is, I feel more like panic than excitement. I feel I'm going into an area that is not safe for me, an area where she is competent and I'm not. I feel I'm going to get criticized. She wants it to be a pleasure for us, but it is not a pleasure for me. And I don't feel she's right and I'm wrong. I'd far rather spend the afternoon sailing or even just fixing cappuccinos and reading the paper. Why won't she do that with me?

I believe there has been a massive consensus recently, in literature and in living rooms, that the solution to the intimacy gap is for men to develop their feminine side. Men need to become better at feeling and at expressing their feelings. Men need to learn to listen to feelings and not always be trying to fix them or solve them. Men need to become more introspective, to be more honest about their pain, to learn the good, enriching side of feeling vulnerable, confused, sad, even humiliated, rather than always suppressing those feelings and adopting a tough exterior.

The women's movement is two decades ahead of the men's movement, common wisdom goes. Men need to catch up with women in better integrating their yin and yang sides. What's more, women are available to awaken and nurture the feminine side of men. We'll help!

No doubt there is some truth in this picture. But there is a lot wrong with it too. Especially because our focus here is not society, but your personal relationship. It might be nice when, sometime in the next millennium, men and women have both become more balanced and more accepting of each other. But that has nothing to do with you and your partner right now. For better or worse, we are still smack in the middle of the revolution. I believe it is important to begin by accepting that.

The true problem with this widely accepted diagnosis that men ought to become more feeling is that it is polarized! Women have it all together, and men are retarded in their psychological and spiritual development. Black and white, either/or solutions are a trap that our minds set up in order to make it easier for us to win. What such thinking actually does is lead us into a dead end in which everybody loses—because there is no good solution, only two non-solutions: women get their way or men get theirs.

What happens when we try to develop empathy for the other point of view and soften the urgency about our own? Does some third alternative emerge that allows us *all* to feel satisfied?

I had a rather dramatic personal experience of a shift like this in my own marriage. I will share it because it is a fine example of a polarization melting away and because I think it contains important clues to closing the intimacy gap—not for society, but in your own relationship.

As I tried to soften my own point of view and listen with empathy to the men I was interviewing, I realized that I have been trying for years to manipulate intimacy into happening in my own marriage. From time to time, I have talked to Mayer about what I want. I've set up romantic dinners and weekends away, always plotting for those special, intense moments of complete merging. Without being conscious of it, I have been living with the belief that if I can only somehow do or say the right thing, I can create even *better* special, pleasurable moments and more closeness between us.

During the course of these interviews, it began to dawn on me what I had been doing. I was able to see how content Mayer is with our relationship, and how lucky he is not to be burdened with this subtle worry that some little extra pleasure is missing. I saw that by holding on to an idea I had in my own imagination, I was diminishing the undeniable intimacy and closeness I could be having every day!

I relaxed. It was a subtle internal shift, but it made a huge difference in my life. I began to take in exactly what was really going on between us, instead of always trying, in subtle ways, to affect it, to push it. The relief made me laugh with pleasure—and laugh at my own blindness and folly.

By acting entirely on my own, by relaxing and letting go of an idealized image, one of me brought the two of us much closer together.

Companionship is an important form of intimacy. The very fact that you share so much of your life with one person is a truly amazing gift. You always have someone with whom to eat, relax, share your home, travel, go for a walk, see a movie, even sleep. You can talk, but you don't have to. You can always be yourself, nothing to prove, nothing to get. Being together is completely effortless and comforting. You know so very much of each other's lives, both inner and outer. It's a lot to be grateful for, and to enjoy.

Companionship can be deeply pleasurable on a daily basis—if you aren't too preoccupied to let it in.

CLOSING THE INTIMACY GAP—BY YOURSELF

So what can we conclude? How can one of you have an impact on the intimacy gap in your relationship?

The solution is not for men to change one hundred percent and become paragons of physical affection and verbal expression. It's a nice fantasy for women, but we'll waste a lot of time if we wait for this to happen, time we could be using to pursue more mutually rewarding solutions.

Here's a very different suggestion for closing the Intimacy Gap, a way for you to get your intimacy needs met, no matter which side of the Gap you are on.

(I have assumed "traditional" male/female desires here. If the roles are reversed in your relationship, simply transpose what I say.)

1. Recognize that the intimacy gap is equally felt by both sides.

No matter which side of the intimacy gap you are on, your partner experiences a problem too, just as frustrating as yours.

Women feel deprived of a kind of intensity of closeness and overt expressions of love. They feel taken for granted.

Men feel deprived of the ability to relax into the relationship and trust it. They feel unappreciated for all they *do* to contribute to the relationship.

Women feel a double bind: If I ask for intimacy, he backs off. If I don't ask, he spaces out. Nothing I do gets me the results I want.

Men feel a double bind: If I ask her to back off and let us relax together, she gets sad and angry. If I don't ask her to back off, she's on my case all the time. Nothing I do gets me the results I want.

(Remember, you experience a double bind only when you are trying to get the other person to change. If you focus instead on changing yourself, the double bind disappears. And so may your partner's resistance. More about this in a moment.)

Men express a different kind of double bind also: If I act strong and together, she wants me to "be vulnerable." If I become vulnerable, she sees a hole in the strong person she wants me to be, and she doesn't like it.

If you are frustrated with your partner, remember, your partner is also frustrated with you. Soften the urgency about your position and develop empathy for your partner.

2. Don't make your partner wrong.

Recognize that your partner has a right to be the way he or she is.

Men: Don't make your wife wrong for wanting affection and verbal affirmations of your love. She has a right to this desire.

Women: Don't make your husband wrong for wanting to relax into the relationship and feel the comfort and security of it, and for wanting to show his love through his normal actions. He has a right to this desire.

Don't badger your partner. If you want to ask for something specific with regard to intimacy, use the guidelines for asking for what you want in Chapter Five.

3. As much as possible, create what you want in your relationship by yourself. Take care of your own needs.

Women: You are the partner who is more affectionate and demonstrative, so go ahead and be that way with pleasure. Tell your partner your loving feelings. Initiate hugs. Touch your partner affectionately. Enjoy this, and let it be okay that you are the one who does most of it.

As the man I quoted above said, one reason he is disinclined to say "I love you" all the time is that he feels verbal affirmations are "handled" by his wife. He enjoys her being lovey-dovey, but he does not feel he has to duplicate what she does. He appreciates that she speaks for both of them. See if you can feel okay about playing that role for the two of you, even if your hugs and words are not reciprocated as much as you would like.

Also, *ask for loving comments from your spouse.* Don't be annoyed that you have to ask; do it graciously. For example, "Do you like this outfit?" "Do you like my hair this way?" "This was a pretty yummy pasta, wasn't it?" "I thought I put on a great birthday party for Rachel, don't you?"

If you ask without the slightest hint of annoyance that you had to ask, and with no implied criticism, you'll probably get a thoughtful response. If you can get over feeling deprived because you had to ask, *you'll be getting what you want!*

Or, just say what you wish he would say; put it out there yourself. "I love the way I get the kitchen so tidy every night. It makes me feel good." Or, "I'm glad I'm so generous with Mrs. Smith. I feel good that I can help her." Your partner will probably agree with you or acknowledge your comment. That's what you want. It's one hundred percent better than nothing—which is probably what you'll get if you wait for him to say something. Let it be just fine that you had to initiate the comment.

Men: If you would like it to be okay with your spouse that you don't give her verbal affirmations and affection a lot, try explaining this to her in the way we've been discussing it here. Tell her how much you enjoy the comfort and security of your relationship, and that just because you don't talk about it very much, you don't take it for granted. Tell her how much you enjoy relaxing with her even when you are not talking. If they speak for you, maybe you could even read her what some of the men in this chapter said about this.

Also, ask for the appreciation you would like to hear from her for all that you do for her. For example, "Do you enjoy that I fix you breakfast every morning?" "Is it a relief for you that I take care of the bills every month?" "I take excellent care of the cars, don't you think?" "Isn't it a comfort to you that I'm able to bring home such a good paycheck?" If you can ask without the slightest hint of annoyance that you had to ask, and with no implied criticism, you will probably get an enthusiastic response. If you can get over feeling deprived because you had to ask, *you'll be getting what you want!*

Or, you can just say what you wish she would say. "I feel good about the way I communicate with our son. I think I'm really good at it." She'll probably agree, and that is one hundred percent better than nobody saying anything about this.

4. Look for the contribution your partner's style can make to your personal growth and your mutual happiness.

We are in an era when we recognize the value of balancing our own masculine and feminine aspects.

Women: Is your partner a model for you of independence, self-sufficiency, self-confidence, clear thinking, personal drive? (You add to this list. What could you learn from your husband?) Could you be taking better care of yourself in certain ways? Might you move toward depending on him less? Are there ways you show your love through everyday actions? Would these skills make you feel better about yourself? Would they push you toward being a more well-rounded person? Would they contribute to your relationship?

Men: Is your partner a model for you of warm human relationships, of honesty about feelings, of the ability to express feelings, of ways to be nurturing? (You add to this list. What can you learn from your wife?) Could you be paying more attention to your inner life, expressing emotions more than you do? Could you learn to value being vulnerable? Might you become a better listener? Are there ways you could show your love more through verbal and physical affection? Would these skills make you feel better about yourself? Would they push you toward being a more well-rounded person? Would they contribute to your relationship?

5. Give some attention to giving your partner what he or she wants.

Try moving in your partner's direction as much as you can.

Women: Your husband would love for you to notice and thank him for all the contributions he makes to your family. Express your appreciation that he takes out the trash, plays with the kids, reads to you from the paper, opens jars for you, . . . Even if you see these actions as his "duty," acknowledge and thank him for being the great guy he is. And take pleasure in what he does.

See if you can relax and enjoy the way life really is around your household. Let go of the fantasy of what you wish the relationship were like, and let yourself enjoy what it actually is.

Try going even further. Try deliberately being just a bit more independent and separate and self-sufficient. Do something you'd love to do for yourself entirely on your own. Or, when your partner is reading the paper and you would like to talk, decide to enjoy some reading yourself at that time.

Experiment with an open mind. See what you learn. See if anything shifts for you. You may think you can predict the outcome of your experiments, but until you actually do them, you'll never know whether your prediction was right.

Men: Try moving in your partner's direction as much as you are comfortable. Your wife will be thrilled if you tell her what you love about her, touch her affectionately, or bring her an unexpected little gift. What she loves most is verbal expressions of your love. Just little ones will work wonders. The suggestions "for men only" in Chapter Five will give you ideas.

One man I interviewed said this:

> Telling your woman you love her out loud in different ways is so important to women. I've had to learn to do it. My wife coached me. But this is definitely something I'll teach my son. If it means that much and it's so easy to do, do it!

Try going even further. Initiate a conversation with your partner in which you talk about something that is troubling you, or something that you regret from the past. Or apologize to her for something you did that was thoughtless, even if it was a long time ago. In other words, try sharing something with her that makes you feel vulnerable. When women do this with each other, they feel a connection. Maybe something like that will occur for you and your partner.

Experiment with an open mind. See what you learn. See if anything shifts for you. You may think you can predict the outcome of your experiments, but until you actually do them, you'll never know whether your prediction was right.

A WORD TO WOMEN

In my workshops, women often raise similar questions as they begin to experiment with closing the Intimacy Gap on their own. For example:

> MARLA: When I ask my husband whether he likes my hair or whether he enjoyed my meal, I know that his inner reaction is "Why is she so insecure? Why does she always need this reassurance from me? Of course her hair looks good. Of course her meal was good, and she knows it!"
>
> What he will *say* is something like, "Yes, I really like your hair," in a slightly annoyed tone of voice.
>
> So I'm not *really* getting what I want.
>
> Sometimes, I may in fact be a little insecure regarding whatever it is I am asking about. But there is nothing wrong with that. That's what a husband is for, to give honest feedback and offer reassurance. But a lot of the time, I have no insecurity at all. I just want him to notice and to share my pleasure. He has a really hard time getting this. He hears my little nudges as my insecurity, and he gets impatient. I'm just trying to connect with him!

If you experience the same frustration, here are a couple of suggestions that may help.

Try modifying the way you ask. Do not make your question sound like it has only one answer: "Do you like my hair this way?" or "This was a good recipe, wasn't it?" Instead, ask it as though you are genuinely interested in your partner's opinion and you haven't formed one yourself yet. "Honey, I'm experimenting with a new hairstyle, and I'd love your opinion." Or, "Did you like the way I prepared the vegetables tonight, or do you prefer them the old way?"

Or, when what you really want is his participation in a little victory, state your own feelings first. Then ask him directly what he feels, again giving him the option of several replies. For example, "I feel just fabulous about how this party went. I loved it. I feel like I did a really good job! I worked hard too! What do you think?" Try to ask an open-ended question, not a specific one like, "Did you have a good time?" Don't give him the option of saying just "yes" or "no."

Here's another example: "I just love these new curtains I made. I think they add a real warmth to the room. I'm interested in what you think."

These question-styles are a little more "technique-y" than I usually like to suggest. But for many people, they are an effective solution to a common problem.

I experience this very syndrome with Mayer sometimes. I tried discussing it with him directly. I pointed out to him that whenever he builds a fence, or refinishes a gorgeous piece of furniture, or cooks a fabulous meal, he always wants my comments. Usually, I offer them without solicitation. If I don't, he asks. He thrives on my involvement, my appreciation, my praise. Is he insecure? Usually not. Does he want me to share in his pleasure? Yes, always!

When I used specific examples of *my* loving comments about him, I was able to help Mayer see why *his* comments about what *I* do mean so much to me. I told him I am quite happy to continue to ask when I want his involvement, but I would greatly appreciate it if he would take me seriously and not belittle me for asking.

Here is another common sentiment:

> CAROLYN: When I spend a lot of time dressing up for an evening and I come downstairs and my husband says nothing about it, I don't think I will ever feel good about that!

But the rest of the women in her workshop agreed that Carolyn will be much happier if she does get used to it. As Shannon said,

> You know you look great! That's important all by itself. Besides, when you get to where you are going, some woman will almost certainly tell you how beautiful you look. Women don't dress for men; we dress for other women!

Shannon had a great point. Look for affirmations where you are likely to be successful. Let them fill you up, and stop expecting them where they are least likely to appear. That's taking care of yourself! And showing good will toward your partner!

Who knows why women crave connection through verbal affirmations and affectionate touch? Who knows why men are not inclined to be affectionate and affirming?

It's the subject of endless conversations, articles, and books. However, though theories about *why* men and women are the way they are may be fascinating, they are useless with regard to your individual relationship right now. We'll never know whether we are right about our theories anyway. Over time, changes in our propensities may slowly occur. We can even encourage them, as the men's and women's movements are doing. But in your relationship right now, you'll be happier if you accept the stage of evolution you find yourself in, and make it work for you and your partner.

Now let's look at some other ways you can bring the two of you very close together, all by yourself.

CREATING INTIMACY

When I asked one woman, "What is intimacy?" she replied, "I have an image of peacefulness, interspersed with sparks."

Intimacy is the flow that happens between two people who know each other well, and who love each other. That peacefulness, that ease and comfort of being together, is a great treasure, hard to come by and greatly to be enjoyed.

In addition, when all of the conditions are right and circumstances flow together in a certain way, heightened emotions, feelings of deep connection, ecstatic experiences, the little jewels of life, do come along.

Usually, you can't make these ecstatic moments happen, but you certainly can create a climate in which they are more likely to occur. All that we have suggested in this book so far—balancing your inner give-and-take scale, creating a pleasant atmosphere in your home, and solving problems by yourself—are major steps in the right direction. Let's look at a few other specific conditions that will help to foster closeness and intimacy.

Time

For starters, you have to spend time together.

If you are so busy or your lives are so separate that you meet only briefly on the run, both the peaceful kind of intimacy and the "sparks" will elude you.

Some couples find it extremely hard to create good times together, because of their work schedules or other constraints. Dual career couples with small children have the biggest challenge. But whatever the obstacles, if you don't spend good time together on a consistent basis, you won't cultivate feelings of closeness.

If you see each other very little, how can *you* make a change that will give you more time together? Can you telephone your partner during the day? Can you suggest getting up early and having breakfast out one morning a week? Can you meet at a coffee shop for forty minutes after work but before you go home to be with your children? One woman got a car phone so she could take care of business during her commute instead of having to deal with it when she got home.

If you have spent almost no relaxing time together—time that is specifically for play and pleasure, time during which there is no particular agenda, time for day-to-day exchanges, regular routines and rituals—you can't expect one weekend away to compensate for lost time and instantly make you close again.

"Togetherness" is an essential component of intimacy.

Self-Disclosure

Intimacy requires that you be open and honest with each other. My strict definition of intimacy that has stood the test of time in my workshops since 1980 is this: Intimacy is the experience of stripping away your outer, more public ways of being, and of sharing your inner life with another person. By this definition, if you aren't sharing fully and honestly what's going on with you, you might have something like intimate-style behavior, but you don't have intimacy.

Your defenses and facades may be appropriate at work or in other relationships in your life. But with your intimate partner, over a period of time you need to develop enough trust that you can be authentic with each other. If you are hiding aspects of yourself from your partner or withholding important feelings, you are preventing intimacy.

Developing openness and honesty is a process that continues for years. It may be an experience of deepening honesty that will create an especially intimate moment for you, even years after you have been together.

One woman told me that she had once been arrested for shoplifting, years before she met her husband. She was mortally embarrassed about it, but had long since put the incident behind her and attributed it to immaturity. But she had never shared this embarrassment with her husband. After they had been married for twelve or thirteen years, he got arrested for fishing without a license, and in the tumult that followed that incident, she told him about her old story. So traumatic had it been for her that she still became quite emotional about it—all these years later. Her husband was able to comfort her and assure her of his continuing love, and she was able to convey genuine empathy for his mistake. She told me it was one of those moments of special closeness.

Being honest with your partner about something very difficult for you gives your partner the opportunity to demonstrate love and support to you. The most precious love your partner can give you is the love you receive when you are having trouble loving yourself. If you never discuss with your partner what troubles you about yourself, you never give him or her the opportunity to provide that extra measure of love.

Self-disclosure is the direct route, actually the only route, to self-love. And you are bound to feel very close to whoever holds your hand through the process of increasing self-acceptance. Give your own mate that opportunity by sharing the most vulnerable parts of yourself with him or her.

Charlene acted by herself to invite an intimate moment with her husband, Walter. Sensing the need for it, she created an environment in which Walter would feel safe to open up to her.

Walter had taken on a responsibility at work that he felt terribly inadequate to handle. So desperately did he want to succeed that he carried on confidently to Charlene. But she could sense his insecurity. Wisely, she didn't assault him with it, or ask him directly. Instead, she asked him if he wanted to take a long walk in a nearby park on a Sunday afternoon. She talked a little about something that was troubling her, and then she was quiet. When he got around to the subject of work, she let him talk. Gradually, his fears came out. Still, she didn't advise him or make suggestions. She just kept listening attentively. Finally, they sat down on the grass and he was able to let the full dimensions of his fears come out. Charlene expressed empathy and support and assured Walter that she loved him and would support him fully, whatever he decided about this job. The next day, he asked to be relieved of the responsibility, and celebrated—and thanked Charlene—by taking her out to dinner.

By creating a safe, secure environment for Walter to talk, Charlene had set up the conditions that allowed an intimate moment to arise. Sometimes, this safe environment is hard to create, especially when the topic under discussion is your relationship. But Charlene's model is an important one to keep in mind. If you and your partner are feeling distant or are having trouble discussing something, is there a way you could make your partner feel less threatened?

One couple I interviewed told me that to create a safe environment for talking honestly, men should tie their hands behind their backs, and women should put tape over their mouths. Not a bad idea, especially if viewed symbolically, because men tend to intimidate women with their sheer strength, while women tend to intimidate men with their verbiage. Next time you have something difficult to discuss, keep this image in mind.

Honest, open talking about difficult or sacred subjects is the heart of intimacy.

Timing

As one man put it to me in an interview, timing is everything.

By now we should all know that men do not like to be assaulted with kisses the moment they walk in the door. Give him time to put down his packages, hang up his coat, and maybe even sort the mail. Then he'll welcome a big, warm hug.

It is difficult to feel close and intimate and to express your happiness to each other when you are stressed, overworked, tired, worried about something, or in a bad mood. Sometimes support in hard times will feel extremely loving. But often, it doesn't work at all.

Intimacy has its own rhythm. Over a long relationship, there will naturally be times of more and less closeness. If you can keep perspective and trust through the hard times and not become overly anxious about them, warmth and closeness will come back to you, maybe when you least expect it.

Romance

If you are a man seeking more intimacy, by all means try the standard methods: Tell your partner that you love her and why. Compliment her about something specific. Bring her an unexpected thoughtful gift. Take her out to dinner. Women, you can use these methods too. Just be sure you are giving without any implied criticisms or strings attached.

Don't forget about the "Seven Steps to Bring the Two of You Together" at the end of Chapter Four.

Take advantage of everything good and exciting that happens to you. Celebrate occasions of all kinds. Create relaxing times together on a regular basis. Go away for weekends or overnights. Attend personal growth workshops or marriage enrichment weekends. All of these more or less obvious ploys often work—especially if you have created a happy atmosphere in your marriage, and learned to manage problems so they don't dominate your relationship—by using the philosophy in this book.

EXPERIMENT #21

Closing Your Intimacy Gap

and Reigniting Your Love

Are you experiencing an Intimacy Gap with your partner? If so, which type of intimacy are you missing? The relaxed, easy, flowing kind? The "demonstrate your love to me, don't take me for granted" kind? The heightened, intense closeness kind? Or do you feel there could be more deep honesty between you and your partner about what is going on right now? Write a paragraph in your journal answering this question, or discuss it with a friend.

Choose the suggestions in this chapter that seem most appropriate for your own needs, and experiment.

❤ ❤ ❤

Let's take a moment to review what we have said thus far.

First, we looked at two general principles that are at the foundation of working on your relationship alone:

1. Look at your own role in your "problems" *without judgment.* Try to avoid viewing either of you as "right" or "wrong." Move away from blaming your partner, and realize that your partner is not likely to change. Start by accepting the situation you have. As much as possible, stop anguishing about it, and stop trying to manipulate or change it. Relax. Maybe even smile.

2. When you are angry, don't just be angry; do something about it. Creatively look for possible solutions to whatever made you angry. They must be solutions that do not involve asking your partner to change. View anger as a signal to make some kind of a change that is completely within your control to make.

Next, we looked at specific strategies you can put to immediate use to change the atmosphere in your home: "Act as if" you are feeling friendly and warm toward your spouse; think good will; focus on what you like and not what you don't like; view your "incompatibilities" as "complementary"; deliberately create time for just the two of you, even if it has to be in small segments. And we looked at seven steps that incorporate these principles.

Then, we learned eight techniques with which you can actually solve specific problems by yourself, approaches like acting on your own, reversing your usual response, depolarizing your power struggle, expressing empathy out loud to your partner, and asking for what you want in a way that is likely to be effective.

Finally, we focused directly on ways you can feel closer to your spouse, appreciate the companionship, and increase the intimacy between you.

What all these specific strategies add up to when taken together is a shift in attitude from frustration, anger, and blame to friendliness, tolerance, understanding, and kindness; a shift from helplessness to personal power. If you can bring yourself to make this shift, no matter whose fault anything is, the atmosphere in your home will change. You will feel more control over any situation that is making you unhappy. And you will almost certainly begin to see positive changes in your spouse. You have no idea—and no control over—what those changes will be. That's the fun of this system: If you are willing to experiment, to try something new, you are bound to be surprised.

One fear you may have is that your mate will take advantage of your generosity of spirit, and that you will simply become your partner's doormat.

As you will see in the next three chapters, adopting an attitude of good will is worlds apart from "giving in" to your partner or "putting up with" what you don't like. In Part Four, we will demonstrate this directly by examining the philosophy behind working alone. While Part Three suggested strategies you can put to immediate use, Part Five will discuss the long-term attitudes that underlie these strategies (though we will still be practical and concrete).

PART FOUR

LONG-TERM STRATEGIES FOR KEEPING YOUR RELATIONSHIP ROBUST

CHAPTER SEVEN Practice Taking Care of Yourself

Another way of putting all that we've said so far is this: To work by yourself toward a marriage that pleases and delights you, you have to pay attention to two concerns that have emerged as consistent themes throughout this book:

1. You have to stand up for and take care of your own needs, and
2. You have to stand up for and take care of your mate.

The strategies we discussed in the last two chapters, for creating a loving atmosphere in your marriage and for solving problems, make use of these two overarching principles. In this and the next two chapters, we will focus on the principles themselves, and discuss ways you can strengthen them in your marriage.

Recall the "inner balance scale" we discussed when we talked about "acting on your own" in Chapter Five: You need to keep a balance within yourself between giving and taking. Don't worry about your spouse's scale, over which you have no control, or the balance scales between you (Is my partner giving as much as I'm giving?). If you can keep your own scales balanced (Am I taking care of myself, and am I taking care of my mate), you will have mastered marriage.

Of course, keeping the scales balanced is tricky! When do you accept and tolerate what you don't like with a spirit of good will, and when do you draw a line in the sand and say, "This is unacceptable. I have to take care of myself?" When do you meet your partner's needs even at your own expense? And when do you meet your own needs, even if it is at your partner's expense? Where is the line between being sweet and generous, and being exploited or taken advantage of?

The next three chapters give you the tools you need to make those judgments.

Let's start with this question: How can you take better care of yourself in your marriage?

In this chapter, I will answer this question by introducing six affirmations. Even though they can be summarized in a sentence, each of these affirmations contains deep wisdom that will enhance the quality of your life and your marriage as you are able to internalize them.

The affirmations are a way of encouraging you to strengthen these inner resources: self-acceptance, self-reliance, courage, perseverance, conviction, and limit setting.

As you read through the explanation of these affirmations, some will seem more appropriate for your situation than others. Begin with one or two that seem most relevant to you and your relationship.

SELF-CARE AFFIRMATION #1 (TO STRENGTHEN YOUR SELF-ACCEPTANCE)

I'm Doing the Best I Can.

After the first year of medical school, Theodore decided to drop out. He longed to become a doctor but was having a terrible struggle with school, and his honest assessment was that he wasn't dedicated enough to make it. He decided to become a physical therapist instead.

Shortly after that, he found himself seated next to a priest on an airplane. During the conversation, he told the priest that he wasn't sure whether on not he believed in prayer. The priest had an interesting suggestion. "Try it," he said. "See what happens."

Theodore couldn't argue with the logic of the experiment, so he went home and prayed. With his recent "failure" at medical school in mind, he prayed, "Show me how to be successful."

To his amazement, an answer came back to him: Success is doing the best you can.

Theodore felt enormously relieved by this answer. He saw that he was not failing after all, because he was doing the best that he could. He forgave himself for what he had seen as a failure. He felt much better.

I don't know whether Theodore continued to pray. But I love his story for what it tells us about forgiveness, compassion, and self-acceptance. He could be compassionate toward himself because he was doing the best he could. How could he possibly ask more of himself? Theodore was able to accept something he didn't like, and to stop feeling bad about it.

Unless you are a most unusual person, you have a reservoir somewhere inside you of feelings like Theodore's feeling of failure: self-doubt, self-blame, and maybe even self-hate. This reservoir contains little pools of low self-esteem, painful regrets from the past, insecurities, fears of failure and rejection, envy, hurt, un-achieved goals, unspoken dreams, un-cried tears. You live, day in and day out, with these constant companions. We all do.

Maturity is the process of learning to manage the pain in our lives, whatever form it takes.

Notice I did not say eliminate the pain, but manage it. The immature approach is to try to eliminate pain. These regrets and insecurities are way too hard to look at, way too painful to feel, way too big a drag on life. So, the imaginative side of you thinks, simply get rid of them. Of course you can never be successful, but you can spend years fooling yourself.

How can you try to eliminate the pain in your life? You can "deny" it, simply ignore it—act and think as though it isn't there. You can laugh it off. You can become so busy and successful that you never have time to feel it. You can compensate: For example, if you feel afraid and insecure, you can become a braggart or a bully.

But if you use these remedies and never look squarely at your pain and address it, you will spend your entire life running away from yourself. That race will take an enormous amount of your energy, and it will keep you forever separated from your true, beautiful self. Worse, it means you can never love your whole self; you will be able to love only those parts of yourself that you allow yourself to see. And of course, if you can't love and have compassion for yourself, it will be virtually impossible for you to love and have compassion for another person. For example, think how much compassion Theodore will be able to have now for someone else who is falling short of cherished goals—because he himself made the shift from loathing to accepting his experience.

All religions, all spiritual movements, all personal growth and humanistic therapies (that are not perversions of their origins) have the same ultimate goal: Love yourself. Accept yourself, just the way you are. It takes a lifetime for most people to experience this simple truth, if they ever do.

You are fine, exactly the way you are right now. Even if you don't exercise enough. Even if you don't have the possessions or status or job you wish you did. Even if you have doubts about your marriage. Even if you dropped the pass that would have won the Superbowl game. Even if you hurt or failed someone. You are doing the best you can. You are wonderful just the way you are. You can't change reality; you can only either fight it or accept it. Accepting it, however unpleasant, is the only route to inner peace.

Religions and therapies convey this concept in a variety of ways. Christianity says, God loves you: Christ died for your sins—another way of saying, No matter what your shortcomings, you are okay. Buddhism says suffering is caused by desire and attachment. Let go of needing to be or to have something else. Again, no matter what your shortcomings, you are okay. (Even if you are attached to letting go of your attachments, you are okay.) Gestalt says, be here now. Keep your awareness in the present. Whatever is going on now, you are okay, exactly the way you are now. Even if what is going on right now is that you are belittling yourself for being too lazy, or wishing you had more money, or dreaming about the future, that's what is going on right now, and that is okay. No matter what, you are okay.

It is a very difficult concept to get.

Most of us still regret, judge, or belittle aspects of ourselves, even though, at any moment, given all the circumstances of our lives, we are doing the best we can.

Is it possible to "work on" getting better at self-acceptance and self-love?

Most of the "work" is involved with getting to know yourself, being willing to look at the painful parts that you have been denying or covering up with some other behavior. If you are open to self-searching, and you ask for support from others, you can always be on a path of discovery.

Especially these days, the opportunities for introspection and self-development are numerous, with all the workshops, therapies, and self-help books on the market. But here is a list of questions that will give you either a start or a boost in exploring more of your inner life.

EXPERIMENT #22

Get to Know Your Inner Self Better

Use these questions for journal writing or for discussions with a friend. If your partner is interested, these questions can form the basis for an intimacy-building conversation.

What do I want?
What hurts?
What makes me angry?
What am I afraid of?
What makes me happy?
What do I like about myself?
What do I dislike about myself?
Could I learn to feel okay about the things I don't like about myself?
What do I do well in my marriage?
What could I do better in my marriage?
What are my dreams?
What are my goals?
How am I going to reach my goals?
Things I would like to work on in myself right now.
Things that disturb or upset me.
What have I learned from my past?
Ways I am like my mother.
Ways I am like my father.
Do I behave or feel toward my spouse the same way I behaved or felt toward either parent?
What are my primary personality characteristics? Can I attribute these to the situation in my family when I was growing up?
Do I want anything to change in my life? If so, what is stopping me from making changes, or from starting to make changes? What do I get out of keeping things the way they are?
How do I feel right now?
How do I feel about my past? my present? my future?

Self-love is an ideal for everyone. You can work toward it by getting to know yourself well and finding whatever means you can to feel good about *all* of you, to stop putting yourself down for even the smallest thing.

But when you finally experience genuine self-acceptance and self-love, forgive yourself for everything, and truly understand that you are doing the best you can and that that is all you—or the universe—can ever ask of you, this feeling usually appears in your life as a gift, as if by grace. And that can happen at any time. You don't have to work for it; you just have to let it in.

"I'm doing the best I can" is an all-important tool in taking care of yourself in your marriage. First, it is a wonderful way to help you to feel good about yourself, to give yourself a pat on the back, to give yourself a little reward, like an afternoon with a magazine, or a nap, or a trip to the mall. You will be a stronger marriage partner when you value yourself and feel comfortable with who you are and what you are doing.

Second, "I'm doing the best I can" helps you remember that you are *not* entirely responsible for what is happening in your marriage. You may be telling yourself, "If I could just communicate what I want better," or "If I could just make my partner understand," or "I ought to be willing to do what my partner wants, but I'm not." But in fact, *sometimes* the best you can do is not enough to resolve a problem. That's okay. It is not your job to fix all the problems in your marriage. It is only your job to do your part. If you are doing your part and there is still a problem, relax. Let go. All you can do is the best you can do. When you are doing the best you can, you are a complete and total success.

EXPERIMENT #23

Self-Love

Create a private, uninterrupted time for this experiment, an hour or more if you can. Find a comfortable, pleasant environment. You may want to put on some soft, soothing music and have a snack ready.

In your journal, list all the things you love about yourself. Little things and big things. Qualities and characteristics about yourself, circumstances of your life, achievements, talents—list everything.

Now, on a separate page, list all the things you don't like about yourself and your life. Qualities about yourself, regrets, insecurities, fears, circumstances. Write it all down. Clean it all out.

Choose one item from the first list. Choose a word, phrase, or sentence that sums up that item. Close your eyes and relax. Say that word or phrase to yourself, or out loud if you wish, and right after it say, "I'm doing the best I can." For example, "I'm an excellent mother. I'm doing the best I can!" Repeat these sentences. See if you can hang on—even if only for fleeting seconds—to feeling good inside. If your mind wanders, that's okay. Just come back to your sentences.

Now, choose one item from the second list. Choose a word, phrase, or sentence that sums up that item. Close your eyes and relax. Say that word or phrase to yourself, or out loud if you wish, and right after it say, "I'm doing the best I can." For example, you might say, "I'm falling behind at work. I'm doing the best I can." Say those two sentences over and over together. Again, if your mind wanders, that's okay. Just come back to your sentences. See if you can get the feeling that whatever it is you don't like is *really* okay. It just is. Don't "try" for this feeling. Just keep saying the phrases over and over and see what happens.

Alternate meditating on an item from the first list and an item from the second list, always adding, "I'm doing the best I can," to each item.

As you do this experiment, feelings may arise in you. You may find yourself smiling or crying. Whatever happens, let the feelings be there. Just experience whatever you experience. There is absolutely nothing else you have to do.

If you find the experiment to be appealing or intriguing, come back to it from time to time. There is no "result" to look for. Just keep doing it. That's all.

SELF-CARE AFFIRMATION #2 (TO STRENGTHEN YOUR SELF-RELIANCE)

If I Don't Take Care of Myself, Who Will?

No one cares about the quality of your life the same way you do.

You may be fortunate enough to have friends and family who care deeply about you; who talk things through with you; who offer you support, advice, and good cheer. Maybe they even lend a helping hand from time to time. All of that helps. Still, their ability to help goes only so far. No one else can climb inside you and find out what you truly want, what your fondest hopes and dreams for yourself are. And no one else can make those dreams come true. No one else can take a nap for you when you need a rest. No one else can take piano lessons for you if you want to learn to play the piano. No one else can exercise for you if you want to add exercise to your daily routine. No one else can make you feel perfectly fine inside if you don't exercise or don't play the piano—even though part of you wants to.

The insidious thing about not taking care of yourself is that, if you don't do it, no one else in the world may ever notice. If you don't feed your children and buy them clothes and support them when they need your help, they'll notice. If you don't keep your agreements with your partner, your partner will be unhappy and will let you know. But you can fail to take care of yourself and your own needs for years, and no one else will care.

If your spouse has strong preferences and you generally agree with them anyway, or if your spouse has a tendency to be controlling or self-centered, you may start to disappear, gradually over a period of time, until one day you wake up and discover that there is very little of the original you left in your marriage or in your home. The loss of yourself wasn't too painful as it was happening. By going along all the time, you avoided conflict and kept everyone happy. But when you suddenly see that your needs have been overlooked for a long time, you may start to feel angry and hurt.

But remember, you can't blame your partner for taking good care of himself or herself, even if it is at your expense. Let your spouse be a model for you! You are the only one who fully understands and cares about your needs enough to do something about them. And it's never too late. Some of the best advice I know I read on a raffle ticket: "You have to be present to win!"

Of course, great excuses are plentiful: I don't have time. I keep forgetting. I'll do it later. I *am* going to do it—but not yet. The best excuse of all is, taking care of myself is not as important as all the other things I have to do—for other people.

Some of us even got a weird message somewhere along the way that it is *virtuous* to be self-neglectful, even self-abusive. I once worked with a woman who took excellent care of herself. She took all her allotted coffee and lunch breaks and always went home right at five. I viewed myself as more dedicated and committed to our mission. I worked through lunch and stayed long hours overtime to help clients; but I also complained about how exhausted I was and how intense the job was. My friend would tell me to let up, but I just felt she didn't care as much as I did.

It wasn't until years later, looking back on the situation, that I realized the self-imposed nature of my stress. I could have made the choice, as my friend did, to balance my life. I poured my whole self into the job as a way to prove to the world—and to myself—that I was a valuable person, an excellent worker. I felt that if I killed myself to do an outstanding job, other people would like and admire me.

It took me years to learn that neglecting yourself, your needs, and your desires is not virtuous. If you spell "stressed" backwards, you get "desserts." You get to choose which you want!

Self-neglect is often gender-related. Men tend to be self-reliant and give a lot of attention to meeting their own needs. Women tend to take care of others first. Women also live with a pervasive cultural myth that a prince is going to sweep into their lives and take care of them. For both of these reasons, women often need lots of encouragement to take care of themselves.

Many women do with their families the same thing I did at work. It is a huge job to run a household, take care of children or teenagers, and be generous and loving to a spouse, especially if you are also working, as so many women are. It is so easy to put the family's needs first—and second, and third, and fourth, and fifth—and never get around to your own needs.

What treat would you love most right now? A massage? A dinner out? An afternoon to shop just for you? A weekend to curl up with a long novel? An afternoon at the movies? A long walk in the woods? Lunch with a friend? Would you like to create a private space in your home that is just for you? Put it somewhere on your priority list, and not all the way at the bottom! If you never do anything to recharge you own batteries, you will have nothing left with which to serve others, and everyone will suffer. Don't look to anyone else to make your life interesting and fun. If you don't take care of yourself, no one else will either.

When you begin taking care of yourself in your marriage, your mate will almost certainly respond positively. One man I interviewed had fallen in love recently with a woman he met in an Internet chat room! He told me this:

> The first time we made love, she took clear responsibility for her own sexual satisfaction. This surprised me. From what I can tell, women usually wait to see what a man will do and then either complain about it or feel disappointed. She freed me up right away from the pressure to perform and provide. It was wonderful to be free of that. I relaxed and we enjoyed ourselves immensely.

We could view this woman's clear communication, verbal and nonverbal, as a model for all our relationships. It is almost always true that when you take care of your own needs, you take pressure off your partner, a welcome gift to him or her.

Take a moment to do this experiment, even if just mentally, before you read on.

EXPERIMENT #24

Self-Care

Make two lists in your journal:

1. How are you failing to take care of yourself in your life right now?

2. How are you failing to take care of yourself in your marriage?

These are typical responses that have emerged in our workshops after discussions:

Failing to take care of myself:

Don't exercise enough.

Should get a job I like better but keep putting it off.

Let errands go for weeks, like getting myself a new toothbrush.

Careless about parking and get too many parking tickets.

Don't eat well.

Let things go around the house until they get worse—like a roof leak.

Work too much. Don't let myself take time off.

Won't spend money on myself, like getting a manicure or new clothes.

Don't go to bed when I get a cold.

Failing to take care of myself in my marriage:

I like to make love at night, but for some reason I never initiate it. My mate prefers mornings, and we do that a lot. I know he'd respond. I just never ask for what I want.

My wife plans too many theater and concert events for my taste. I go to them all, but so many nights I'd rather stay home and relax. I need *not* to go sometimes. She could take a girlfriend.

My husband's second job keeps him away from home too many evenings. I need to ask if he'd be willing to let it go.

I love getting together with my women friends and almost never do it anymore—because I want to be home with my children and my husband. I need to find time for my friends and make it sacred, even if it is only on the phone.

We go to my in-laws every weekend. I need to insist on cutting back on this. We need some weekends to ourselves.

I want us to cuddle and be affectionate more, and I need to talk to my husband about it and initiate it more. I've just let this go for years.

I feel like my wife assaults me when I come home, and doesn't give me any time to unwind. I just go along with it because I don't want to hurt her. I need to claim some time for myself in the evenings.

I'd rather read in bed at night, but my mate always turns on the tube and I get lazy and watch it. I could go in the other room to read or ask him to use earphones.

You may be well aware of the ways you fail to take care of yourself in your marriage. On the other hand, it may not be obvious to you. As they adapt to marriage and accommodate each other in a spirit of good will, married couples sometimes lose sight of their individual desires over a period of time. If one person has a fully developed idea about something, and the other, a tender green shoot of an idea, the stronger opinion is likely to influence the weaker one. So you may need to dig a bit in doing the above experiment. If you have some vague ideas about your needs and wants but can't pinpoint them, as always it will help to write in your journal or talk with a friend.

In a workshop, we helped Mark to uncover a desire he wasn't aware of. He had told us that his wife was an interior decorator and that he felt lucky to live in a home decorated with her beautiful taste. Later, he told us a story about having friends over in which he actually apologized for the formality of the home and even for the colors in the living room. When we asked him about this inconsistency, he became pensive. I asked him to describe the place he had lived in before he got married. He did so with great pleasure; his place had been rustic and informal.

It wasn't until two weeks later that Mark told us he gradually realized that while he liked seeing how much pleasure his wife's decorating gave her, he saw that there was nothing of him anywhere in his home. We encouraged him to claim a room for himself. I learned later that he had taken a full year in his spare time to complete major renovations to the basement and had created his kind of space there. He was clearly thrilled about it.

There is no simple answer to learning to take better care of yourself. One thing that can help is to find a role model. Some people have a natural instinct for self-care or learned self-reliance and independence in their families. I know a woman who is one of the most self-nurturing people I have ever met and stands as a model in my life. Once, for several weeks ahead of her birthday, she selected gifts that she really wanted for herself. She wrapped each one beautifully, and when she woke up on her birthday, she opened all her presents!

Find a model in your life of someone who knows how to take care of him or herself, and start taking lessons!

It is most important to be compassionate with yourself. As you make the effort to take better care of yourself, remember that you are doing the best you can. Don't make a list of ways you should take better care of yourself and then use that list to beat yourself up for not being perfect.

EXPERIMENT #25

Taking Care of Yourself

From your lists in Experiment #24, select one way of taking care of yourself from each list. Write them on an index card, and put the card with your toothbrush or make-up, or in your briefcase—where you will see it often. Be patient and gentle with yourself, but see if you can make progress with this goal, just by being reminded of it often.

Plan a reward for yourself. When you achieve your goal, go to a movie or buy yourself a gift, something you wouldn't otherwise do for yourself.

SELF-CARE AFFIRMATION #3 (TO BUILD YOUR COURAGE)

I Can Do This.

Stories of courage are usually dramatic. You need courage to jump out of an airplane with a parachute on your back or to walk across a bed of hot coals. You need courage to go back to school in your forties or fifties, to travel alone, or start a new business.

But far less dramatic events in our everyday lives require great courage also. You need courage to forgive someone who has wronged you. You need courage to admit that you have been wrong. You need courage to look at your own attitudes and behavior, to see whether you might be defeating yourself in some way. You need courage to take initiative in your marriage, especially if you haven't done so for years.

Our group had been encouraging Allison to take a vacation with a friend of hers. Her husband, Herb, was in the second year of starting his own business. It was enormously consuming for him. Allison had been talking about taking a vacation for several years, and Herb just kept saying, "Maybe next year." Allison was desperate for a break; but she was full of reasons why she could not go away and leave Herb by himself and why she would not enjoy a vacation without him. We asked her to think about her vacation every chance she got during the next week. Whenever the excuses came into her brain, she was to say to herself, instead, "I can do this."

We taught Allison about "Olympian thinking," a concept developed by former Olympic athlete Marilyn King. Marilyn says that, in order to achieve anything, you must have vision, passion, and action: You have to know exactly what you want, you have to want it deeply and passionately, and you have to do whatever actions are required to bring it about. If you have any two of these components for success and not the third, you will not accomplish your goal. For example, suppose you want to learn the guitar. You have a clear picture of yourself playing your favorite songs (vision). You sign up for lessons (action), but you find that you are not practicing very much (no passion). Finally, you'll stop, because you don't want to play the guitar enough to overcome the obstacles to practicing. Or, suppose you have the vision and the passion, but you never get around to signing up for lessons. No action, no success.

We asked Allison to apply the three-step test to her vacation. She knew exactly what vacation she wanted: She and a friend would go to a specific village in Mexico and stay in a condo recommended by a friend (vision). She wanted this vacation desperately (passion). Her problem was that she found it too hard to bring up the idea with Herb. She had vision and passion but no action. She needed courage.

After three weeks of our coaching Allison to tell herself, "I can do this," she came to the group with this report:

> I presented the idea to Herb. It is one of the hardest things I've ever done. Herb was aghast. He didn't even say anything; he just sort of sat there and looked at me. So I quickly retreated. I said it was just an idea, and that we could forget it. But the more I thought about my vacation, the more reasonable it seemed to me. I understood why he was such a workaholic, but I didn't have to do that too. And when I tried to give up the vacation, I got sad. I realized I *really* wanted to go on this trip. So the next day, I just told him that I was going to do it. He got mad, but it was a short fight.
>
> A couple days later, we had a good discussion about it. He told me he realized he was jealous, and he agreed I should go. He said he was clear he did not want to live his whole life the way he was now, and that he wants us to plan a joint vacation over Christmas, and that no matter what, he will go. I'm thrilled. And I think this will be very good for us in the long run.

When you are trying to work up the courage to do something, break it down into small steps and realize that you need courage only for the very first baby step. You may think you know what will happen after you take that step, but the truth is, you don't. A baby step is not so formidable, and you have no idea where it will lead. Think of your baby step as an experiment; you need to try it just to get data, and you don't have to continue beyond it if you don't want to. Beyond baby steps lurk lovely surprises you will never discover if you always stay right where you are. To open up the possibilities of miracles in your life, you need a little willingness, a little courage: "I can do this."

The simple phrase, "I can do this," can make an actual physical difference in your life. According to psychiatrist and writer Daniel Amen, when you think negative thoughts like, "I can't do that," or "Things in my marriage will never change," your brain actually releases chemicals that make you feel bad. On the other hand, when you think positive thoughts, your brain releases chemicals that make you feel good. Positive thoughts like "I can do this!" help to sustain and fulfill themselves!

The only way to eliminate negative thoughts and emotions is to replace them with positive thoughts and emotions. When you are discouraged, if you think about why you are discouraged and how bad your situation is, you'll continue to feel discouraged. If you can make yourself think positive thoughts instead, like "I can do that" or "Won't it be wonderful when I succeed," you will push the negative thoughts right out of your head, and your brain will actually help you to feel better.

Norman Vincent Peale was ahead of the psychologists with his *Power of Positive Thinking*. We now have proof that positive thinking contributes to your health and well-being. (Critics of positive thinking allege that positive thinking by itself is not enough to bring about change. This is beside the point; positive thinking is a critical first step. And it actually can make you feel better!)

Alan Loy McGinnis, author of *The Power of Optimism,* distinguishes between cheerfulness and happiness: "We can choose to behave cheerfully in dismal or dispiriting circumstances, in part to sustain our own strength, in part as an act of courtesy to the people we love." People have been able to overcome devastating circumstances with "cheerfulness" and positive thinking. W. Mitchell, author and speaker, was burned and paralyzed in two separate accidents. Yet he starts his book off by saying, "I have a great life. You can have a great life too. . . . It's not what happens to you, but what you do about it that matters." Rose Kennedy, who endured more tragedy in her life than most of us can imagine, said, "Birds sing after a storm. Why shouldn't we?" And Helen Keller said, "No pessimist ever discovered the secrets of the stars, or sailed to an uncharted land, or opened a new heaven to the human spirit."

What step do you need to take to improve your marriage or to take better care of yourself? *You can do this!*

EXPERIMENT #26

Courage: Vision, Passion, and Action

What would you like to change about your marriage? What would you like to do for yourself? Select one inner goal you have been unable to accomplish or one idea you have been unable to try out.

Apply the three components of success: (1) Do you know exactly what you want? Can you visualize it with absolute clarity? (2) Do you want this thing with a deep, unambivalent passion? Do you want it so much you can taste it? (3) What is the first small baby step you would need to take to get this goal off the ground? Are you willing to take some action toward achieving your goal?

If you lack clarity and vision, picture this goal in your mind's eye. Or, write about it, talk to a friend, or create a collage of it by cutting out magazine pictures.

If you lack passion, consider giving up this goal. If you can, great. Move on to another goal. If you can't, maybe your passion is greater than you think. How can you cultivate your passion?

If you lack action, design one small baby step, and start telling yourself on a daily basis, *I can do this!*

SELF-CARE AFFIRMATION #4 (TO BUILD YOUR PERSEVERANCE)

Things Take Time.

As we have been saying, to create a thriving marriage with the mate you have, you need a "can do" attitude and the willingness to experiment. But there is another critical ingredient we have so far neglected to mention: perseverance. Major changes in you or your partner don't happen overnight; they may occur slowly over months or years. You have to learn to persevere even when immediate success is not apparent.

Perseverance is a combination of patience and persistence. Either one by itself won't work.

Patience without persistence is what most of us do when we realize our marriage is not all we wanted it to be: nothing. Patience without persistence goes by other names: apathy, laziness, indifference, denial. If you make no changes but you are patient for years, you will keep on getting what you already have.

But persistence without patience won't work either. If you are only persistent, you may become demanding, anxious, restless, and dissatisfied.

Persistence with patience is a magic combination. It means that you stand up for yourself and act lovingly toward your spouse, without the expectation of any particular or immediate outcome. You persevere. Your self-love and your good will become an end in themselves, and any wonderful results that they bring about are a bonus.

Two pieces of spiritual advice I have been hearing for years always seemed to me to contradict each other. On the one hand we are told, to achieve a goal, visualize it in full detail. Act and speak as though you have already accomplished it. Don't let a single negative thought creep into your head. Discipline yourself to hold the vision, rehearse it over and over, and be unswervingly committed to it.

On the other hand, we are told, don't become attached to any particular outcome. Open yourself up to a whole variety of possibilities. The universe will give you, not what you want, but what you need. Trust that there is a gift in any outcome. Any attempt to control the universe will be futile.

I have learned that although these thoughts seem to be in conflict, they are not. The secret to success is to hold on to both of them. You can't sit back and do nothing and expect to be taken care of; you have to do everything in your power to further your own cause. At the same time, you have to realize that you are not the only power in the universe and you can never have complete control. So you visualize with passion and determination—and with graciousness and humility, all at the same time. Persistence and patience.

As long as you are doing all you can to make your marriage into what you want it to be, you can relax. You are responsible for the activities of self-care and good will, but you are not responsible for the results. You have enormous control over what you do, but none over what you do *does.* If you lack patience and the ability to forego specific outcomes, you run the danger of giving up on yourself or your spouse too soon and losing out on the rewards that would have been there if you had been patient.

There does come a time, sometimes, when you should give up. That will be the subject of Chapter Ten, Evaluating Your Relationship. But if you are committed to your partner, then your job is to do all you can—and be patient, that is, to persevere.

We discussed perseverance when we said, "I can do this!" Let's talk more now about patience.

To be patient is to let go, to surrender, to do your best and then trust that the outcome will take care of itself.

Letting go does not mean that you stop taking care of yourself. It does not mean you stop striving for the goals you want in your relationship. It simply means that you stop being anxious about your relationship. As I said in my book *If I'm So Wonderful, Why Am I Still Single?,*

> Letting go is a state of mind—and body. It is a light, easy feeling of being free of a burden, a quiet that settles over you like a cosmic tranquilizer . . . What you are letting go of is the struggle, the panic, the longing for things to be other than they are . . . Letting go is relinquishing control, giving up the effort to force your [life] in one direction by manipulating your situation and the people around you. It is turning your [life] over to fate, recognizing that fortune never comes in the form you expect, and trusting the natural flow of the universe . . . Letting go is recognizing that you don't have all the answers. You don't know enough to be able to control everything. You can work with the forces in the universe that make things happen, but you don't have to make everything happen yourself . . .

> But here's the rub: letting go is not something you can achieve by an act of will. It is something that happens to you. Like grace, it comes to you not because you earned it or because you did anything in particular to "get" it. Rather, it steals unobtrusively over you, and one day you take a look and discover that—sometime, you aren't sure when—you let go. You gave up. You gave in. You stopped struggling. Or something let go of you.

When you are eager for change, patience is difficult. When I am impatient for results, I always think of the prayer: God, please give me patience, right now! What often helps me through my impatience is the metaphor of learning to ride a bicycle, which we mentioned earlier. You try and fall off, try and fall off—until suddenly you get the feel, and your life is changed forever. Never again will you not be able to ride a bicycle. This type of progress requires perseverance in the face of apparent failure, persistence and patience, the magic combination.

Before I married Mayer, I spent a lot of time with a couple I'll call Peter and Ellie. Peter wanted his wife, Ellie, to stop smoking. He cajoled and pleaded and set up incentives and teased her and talked incessantly about it. One day, I talked Peter into letting go of this issue. After a long conversation, he resolved never to mention it again. For months, I had to give Peter pep talks over and over. He kept telling me that not saying anything wasn't working. But I kept telling him that constantly saying something hadn't been working either. He did admit that life was much more pleasant without the constant fights about smoking. More than two years later, Ellie stopped smoking.

Some time after that, Peter got me aside and told me,

> Patience nearly killed me, but I have to admit, you were right. When I stopped demanding that Ellie quit smoking *for me,* she let go of her intensity about it. She didn't feel controlled, like she was quitting because I ordered her to. I was trying to get her to admit I was right. When I laid off, it opened up a space for her to give it up as a gift to me. And actually, I was very moved when she did it—I still think I was right about the whole thing, but so what? It wasn't being right that worked, it was being patient.

EXPERIMENT #27

Perseverance

What is causing you to be impatient in your life right now? Are you trying to change yourself in some way? Do you feel you have been waiting years for things to change in your marriage?

Think of one area in which perseverance is necessary for you. Do you feel you have an ideal combination of persistence and patience?

Remember, things take time. Persevere. The only way you can fail is to give up.

SELF-CARE AFFIRMATION #5 (TO BUILD YOUR CONFIDENCE)

My Desires Are Reasonable.

One of the ways we defeat ourselves in achieving our goals is to belittle the goals themselves. This is especially easy to do in marriage.

Jessica wanted more closeness with her husband, Brad. They had an easy, enjoyable relationship, but Jessica felt that Brad took her for granted. He didn't seem to take pleasure in her, to gaze lovingly at her, to write love notes the way he did at the beginning of their relationship. Jessica tried to talk about it with Brad, but his response was to get impatient with her. "You know I love you. I adore you, and feel lucky to have such a great relationship." The only time Jessica would hear such loving phrases was in this mildly irritated tone of voice in response to her concern. It wasn't the same as a spontaneous outburst from him about how much he cherished her.

"I'm unrealistic," Jessica told me. "It's a cliché to say you are too influenced by Hollywood, but I honestly believe that watching too many romantic movies has an impact. I *want* that kind of adoration from a man. I want him to be completely smitten with me. But it's unrealistic. At least with Brad it's unrealistic. I'm a dreamer."

Jessica may be right that she will never get exactly what she dreams of from Brad. This may be something she needs to accept and tolerate. But that is very different from saying that her desire is unreasonable. What she wants is entirely reasonable. Most women want more affection and adoration from men. If Jessica puts herself down for what she wants, she will be making *herself* into the problem. She will be blaming herself for being who she is and wanting what she wants.

Everything that ever happened in the history of the world started with a dream. Most dreams are "unrealistic," otherwise they wouldn't have to be dreams. Dream, imagine, fantasize, desire. These are self-affirming activities. These are how you know exactly who you are and how you are different from everyone else. If you censor your dreams, or worse, put yourself down for your dreams, you are "hiding your lamp under a bushel," apologizing for who you really are.

One woman I interviewed told me this:

> I was single for twelve years between marriages. I had a fabulous life as a single person. I loved the way I managed my money, my social calendar, my home—everything. Now, my husband tries to convince me that I spend too much on clothes, that we have people over too often, that I spend too much time keeping the house tidy. I keep trying to tell him we have different opinions on these topics and that we can both be right. But he forever tries to convince me I'm wrong. I didn't wake up to what was going on until one day I found myself telling a friend that I should cut back on my clothes shopping. Why? I have plenty of money. I might want to compromise with him and make him feel more comfortable. But I don't have to go so far as to say I'm wrong about it. My clothes shopping is entirely reasonable!

And, even if they did not have the money for clothes the way she did when she was single, her *desires* would still be reasonable. You can modify your actions and still cherish your desires. You are not wrong for wanting whatever you want! If you want it badly enough, you will find a way to make it happen.

EXPERIMENT #28

Confidence and Self-Affirmation

Make a list of your desires. Dream away. Fantasize. Create your ideal life. Don't censor.

Look over your list and see if there is anything there that you feel is "unreasonable." Now look for anything you know or suspect your mate considers to be "unreasonable."

Look over your list again with the conviction that everything on the list is entirely reasonable. What's more, if you are passionate and dedicated enough about any one of these dreams, you can go a long way toward creating it.

You probably realize that some of these fantasies are not high enough on your priority list to get any attention. At least for now. But if you discover some items on the list that you truly do want and have been neglecting—just because some voice from somewhere tells you it is unreasonable, then start applying Affirmation #3: "I can do this!"

SELF-CARE AFFIRMATION #6 (TO BUILD YOUR ASSERTIVENESS)

I Can Take a Stand.

I interviewed Krysta in her beautiful home overlooking the Golden Gate Bridge.

> Frank is a great guy. Everybody loves him. He's funny, he's a great practical joker. He's pretty macho, which I tolerate, but he's truly generous, and he's very good to me. He likes to do things, so we're always off on some adventure. We have a wonderful time together and a really good life.

I was waiting for the "but."

> But, the problem I have with him is, he has a temper, and he takes it out on the children. He can be really sweet to them but then, almost without warning, he'll descend on them. He yells

and he even uses his belt on them sometimes. It just breaks my heart and causes an uproar in the whole family. I can't talk to him about it. He just won't listen. I think he's sort of embarrassed that he does it, but he'll never apologize or admit that he's out of line. It's so upsetting. I keep saying I have to do something about it, but I don't know what to do.

ME: How long have you been wanting to do something about it?

Oh, this has been going on for about ten years now.

Krysta had made an unconscious choice. It was easier for her to endure heartbreak and to see her children suffer than to take the initiative to solve this problem. Why? Because setting a limit with Frank would be difficult and scary, and Krysta didn't believe she could be successful. Her fears and doubts stopped her cold.

Sometimes, the hardest thing in the world to do is the thing you have to do. You can't *not* do it just because it is hard.

Failing to set a limit not only allows a problem to continue, but it can also eat away at your own self-esteem. You begin to believe that you are powerless. It is hard to feel good about yourself when, day after day, you are not willing or able to take care of your needs in this critical way. You have to live with a constant ambivalence: I love him *but* . . . We have a good life, *but* . . .

As I talked further with Krysta, I learned that she was trying to get herself to stop feeling so much fear about confronting Frank: She was waiting for her fears to diminish.

Krysta was working on the wrong goal. The elimination of her fears was an unlikely outcome; what she needed to figure out instead was how she could act in *spite* of her fears.

Here are some guidelines for drawing a line in the sand in tough situations—a step-by-step plan that will help you to take a stand, even though you still have fears about setting limits and doubts that your strategy will work.

Enlist the help of a friend or your support person. Think through all these steps together first. Stay in close touch with your friend throughout all the steps.

1. Admit that this is an extremely difficult job you have to do. Write a paragraph in your journal about exactly what your fears and doubts are. Then write this sentence: I can be afraid and full of doubt and do this anyway. I can take a stand.

2. Decide exactly what you want to declare to your mate. When you draw a line in the sand, you are not asking for something, and usually, you are not open to negotiation. So you need to have your absolute limit very clear in your mind.

3. Decide whether you need to establish a consequence. For some limits, you don't need one. David's limit was that he would no longer play bridge with his wife one night a week, an activity he had been enduring for years to please her. All he needed to do was give her time to find another partner, and stop going. But when you are setting a limit about something *your spouse* needs to do or not do, you may need to be clear in your own mind what the consequence will be if the situation doesn't change.

If your problem is not serious enough to make you consider leaving your relationship, consequences can be hard to invent. Krysta told Frank that if he hit or verbally abused any of the children again, she would ask a protective services worker to come talk with them both. Since she had never before taken a stand with Frank on this matter—she only cried and distanced herself and made it obvious she was unhappy—her consequence startled Frank, and made him realize she was serious.

Another couple I spoke with, Sue and Rick, were feuding because she refused to get a job. They both agreed they needed her income. But she had been working for two years to start a mail order business and even though it was actually draining their resources, she didn't want to give up and get, as she put it, a "Mc job." Rick told Sue that if she didn't get a job within three months, he would take a second job that would keep him away from home every evening. Sue enjoyed their evenings at home and desperately needed his help with the children. She knew her guilt would be unbearable if Rick were working two jobs. His limit worked with her.

4. Decide whether you want to write a letter to your partner, with the idea that he or she will read it in your presence and you will then discuss it, or whether you want to speak directly to your mate. The advantage of writing your limits in a letter is that you will be giving a clear signal that this concern is different and special, and you really mean it. Also, you avoid the possibility of losing your nerve or becoming fuzzy-headed in the middle of your conversation. But either way can be effective.

5. Mention one or two qualities that you like about your mate first. For example, Krysta might say, "I love the way you are so generous with the kids and bring them thoughtful gifts and take them places. You are a really special father in that way." Even though this may sound contrived, I can't overemphasize the importance of it: Your mate will feel less attacked, and you will establish an atmosphere of good will at the outset.

6. Speak or write only with "I" statements; avoid "you" statements altogether. Never say, "You are too hard on the children. You lose your temper too often." Instead say, "I am not willing to have you hit the children anymore. I feel horrible when it happens. I need it to stop."

7. State your position very simply. Do not give elaborate explanations or illustrations. Do not drag up past incidents. Do not give reasons for your position. Your partner might start arguing with the reasons or explanations and get the whole thing off-track. For example, if Krysta said, "Your outbursts are hard on the children," Frank could say, "No they aren't; discipline is good for them." This is beside the point. What Frank needs to get is that Krysta is not willing to tolerate the outbursts anymore—for whatever reasons. You don't owe your spouse any reasons; you have a right to your position. The more simply you can state it, the stronger it will be.

8. When you take a stand, your mate will react in some way—possibly with anger, defensiveness, pleading, or silence. You are not responsible for your partner's response; you are not *causing* your mate to feel bad. You have to do what is right for you. You can express genuine concern and understanding: "I'm really sorry if this makes you angry," or "I don't blame you for feeling sad about this. I know this is a very hard problem for you." But you should never try to "fix" your partner's pain, or blame yourself for it. You cannot be both the disease and the doctor. The most loving thing you can do for your partner is to be decisive and firm about your position, and understanding about your partner's feelings.

These guidelines will work for both major and minor issues about which you need to take a stand. If there is anything you have been putting up with for years, give this method a try.

If you need to take a stand with your partner about something that is seriously dangerous or threatening, consider asking for professional support. If there has been physical abuse or destruction of property, you can ask a police officer to "stand by" as you let your mate know that you will no longer tolerate abusive, destructive behavior. If you are a woman and are afraid of your husband's response to your declaration, call a shelter for battered women. An experienced person will be able to guide and assist you.

EXPERIMENT #29

Take a Stand

Is there something going on in your relationship that you feel you cannot or should not tolerate?

If so, carefully go through the above eight steps. Take your time with them. I reiterate the importance of asking a friend to work through the steps with you and offer you support with each one.

The key to creating a successful marriage on your own is, as we have said, to achieve a balance between taking care of yourself and taking care of your partner; to equalize the taking and the giving that you, by yourself, do in the marriage.

In this chapter, we have discussed six affirmations that will encourage you to take care of yourself in your marriage:

I'm doing the best I can.
If I don't take care of myself, who will?
I can do this.
Things take time.
My desires are reasonable.
I can take a stand.

Keeping these principles firmly in our minds, we can now look at the other half of the equation: taking care of your spouse. Chapter Eight offers you consciousness-raising and skill-building in the area of good will, the all-important quality that I think is undervalued and even ignored in most relationship literature—and in our culture in general.

CHAPTER EIGHT Cultivate Good Will

In the study of successful marriages that I wrote about in my second book, *Eight Essential Traits of Couples Who Thrive,* as I mentioned before, over and over I saw one outstanding quality that separated couples who thrive from couples who don't. It wasn't that thriving couples all came from stable, loving homes. It wasn't that thriving couples all had excellent communication skills. Instead, I found, virtually without exception, that thriving couples have a spirit of good will toward each other that is absent in couples who do not describe themselves as "thriving."

Good will is an overall spirit of generosity toward your partner. It is the feeling, "No matter what, I am on your side. I am an ally, not an adversary."

If you have used any of the strategies presented in Chapters Four and Five for creating a happy atmosphere in your home and for solving problems by yourself, you have been exercising your good will. In order to be the "big" person in your relationship, to use leadership skills, you have to have good will.

Though good will is a concept that has already woven itself thoroughly into the fabric of this book, we will focus on it directly in this chapter to help you strengthen this all-important aspect of your character. Good will is the single most important tool you need for one of you to bring the two of you together.

Of course it is easy to exhibit good will toward your partner when you are feeling good and are generally happy with your mate and your relationship. It becomes challenging to call up your good will when you are feeling deprived or angry with your mate.

Since it incorporates qualities like tolerance, acceptance, compassion, forgiveness, and generosity, good will *sounds* like it is all designed to benefit your partner. But in fact, good will will do more to make *you* into a happy person than anything else you can do, and it is the ultimate secret to success in marriage and long-term love. You should practice cooperation and good will, not only because this is a nice way to be, but because good will *solves problems.*

> *As the soft yield of water cleaves obstinate stone,*
> *So to yield with life solves the insoluble.*
> —*Lao Tsu*

If you are willing to yield, to give, to be generous and vulnerable, problems will yield.

Although she acknowledged that it wasn't important, Allison tried in vain to get Harry to put the toilet seat down. She attempted to use humor and a variety of clever reminders. Nothing worked, and she was becoming exasperated with the problem. Then one day, she was with a group of frustrated single women who were swapping horror stories about awful dates, men too thoughtless and chickenhearted to call back, and the frustrations of singlehood. Suddenly, she was overcome with gratitude for her wonderful relationship, and the toilet seat problem looked ridiculous to her. She decided that, henceforth, whenever she saw that toilet seat up she would use it as a reminder of how much she loved Harry and how happy she was to be with him. She now viewed the raised toilet seat as a pleasant ritual, a little gift Harry left her as a reminder of his love. She also found that it was quite simple for her to lower the toilet seat herself.

Allison yielded, and the problem disappeared.

Arthur's main complaint about Sherry was that she was a back-seat driver, and not only when they were in the car. She guided and instructed him through everything he did. "If you hold the knife this way when you slice the bagel, it's easier." "Be sure to use the small attachment when you vacuum in the corners." "Don't slump over at the table." It went on and on. Arthur told me that he always "fought back." I asked him why. He thought about my question:

> She seems to think I am incompetent, and I feel I have to stand up for myself. I view myself as quite capable—self-sufficient, actually. I think my fighting back is a way of defending my self-image. Also, of course, I try to get her to stop it.

I asked Arthur to go home and ask Sherry where she would put him on a scale from useless and incompetent (1) to capable and self-sufficient (10). He was astonished that she not only gave him a 10, but expressed great appreciation for all he does to help around the house.

In further discussions, Arthur began to transform his understanding about Sherry's "back-seat driving." He saw that she did not connect her advice to any sense of his being incompetent; she did it more out of habit and her own need to be in control. Arthur began to realize a critical fact: Sherry's back-seat driving had nothing to do with him. Sherry was just being Sherry, trying to control things. I suggested to Arthur that he begin, as an experiment, to do the opposite of what he had been doing. I asked him to thank Sherry each time she offered him advice, and then simply to go ahead with his activity. If it didn't bother him to do so, he could even use her suggestion.

> ARTHUR: The first few times I thanked her, I felt what I can only call a major inner shift taking place inside me. It was one of those "aha" moments that felt like a miracle—because, in a million years, I never could have imagined feeling this way before. It felt like a huge brick wall between us instantly disintegrated. And what shocked me was to see that *I* had created the wall, not Sherry. I see that I can let Sherry be her controlling self and not let it affect me. Her comments are no big thing. I can keep being my competent self. By fighting her on this, I am only creating friction, and I'll never get her to stop. So give in to it!

Arthur's comment is what reminded me of the quote from Lao Tsu, which I'll now remind us of again:

> *As the soft yield of water cleaves obstinate stone,*
> *So to yield with life solves the insoluble.*

Another woman I interviewed, Zoe, told me this story about transforming a problem through the use of good will:

> During my first pregnancy, Fred was so caring and thoughtful. Especially in the last months, he would massage my aching back for long periods of time, cook dinner a lot, and worry about my health. Of course, I expected the same loving treatment during my second pregnancy. But everything was different. He had a new, stressful job with a long commute. I was now working also, and we had a demanding two-year-old. Fred just didn't have anything left to give me. This time, when I asked for mas-

sages, he would tell me he was just too tired, and a minute later, he would be asleep.

At first I felt very sad and deprived, and longed for the good ol' days. I had a good cry. Then I got an idea: I'd pay to get a professional massage for myself! Then I got an even better idea: I'd pay to get both of us professional massages! I might be the pregnant one, but Fred was under a lot of stress too. I got us a babysitter too (even though that was against our stated policy since we thought it was important to spend weekends with our son), and we ended up having a relaxing and enjoyable—and badly needed—afternoon and evening. Both of us felt renewed and closer to each other.

It is important to recognize that good will is not the American way. In this chapter, we will discover specific ways that you can cultivate your spirit of good will. As you read through them, you are likely to hear inner voices that say,

- This is not realistic; she's dreaming.
- Good will isn't fair!
- Yea, but she doesn't know my marriage. This will never work for us.
- She's just telling me to put up with a bad situation. I'll end up being a doormat. My partner will take advantage of me.
- What does she think I am, a saint?

These voices are to be expected because you have been barraged your entire life with cultural values that are the opposite of good will. Individualism, self-sufficiency, and competition drive this country, not good will. To survive in the marketplace, you put your own interests first, withhold information, and suspect other people's motives. Take care of ol' Number One! Be careful, other people may take advantage of you!

Rarely in corporate or government life do we see a spirit of cooperation, mutuality, and understanding. The free market economy depends on competition, and, as pathetic as it is to see, national politics have become entirely adversarial. Even though win/win solutions are almost always possible in our public life, the solutions sought are virtually always win/lose. On both the individual and the collective level, our tendency toward narcissism and self-involvement usually blots out the spirit of good will.

Too bad, because as we have just seen, cooperation and good will solve problems. This would be true in government and business too, but that is another book.

Let me respond briefly to the objections that will arise inside you as you read the specific suggestions for cultivating good will in this chapter.

POSSIBLE OBJECTIONS TO GOOD WILL

Objection #1: It won't work.

This entire discussion of good will assumes that you love your mate, and that you are in a marriage or long-term commitment that you value. If you are truly un-happy in your marriage, the suggestions about offering good will to your partner may make you angry. If you are convinced that good will won't work in your marriage, it won't.

Your response to the suggestions in this chapter will be an important barometer for you. As you read, pay close attention to how you feel. If you are secure in your relationship, your response is likely to be, "Yes, I know she's right. I have done that, and it works for us"; or, "That sounds good. I want to try that." However, what if every time you read a suggestion your first response is, "Yeah—but she doesn't know my spouse. My partner will never even notice if I do that. I don't want to keep being generous. I'll never get anything back?" If your fear is that all the good will you can muster will still leave you feeling deprived or cheated, then Chapter Ten, in which I assist you to evaluate your marriage in the light of all that we have discussed in the book, will be especially important for you.

If you believe in it, good will always "works."

Objection #2: It isn't fair.

This is true. Most often, love and good will aren't fair. If all the giving and understanding in your relationship were completely equal, you would have no need for good will; you would need only a scorecard. Indeed, you need large doses of good will precisely because life usually isn't fair.

A preoccupation with fairness will erode love, for love and attention can never be given out in equal doses. If you want to give only as much as you receive, look to the marketplace, not to your marriage.

When you think up a perfect gift for someone, something highly personalized and appropriate, don't you take greater delight in giving such a gift than in opening your own? Generous, free-spirited giving can bring you much happiness. Keeping score will only bring you stress.

Mayer and I have a close family friend whom we adore. Over the years, we have gone out of our way for each other over and over, including freely sharing professional skills that we usually get paid for. We take great pleasure in giving, taking, and asking each other for help, and experience our sharing as an expression of our mutual fondness.

I was saddened when I received a letter from another close friend who is a "writing buddy" of mine. Concerned that one of us might do more reading or editing of the other's work, this person suggested we begin to keep some sort of track. Rather than beginning to deal on this level, I stopped exchanging help with my friend. I had liked helping each other as an expression of our friendship, but I had no interest in doing it as a business deal. We lost, not only our writing exchanges, but the pleasure of giving to each other.

If you achieve perfect equality in your marriage, will you be happier? I doubt it. Good will is a unilateral action.

Objection #3: You are just telling me to put up with a bad situation. I will become a doormat. My mate will take advantage of me.

Good will won't make you into a doormat if you have some level of balance between taking care of your own needs and taking care of your partner's. The Self-Care chapter came before this one on purpose. If you are someone who already gives a great deal to your partner, and you feel you don't receive enough back, concentrate first on taking care of your own needs within your marriage.

But the main reason good will won't make you into a doormat who just puts up with things is that exercising good will is not a passive activity but an active one. A spirit of good will requires initiative, imagination, and courage. While it sometimes means that you have to become vulnerable, it also puts you in control. "Putting up with" something, and deciding you will graciously tolerate it and make the best of it, are two entirely different things. Good will is empowering. It puts you in charge and gives you a sense of accomplishment, even victory. Any average wimp can grudgingly "put up with" a bad situation while constantly complaining about it; it takes a strong, independent, self-loving person to respond with good will. Offering good will to another person is as much a gift to yourself as to him or her. It makes you feel good about yourself, in control, a *Good Housekeeping*–type seal of approval that says you are managing well.

You are in no danger of becoming a doormat or a codependent if you do someone else a thoughtful favor, forgive a transgression, or graciously accept an unpleasant, unlikely-to-change aspect of a person. You'll be more like the master of the house than the doormat.

Objection #4: I'm not a saint.

The difference between normal human beings and saints is a difference in degree only. Saints behave generously and lovingly toward others more often and more consistently than the rest of us. They are always good and never bad. They devote their entire lives to good causes, and to serving others. Saints are so highly evolved that they require very little in the way of attention to themselves.

Most of us are not ready for this. We wouldn't choose to be saints, and we aren't capable of it anyway. But maybe what we are saying here is that it would not hurt any of us to become a little more saintlike. Even one percent more good will than you practice now is guaranteed to improve your marriage.

Good will is not a philosophy, it's a practice. The more you practice good will, the more you understand it, the more it gets in your bones, and the more you will want to practice it. The goal is never perfection, but progress.

Let us now look at specific strategies for cultivating good will in your life and for strengthening your ability to call it up in stressful situations. Again, we will do this by learning a series of affirmations that will encourage you to cultivate these aspects of good will: acceptance, tolerance, detachment, forgiveness, compassion, and generosity.

As you read through the explanation of these affirmations, some will seem more appropriate for your situation than others. Begin with one or two that seem most relevant for you and your relationship.

GOOD WILL AFFIRMATION #1 (TO CULTIVATE ACCEPTANCE)

This Is Not a Problem; It's a Fact of Life.

Acceptance is a fundamental component of good will.

Accepting your mate is the same thing as feeling unconditional love toward him or her. You are not saying to your mate, "When you are in a good mood, I love you," or "I love some things about you but not other things." No. "I love you" means "I love the complete you, including the parts I'm not so fond of." Accepting those parts of your mate that you don't like may be a stretch for you; it requires good will.

Sue adores Jeff, but hates the amount of time he spends in front of his computer playing with the Internet. "It's such a waste of time. He doesn't do anything useful. And it takes so much away from the time we used to spend together. I just hate it. It's the biggest problem we've ever had in our marriage. Jeff agrees that it creates a time problem, but he doesn't want to give it up. I'm at my wits end. I don't know what else to do."

"It seems like the Internet is not going to go away," I suggested to her. "What would happen if you stopped viewing it as a problem and began to see it as a fact of life, a new, possibly unwelcome fact of life?"

"Yeah," she sighed.

I continued. "A problem is something you have to solve. A fact of life is something you have to adapt to."

When I saw Sue several weeks later, she told me this:

> I realized I had been working really hard to solve this problem. In my fantasy, the solution was that Jeff would see the light and begin to reduce his computer time. The less that happened, the more out of control I felt. I kept imagining the perfect conversation with him in which, if I just said the right thing in the right way, he'd be willing to compromise. When I realized I had no problem to solve, the whole thing shifted for me. When I started thinking about adapting to this fact of life, I came up with different ideas. For one thing, I asked him to show me some of what he does. He was thrilled, and it did give us more time together. And I began to see why he has so much fun with it. Second, I joined a quilting group, so I could be doing more of my thing while he does his. The whole atmosphere has changed around our house.

> Jeff told me that the hardest part of my unhappiness with him was not that I complained about the time but that I was actually putting him down for what he loved. I was belittling him and his hobby. I see now that he has a right to an interest that doesn't interest me, and that part of loving someone is loving the parts you aren't so happy about.
>
> But the best part is this: Ironically, now that Jeff doesn't have to feel so defensive about the computer, he is much more willing to negotiate with me about particular times and the amounts of time he spends with it.

When you fail to accept what is, you will rarely realize that it is *you* who are creating a problem. Usually, you will be convinced that the other guy is at fault.

If Sue complains about Jeff's computer time, it is she who is creating a problem between them, not Jeff. Jeff is just being Jeff, taking care of his own needs. Because Sue is not graciously accepting Jeff's preferences, with a spirit of good will, she is making his hobby into a problem. When one partner is trying to change the other, the conflict is usually caused by the partner who is not willing to be accepting, not the partner who is unwilling to change.

Life is tough. You don't always get exactly what you want. But if you can't change something, accepting it in a spirit of good will is far less exhausting for everyone involved than continuing to fight it.

And, as Sue found out, in the end acceptance is also more likely to get you what you want.

Helen came to me feeling anxious about her sexual relationship with her husband of fifteen years, Harv. "I tell him over and over what I like. He may do it once, but then he goes back to his old ways. Nothing changes." She thought I would be able to give her a formula for getting her messages across to him successfully; that she somehow wasn't communicating in just the right way. What I told her instead is, "Maybe Harv just isn't ever going to be Don Juan. Maybe he will never get it, no matter how many times or in what different ways you tell him." The idea came as a shock to Helen. It had never occurred to her in just that way. As the idea settled over her, I asked her, "How does that make you feel?"

"Well," she replied, "I feel sad, and resentful, and deprived."

We discussed each of her feelings. She realized both that they were appropriate under the circumstances, and that she could live with them. By the end of our conversation, she told me,

> Overall, I feel a great relief. I now realize this problem is not my fault or my responsibility. For years I've been convinced that if I just had the courage or the wisdom to say the right thing, this problem would change. Letting go of that feels like a great weight off my shoulders. Also, now when I ask for something from Harv, it will be to get something for myself, not to try to change him! This feels like a huge difference. To request something I want is simple. To assume that when I ask for something it will get Harv to change feels monumental, and I now see, doomed to perpetual failure.

Accepting someone is not mutually exclusive with asking the person to change. Quite the contrary, acceptance is the starting point for change. Until you stop fighting something and accept it, you aren't dealing with reality but rather a wish you have created in your mind. Also, when you are generally accepting and non-judgmental of your mate, he or she is far likelier to respond positively to your requests for change. A spirit of acceptance in a relationship creates a safe atmosphere that makes asking for change much more likely to be effective.

Sometimes it helps you to become more accepting if you can make an internal shift, so that you begin to view something you don't like in your mate as an endearing idiosyncrasy. Over time, this shift occurred for Sue. She saw that Jeff's knowledge of and opinions about the Internet made him a lively conversationalist, and she began to respect him for his self-taught expertise. She began to tease him good-naturedly, calling him her "nouveau-nerd." It all started when she began to accept the inevitable.

Remember, accepting something is not the same thing as liking it. It just means that you stop spending useless energy fighting something that is not likely to change. Until you make the shift to acceptance, you will never know what other shifts may also take place.

I once heard the psychologist and spiritual leader Ram Dass say in a talk that we don't go into the forest asking the maple trees to become elms and the oaks to become poplars. We accept the forest just as it is. Would that we could apply such wisdom to people.

I want to repeat several of the ideas we just discussed about accepting what we don't like in a spirit of good will:

1. A problem is something you have to solve. A fact of life is something you have to adapt to. Maybe what you are dealing with is not a problem but a fact of life.
2. Accepting a fact of life is not the same thing as liking it. It just

EXPERIMENT #30

Cultivating Acceptance

What is the worst problem in your marriage? What happens to it if you say, "This is not a problem; it's a fact of life."

Try making this shift in your mind, and just live with it for a week or so. See if your attitude toward the "problem" alters.

In your journal, write down your problem in a phrase or sentence. Now write the sentence, "This is not a problem; it is a fact of life." Now write, "Ways I can adapt to this fact of life." Make a list or write a paragraph about ways you might adapt to this fact of life in a spirit of good will.

means that you stop spending useless energy fighting something that is not likely to change.

3. When one partner is trying to change the other, the conflict is usually caused by the partner who is unwilling to be accepting, not the partner who is unwilling to change.
4. Accepting someone else's behavior is not mutually exclusive with asking the person to change. Quite the contrary, a spirit of acceptance in a relationship creates a safe atmosphere that makes asking for change much easier. Acceptance is the starting point for change.

GOOD WILL AFFIRMATION #2 (TO CULTIVATE TOLERANCE)

My Partner Is Not Wrong, Just Different.

A speaker I know, John Warren, tells a funny story about the fights he and his wife used to have about time. "When the invitation says eight o'clock, to me that means that at eight o'clock, my finger is pressing their doorbell," he says. "To her, it means that at eight o'clock, she starts thinking about getting ready. Even when we compromise, it doesn't put us very close together."

Ogden Nash captures this problem in a long poem about people who arrive at the theater before the cast, versus those who fall over other people's feet getting to their center seats just as the curtain is rising. His poem ends thus:

> *Oh, one kind likes to be on time and the other likes to tarry,*
> *Which wouldn't make any difference at all at except that each other*
> *Is what they always marry.*

John goes on to tell that, after several years of horrendous fights about time, he and his wife happened to bring up the topic on a long drive when they had the opportunity to discuss it calmly at length and with the aim of truly listening to each other. They talked about how time was treated in their families. Of course, they discovered huge differences. They asked each other what was good about the other person's approach. He knew that he could benefit by being more relaxed, less rigid. She knew that she could benefit by learning to plan ahead better. They realized that their fights had been an effort to get the other person to admit to being wrong and to repent and reform. Now they saw that they each had a right to be the way they were. No one was wrong. They were just different.

Gender Differences

I recently found myself in a group of women who were engaging in casual man-bashing. It started because one woman in the group had begun an intimate relationship with a woman, and she was ecstatic. "She wants to talk when I do, she's romantic and calls me a lot. She brings me little gifts. She knows just what to do sexually. She lets me talk and doesn't try to solve all my problems. It's just wonderful. I'm getting all the things I have never been able to get from a man."

"Oh how wonderful," the others chimed in. And then it started. "Men are so dumb. They can never "get" what we really want. After the first month, they don't even like to be affectionate. All they ever want to do is read the paper. They think they can say "I love you" once every ten years and that's enough. You can't have long, delicious conversations with men. Men just aren't focused on the relationship. You have to keep getting them to pay attention, and after a while you get tired of the effort." On it went.

"Why can't we get men to change—after all these years of trying?" one woman said, her voice tense with frustration. We began to fantasize massive mandatory classes for men in how to be good human beings.

As soon as I left the group though, I knew what I should have said. "Men are not awful people. They are men. They aren't being malicious and stupid. They are just doing what men do. The problem is not that we haven't taught them well enough how to be what we want. We women are creating the problem, because we are not accepting that men are men and figuring out how to adapt to this fact of life. Men are not wrong; they are just different."

I once asked Mayer if he wished he could be a woman. It looked to me like women get all the goodies. Women form closer bonds more easily. We tend to have closer friends. We feel emotions more easily. We get to wear more interesting clothes. How naive I was! Mayer assured me he wouldn't want to take on any of that, he is quite content with himself and his life, and that putting on makeup every day would never be worth all the bonding and emotions in the world.

Both genders would do well to give up trying to change each other, and instead draw on each other's strengths and, in a spirit of good will, adapt to our incompatibilities.

Does this mean we need to be content with the world as it is? That we can't work toward better communication and greater compatibility between the sexes? That we shouldn't continue to strive for equality and genuine partnership and a society not dominated by oppressive patriarchal values? That we can't envision a future in which the feminine side of our collective psyche has as much prominence as the masculine side now does?

Not at all. Remember, acceptance is the starting point for change. Fighting who men (or women) are today wastes our creative energies. Accepting each other opens up limitless possibilities.

It is important to realize that you can disagree with a person and still not view that person as "wrong." To be sure, sometimes people definitely *are* wrong. We will discuss those situations in a moment. But often, reasonable people differ. There can be two or many valid opinions or legitimate ways to do something.

Marla was in a stable marriage. She loved and admired Philip and enjoyed his companionship. But she always felt mildly cheated because Philip wasn't affectionate and never told her, "I love you."

One evening they had a group of friends over, and she inadvertently overheard someone say, "I just love to see Philip and Marla together. It's so obvious he adores her." The remark surprised Marla and stuck with her.

The next day, Philip was working on the roses in the yard. Marla was thrilled to be living in a place where they could grow roses. She said to herself, "He's working on the roses because he adores me." That night, he fixed the light in the garage. "He's fixing the light because he adores me," she thought.

Philip's way of being in his marriage and his way of showing love were not the same as Marla's ways. But they weren't wrong, only different. An accidentally overheard comment shifted the way Marla viewed Philip and his behavior, and she felt her complaints about him melt away. She had been creating the problem, not Philip. Philip was just being Philip.

As we've observed, men often express their love by doing things. A man feels close to a woman when they go to a movie together or curl up and watch TV or read the paper or make love. Women feel close when they have more direct face-to-face contact. Women express their love by talking, showing affection, sharing intimacies. Men are not wrong; women are not wrong. They are just different.

EXPERIMENT #31

Cultivating Tolerance

Think of something that you don't like about your mate, some way in which you wish your mate were different. Maybe you wish he would spend more time with the children, or that she were not such a talker. Now try saying to yourself, "My partner is not wrong, just different. My partner has a right to behave that way."

Let yourself live with this idea for a week or so. Try discussing it with a friend or writing about it in your journal. Does it change the way you view your partner? Who is creating a problem about this issue?

Even if you want the situation to change, in fact especially if you want it to change, try to stop fighting and resisting it. Accept it. Remember, acceptance is the beginning of change.

GOOD WILL AFFIRMATION #3 (TO CULTIVATE DETACHMENT)

This Has Nothing to Do with Me.

Recall the story earlier in this chapter about how Arthur was being driven crazy by Sherry's constant advice-giving and back-seat driving. Remember, Arthur realized that Sherry's back-seat driving was something she needed to do for herself—because she felt better when she had a sense that she was in control. He realized that Sherry was controlling with everyone in her life, that she was not singling him out for special treatment. She gave Arthur advice, not because she thought Arthur was inadequate, but so that she herself could feel more in control. Her back-seat driving was independent of him. It had nothing to do with him!

Shortly after Arthur and I spoke, he overheard Sherry talking to friends at whose home they were about to spend a weekend. "Do you have enough blankets?" she inquired. "We like fresh fruit. Do you have plenty of fresh fruit on hand?" Arthur laughed. Sherry was just being Sherry. He saw clearly that he was making a mistake to take her back-seat driving personally.

The affirmation, "This has nothing to do with me," is most appropriate when you feel your mate is doing something *to* you. If your mate is advising you, criticizing you, ignoring you, being impatient with you, even yelling at you or lying to you, try on the idea, "This has nothing to do with me. My mate is just being my mate, just doing what my mate does."

Admittedly, sometimes this can be extremely difficult. When your partner is coming at you with a strong emotion or opinion, it is hard not to get hooked into it.

Peter was very upset when I first spoke with him. His partner of one year, Diane, was critical of him. When she got critical, she also became very angry. Peter was too messy, he was too slow, he was too disorganized in Diane's view, and she would yell at him to try to get him to shape up.

I asked Peter, "What if we found out that Diane has a disease called Chronic Yelling and Criticizing?" It is not known exactly what triggers outbreaks of the disease, but fortunately, the cure is known. If the patient hears the phrase, "You are right, I wish I could be better," she begins to calm down.

Peter was very skeptical, and kept reporting to me that their fights were escalating. "I'm not messy and slow," he told me. "She makes me furious."

But I kept coaching Peter. "Let it roll off your back," I suggested. "It takes two to fight. Just don't engage with her. Keep telling yourself, 'This has nothing to do with me.' "

After several months, I got a call from Peter one night. "I finally understand what you mean," he told me excitedly. "I took the afternoon off and cleaned up the whole kitchen and living room—for her. When she came home, she was pleased. She couldn't help but notice, but after three sentences, she started in telling me how I could have done it better. I mean, if this didn't make an impact on her, nothing will. I now see that she'll criticize no matter what I do! It has nothing to do with me."

The change Peter made was that he stopped fighting with Diane. He would let her "run her number," as he put it, and then they would get on to the aspects of their relationship that they both enjoyed, which were numerous. Peter didn't like Diane's criticism, but he learned to accept it and move on. He exercised a spirit of good will toward her by accepting her for who she is.

Eve and Gary had a potentially worse problem. Though they had a strong and powerful attraction to each other, Gary had a huge fear of commitment. Even so, he agreed to marry Eve. Two years into their marriage, Eve learned that he was seeing another woman, and that he had been lying to her about it.

I interviewed Eve several years after they had resolved the crisis.

> Though I considered leaving Gary, I knew deep inside that he loved me, that our relationship was right, and that he was just playing out his fears. I was much more upset about Gary's lying to me than about his seeing this woman, an old girlfriend who didn't threaten me at all. But I realized that lying was Gary's way of surviving in the face of what he had done. Lying was his defense mechanism, the way some of us deny things to ourselves or get judgmental or defensive. He felt terrible and was terrified he was going to lose me. I was angry, but I also felt a lot of compassion for him. I know what an inner struggle it was for him to marry me in the first place. Gary wasn't lying *to me*. He was just lying. That is what Gary does. *It had nothing to do with me.*

The affirmation, "This has nothing to do with me," allows you to pour out good will toward your partner without having your judgments stand in the way. Eve didn't like that Gary had lied. But she was able to separate her judgment about his behavior from her support for Gary, the person. She was able to support him though not the behavior she didn't like. She didn't take it personally, and she didn't take on the responsibility of "fixing" Gary so that he wouldn't lie.

Of course Eve's support of Gary and her loyalty to him after such a transgression moved Gary very much. "Eve made it safe for me to come back," Gary told me. "It was the only way that would have happened."

Eve added,

> I don't believe that affairs should always be treated this lightly. I had a big context in which to see what Gary did, and I knew I would be a fool to throw away what we had. Only because I know what a struggle he was going through could I forgive him and get on with things. I knew his affair and his lying were not about me but about him.

When you are in a close intimate relationship with someone, it can be monumentally difficult to extricate yourself emotionally from something that person has done, or does consistently. It calls for a lot of good will. But sometimes it is essential.

Charles and Hong were having a hard time because Hong couldn't settle on a career that worked for her. Charles felt that, to be supportive, he should keep offering suggestions and then be sure that Hong followed up on them. When Hong didn't follow up, or a lead didn't work out, they both felt they had failed. I suggested to Charles that he try the affirmation, "This has nothing to do with me." When he could stop feeling responsible for Hong's work life, they both felt freed up. He smiled, "Now I just tell her, 'I love you. Let me know if I can help. Good luck.' "

EXPERIMENT #32

Cultivating Detachment

Does your mate have an annoying habit? Does your partner consistently do something *to* you that you don't like? Is your partner trying to blame you, change you, "fix" you?

Try imagining that situation, and then say to yourself, "This has nothing to do with me."

In your journal, write about what that sentence means to you, or discuss it with a friend.

If the idea makes sense to you, keep the affirmation in the front of your mind and say it to yourself the next time your mate tries to hook you. As you say the affirmation to yourself, don't say anything to your mate.

The secret to success in detaching from something your partner does, for reasons of his or her own, is silence without hostility or judgment. Let it be okay that your mate does this thing; just don't let it affect you.

This is a hard one. Keep working at it.

GOOD WILL AFFIRMATION #4 (TO CULTIVATE COMPASSION)

She's Doing the Best She Can.

or

He's Doing the Best He Can.

You will be able to feel forgiving and compassionate toward your mate more easily if you can see that, circumstances being what they are, your mate is doing the best he or she can.

When Eve was telling me about the time she had to deal with Gary's affair in the above story, she said,

> All my friends told me I should be furious with Gary. At first I felt embarrassed about forgiving him, afraid I was just being a

wimp. But the difference between me and my friends was, I knew so well the whole struggle that got Gary to where he was, and I saw this as the last step in his fight to let go of his old ways. I know he was genuinely sorry, and that he was, in fact, doing the best he could. He talked to me about how it all happened and what he learned from it, and because I know Gary, I felt confident that the lessons would stick.

A spirit of good will requires that you take the focus off yourself and put it on the other person. Hurt, resentment, anger, and the urge for revenge keep the focus on you. Compassion and forgiveness put the focus on the other person. Eve was thinking not about herself, but about Gary. This requires courage and vulnerability.

Marriage is not a 50/50 proposition, it's 100/100. That is, both partners need to give one hundred percent of what they have to give, at all times. But we must realize that two partners bring *unequal* resources to a marriage. One person's one hundred percent might be $40, figuratively speaking, while the other person's could be $80. In an ideal relationship, the partners' love, support, and understanding of each other will expand each partner's "best," just as Eve's courageous and generous support of Gary helped him to grow. To feel compassion and extend good will when you are feeling upset with your partner, you must always ask, What does your partner have to start with?

Lorraine Hansberry's character in her play *A Raisin in the Sun,* says it beautifully:

> "Love him? There is nothing left to love."
>
> "There is always something left to love. And if you ain't learned that, you ain't learned nothing. . . . What he been through and what it done to him. Child, when do you think is the time to love somebody the most; when they done good and made things easy for everybody? Well then, you ain't through learning—because that ain't the time at all. It's when he's at his lowest and can't believe in hisself 'cause the world done whipped him so. When you starts measuring somebody, measure him right, child, measure him right. Make sure you done taken into account what hills and valleys he come through before he got to wherever he is."

To convert resentment into compassion you have to look beyond the immediate situation to the person behind it. What is the source of this person's behavior? What led up to this event? Given the circumstances, is this person doing the best he or she can?

Jill was concerned that her husband Ricardo didn't pay enough attention to their two young children. He had been eager to have children, but now everything else was a higher priority for him. Jill explained why she thought spending time with the children was important. She set up specific situations for him to be with them. But nothing changed. When she first mentioned her problem in a workshop she sounded desperate, not so much for herself as for her children. She fantasized catastrophic outcomes for the children, such as fear of abandonment when they became adults.

We asked Jill to go home and write a page or two in her journal about what might be contributing to Ricardo's behavior. The next week, she reported back that she had thought about four possible contributing factors:

1. Ricardo's father gave very little attention to him when he was a child, so he did not have a good father model.
2. Ricardo was anxious about his job and eager to succeed, and this took a lot of his time.
3. Ricardo had never spent time with small children, and didn't really know what to do with them. People kept telling Jill that he might become more interested as the children grew older.
4. Ricardo believed that taking care of children was women's work.

Of course, Jill didn't know for sure that these were contributing factors; this was only speculation on her part. But the ideas seemed reasonable to her, and they helped her to look beyond Ricardo's specific behavior to the person behind it. Ricardo was doing the best he could.

We also reminded Jill that acceptance is the starting point for change. Hers was a good example of the principle that resisting something actually causes it to persist. By fighting against Ricardo's behavior and trying so hard to change it, Jill was possibly strengthening Ricardo's resistance to fathering, making him even more afraid of it. We presented her with a picture of graciously accepting Ricardo for who he is, actively thanking him for all that she appreciates about him, and dropping the whole fathering issue altogether. We asked her to try this for three months. She told us that she felt a great deal of relief just hearing what we said. Then she went home and tried it.

Over the course of the next several weeks, Jill reported to us that she believed in the principle of compassion and forgiveness, but found it hard to practice. She kept hearing herself be critical of Ricardo in spite of her best efforts, and she kept feeling anxious and resentful.

As we have said, compassion and forgiveness are not a "belief" or a "principle." They are a practice. You can't learn them in a week; you can only begin to practice them. The more you exercise forgiveness and compassion, the better you will feel, the better results you will get in your life, and the better you will become at doing it. The goal is not perfection, but progress.

One thing that helped Jill was hearing how other people in our group made progress by offering forgiveness and compassion to others. On the fourth week, she surprised us all by telling us this:

> All my life, I've had a problem with being shy which is a big liability in my work [she was a real estate agent]. I went to a shyness workshop a few years ago and got a lot of help with it. I started thinking how long and hard and slow my efforts to overcome my shyness have been. I've made a little bit of progress, but I keep sliding back. So this week, I suddenly saw Ricardo's trying to be a good father in the same light! I believe he wants to be a good father, but it's just not that easy for him, especially with all else he is trying to do. Finally, I felt like I see what you mean that he is doing the best he can. I of all people know how hard it is to change habits. I need to give him some time!

By starting with our experiment, Jill discovered her own road to compassion.

Her road is a good place for all of us to start. First have compassion for yourself. You too are doing the best you can. If you can be loving toward yourself for your weaknesses, you'll have an easier time accepting your partner in exactly the package you see before you.

Again, the secret to converting resentment into compassion is to look beyond the specific situation you don't like to the person behind it. Maybe your mate is already giving all he or she has to give.

Let's get a bit more specific, then, about looking at the person behind the situation. You might think about (*a*) the person's family history, (*b*) previous experiences you know about, and (*c*) the person's general personality type. Here are a few questions that will help you look at each of these factors. You can answer to the best of your own ability, or you might actually want to ask your spouse to comment—casually—on some of these questions. Any one of them might lead to an interesting, rapport-building discussion.

What is the family history behind this situation I don't like?

1. From what you have heard, what was it like for your partner to grow up in his or her family?
2. How is your partner like his or her mother in attitudes, behavior, and beliefs?
3. How is your partner like his or her father in attitudes, behavior, and beliefs?
4. Is your partner heavily influenced by any siblings or by his or her relationship with any siblings?
5. How does you partner feel now about his or her family?

Are my mate's previous experiences influencing this situation?

1. What do you know about your mate's previous experiences regarding this issue?
2. How might these previous experiences be influencing your mate?

Is my mate's general personality type influencing this situation?

1. What are the two or three most dominant qualities in your partner's personality?
2. Complete this sentence with as many different adjectives as seem appropriate: My partner has a strong tendency to be ______. For example, your partner might tend to be perfectionist, helpful, achievement-oriented, melancholy, overinvolved, optimistic, quick to anger, good-natured, well-organized, left-brain, right-brain, . . . etc.
3. What is your partner's astrological sign? How does he or she match or fail to match the characteristics that are traditionally assigned to that sign?
4. In general, men have a tendency to invalidate or ignore feelings and move directly to solutions; to cope with stress by becoming silent and withdrawn; and to show their love by being good at what they do or by doing big, impressive favors. Women have a tendency to value and express feelings; to cope with stress by asking for support and talking things through; and to show their love with small favors and affectionate gestures.

In what ways does your mate correspond or fail to correspond to these generalities?

What did you discover by asking these questions? Maybe your mate isn't being malicious, thoughtless, ungrateful, or deliberately neglectful of you. Maybe your mate is just doing what he or she has always done, being who he or she has always been. If so, can you be more accepting of the qualities you don't like, understanding that they are part of your mate's general makeup?

In his book *When "I Can't Help It" Is for Real,* psychiatrist Daniel Amen describes pioneering research that shows conclusively that disorders in certain portions of the brain correspond to specific dysfunctional behaviors.

For example, a disorder in the brain's cingulate system will cause symptoms like addictions, obsessive-compulsive behaviors, and eating disorders. People who are excessively moody, or who have trouble recovering from a loss or upset, may actually have a disorder in their brain's limbic system. These brain disorders, much more common in the general population than previously believed, may be a result of genetics, environmental factors, or injury. Psychiatrists now know how to correct unwanted tendencies and behaviors by restoring normal brain functioning, using either behavioral or chemical therapies. Dr. Amen's book is filled with extraordinary stories of people who have "cured" everything from excessive moodiness to anxiety, impulsiveness, inability to concentrate, low levels of imagination, and even violence, using simple, widely available therapies. Dr. Amen expects this very new clinical approach to revolutionize psychiatry over the next ten years.

The most satisfying aspect of his practice, Amen says, is watching patients and their families suddenly transform their criticism and impatience into compassion when they learn that the person with the problematic behavior genuinely *can't help it.* For example, Robert seemed to his family to be lazy and unmotivated. He never completed what he started and could never stay with a project. "Just be disciplined!" they would tell him. "Make yourself do it!" But tests done on Robert revealed that when he tried to engage his brain, it quite literally stopped functioning! Both he and his family became compassionate and understanding instead of critical and belittling—and chemical and behavioral therapy corrected his problem.

I mention this here not only to suggest the possibility that certain patterns you don't like in your spouse may be things he or she could be treated for, but more because this psychiatric breakthrough is useful as a metaphor. Whether or not it is because of a specific brain dysfunction, your mate can't help being who he or she is! Your partner's habits, thoughts, attitudes, and behavior are there for reasons that have nothing to do with you. If you ever hope to be happy together, you have to begin by accepting your mate with grace, compassion, and understanding. Believe that your mate is doing the best he or she can, and be supportive, not critical. Your patient support could work miracles for both of you.

EXPERIMENT #33

Cultivating Compassion

What is your pet peeve about your partner? What would you change about him or her if you had a magic wand? Or what has your partner done recently to anger or annoy you?

Now, reach beyond the situation to the person behind it. In your journal, to yourself, or with a friend, ask yourself each of the questions in this section about the source of your partner's behavior.

If you believe your partner is doing the best he or she can, might you find a way to offer support rather than criticism? What could you do or say that your partner would find supportive?

Write a little "essay" in your journal entitled, "I Have Compassion for (Partner's name)."

Now, repeat this entire experiment with yourself in mind, rather than your partner.

Whenever you feel self-critical or critical of your mate, say to yourself, "I am doing the best I can." or "My mate is doing the best ______ can."

Practice compassion.

GOOD WILL AFFIRMATION #5 (TO CULTIVATE FORGIVENESS)

My Partner Was Wrong. I Have a Choice.

When your partner does something thoughtless, inconsiderate, or hurtful to you, you will probably feel sad, angry, hurt, betrayed, and/or cheated. That is normal and appropriate—but it doesn't have to stop there.

You also have the option of forgiving your spouse and feeling compassion toward him or her. Anybody can feel angry after being wronged; it takes a more evolved, more conscious person to call upon good will in these difficult situations.

I once drove to a conference with Paul, a man I did not know very well. For a long stretch while we were driving on a curvy mountain road, a car was tailgating us at a very close distance, truly dangerous and annoying.

"Stupid driver," Paul said. "I'll get him!" Then to my amazement, Paul slowed down quite deliberately. The closer and more impatient the driver behind became, the slower Paul would drive.

"Maybe you could just pull over," I meekly suggested.

"Pull over! Not for that (unprintable epithets). He's got what's coming to him. Look what he's done to us, spoiling our leisurely drive! He needs a taste of his own medicine."

I could see Paul did not realize that he had a choice. He was a slave to this other driver, with only a knee-jerk reaction possible: revenge. Someone did something to him; he could only be angry, as surely as the tail follows after the dog.

Confucius said, "If you set out on a journey of revenge, dig two graves." Paul was, of course, digging his own grave, escalating the hostility, and giving himself an ulcer. He saw both the situation and his response to it as one unit. He was trapped.

His last comment still rings in my ears: "You can't afford to be too sweet in this world. You'll end up a doormat!" He spat out the word "sweet" as though it were a poison.

Too sweet? Too much good will? Too much forgiveness and compassion? I don't think so. Certainly you can be too unassertive, too unable or unwilling to set boundaries and establish standards for yourself. That's when you end up a doormat. But there is no such thing as too much good will. Good will is a warm, pleasurable feeling. You can't have too much of it any more than you can have too much contentment or too much good health. And what's more, the more of it you spread around, the more you will receive back.

People screw up. People make mistakes. People do nasty things, dreadful things. Why? Probably because other people have done nasty, awful things to them in the past. You can either continue that cycle, or reverse it by offering your compassion and forgiveness in a spirit of good will. You always have a choice.

Paul's story seems extreme. Yet we have all fallen into this same trap.

Your husband is late for dinner. He forgets to pick up the dry cleaning. Your wife schedules way too many evening activities for one week. It's okay to be angry. But get over it. Don't keep nursing your wounds; let them heal.

Hanging onto past hurts is a version of the booby prize. You get to be right! Your partner screwed up, and you have a perfect right to feel hurt or angry. Agreed. But what does it get you? Would you rather be right, or feel happy and close to your spouse? The choice is yours. Call up your spirit of good will, forgive, and move on.

In *The Way of Marriage*, Henry James Borys shares the following incident from his journal:

> This morning I wanted to make love, but Susan did not want to. She was unusually touchy about it and said that all I wanted was sex, without regard for her. Her comment seemed unfair. I felt hurt by it. I had not exactly thrown myself at her, I had just shown a little affection.
>
> Once Susan was fully awake, she apologized. I told her that it was okay, yet I noticed a thought lurking in the back of my mind: She had hurt me. Did she know that?
>
> No good ever came of such a thought.

Borys made a choice. In that moment, he let go of the booby prize, made an active decision to quiet his knee-jerk response, and exercised his good will. He let the past be the past and stopped worrying about who was right and who was wrong.

Whenever your partner is genuinely wrong, whether or not you get an apology, you have a choice. You can carry the hurt around, or you can exercise your good will and forgive. The choice is yours. Let yourself be angry for a while. But then, exercise your good will, forgive, and forget.

Do not confuse forgiveness with allowing yourself to be abused. If your mate did something—or consistently does something—that is truly inappropriate, you may need to draw a line in the sand and make it clear that you will not tolerate this behavior. If you "forgive" inconsiderate or abusive behavior over and over, this is not compassion; it is fear, denial, or self-negation.

But in the normal course of events, see if you can adopt a generous attitude toward your partner's shortcomings. Remember that you do not have to respond "automatically," in the expected way. You have a choice.

EXPERIMENT #34

Working on Forgiving

What has your spouse done lately to hurt you?

If nothing leaps immediately to your mind, don't belabor the question. Come back to this affirmation the next time you need it.

If you think of several ways you've been wronged, choose one.

In your journal or just thinking to yourself, what is your response? How do you feel?

If you feel angry and resentful, and you don't feel forgiving, you won't be able to change that feeling just because you know you have a choice. That's okay. Feel angry and resentful. *You are doing the best you can!*

Go back to Experiment #33. See if you can reach beyond the deed to the person, and experience some understanding and compassion.

Ask yourself what you are gaining for yourself by carrying this hurt and anger around. (Is it the booby prize?)

Keep telling yourself you have a choice. If and when you choose to, you can soften and forgive your mate, but not before you are ready.

Be patient with yourself. Even when you find it impossible to forgive, you are doing the best you can.

GOOD WILL AFFIRMATION #6 (TO CULTIVATE GENEROSITY)

How Can I Be Generous to My Spouse Today?

When I got married, my mother gave me this advice: "If people would spend less time in their marriages trying to get their needs met and more time going over to rub each other's shoulders, we wouldn't have so many troubled marriages."

As we've been saying, what's ideal is a balance. But my mother was making a comment about our times.

We have been preoccupied for decades now with getting our own needs met. The '60s was the lifestyle revolution: Don't make me conform! In the '70s we asked, Now that I have established the right to be myself, who am I? It was the Me Decade, complete with the Gestalt prayer that began, "I am not in this world to meet your needs." Women launched the contemporary Women's Movement with declarations like: "A woman without a man is like a fish without a bicycle." In the '80s we were busy catching up with the Joneses in a consumer frenzy that got out of control. And we became so obsessed with avoiding the dreaded "codependency" that plain old *giving* got a bad name, giving out of the goodness of our hearts that has nothing to do with "helping" other people to cure or improve themselves.

The search in the '90s for meaning beyond materialism is a turn in the right direction. But the question is still, what is *my* meaning, what are *my* needs?

Can you imagine a decade of generosity?

Thoughtfulness is a lost art. To suggest spontaneously giving your partner a shoulder rub sounds quaint. Yet nothing captures the essence of happiness so easily or creates it so quickly. As Henry James Borys put it, "Giving, not taking, is how we liberate the happiness hidden in our being."

In one workshop we spent time discussing generosity. The next week, Kurt wanted to talk.

> I can see that I am not a very giving person. I watched myself this week. I don't want to give to Charlotte. She had to put a mailing out this week and asked for my help. I worked a little bit, but I complained about it because I had work to do, so she finally got disgusted with me and let me go. She got on my case about it later. It was kind of an amazing thing because of course

> she had no idea we were talking about giving right now in this course, but she said something like, "You always worry more about your own needs than mine. You don't want to give anything in this marriage." She always says I don't see things that need doing. I think she's right. I see the importance of being generous, but I don't think I'll ever be very good at it.

Kurt raised an important point. Some personality types are naturally giving and helpful, but for personality types that are not that way, learning to give may not be easy.

So how do you learn to be giving if you are not naturally generous? By giving.

Like the other aspects of good will, giving is not a theory, but a practice. The more you do it, the more you will experience the pleasure that can come from giving, and the more you will choose to give. The goal is not perfection, but progress. If you are not naturally generous, don't try to change your whole personality. Start by being spontaneously generous once a week.

You can be generous by

- responding cheerfully to requests made of you
- doing your share without having to be asked
- seeing something that your partner would appreciate your having done, and doing it without having to be asked
- surprising your mate with a completely unexpected gift or generous act

These can be tiny little things: Cut out an appropriate cartoon for her, polish his shoes for him, clean up an area of the house, hide a love note in his lunch or her makeup drawer, do her share of the dinner or clean-up when she is tired, have his favorite CD playing when he arrives home, buy her a funny greeting card, dim the lights and put candles on the table, give your mate a foot massage or back rub . . .

Generosity can be big, too. One man told me that when they go on a weekend drive or a trip, he willingly stops at every antique store, even though the first three would be enough for him. Mayer once drove two hours to retrieve something I had left behind.

Love and marriage involve a lot of giving. You can't run your life in a relationship exactly the same way you would run it if you were alone. There are two of you to consider now, two equally important sets of needs and desires. If you don't want to be giving and generous, don't get married. If you are giving and generous and you are married to someone you love, your rewards will far outweigh your losses.

Some people like to talk about the necessity of making "sacrifices" in a loving partnership, conjuring up a picture of long suffering and self-deprivation. But a sacrifice is an *offering*. You make an offering only to something or someone whom you value and cherish. My *Random House College Dictionary* calls sacrifice, "the surrender of something prized or desirable for the sake of something considered as having a higher or more pressing claim."

Kurt could have made a "sacrifice," an offering to his wife who needed help with her mailing. If he had, he would have given up his own work for a few hours (something prized and desirable) in favor of giving his wife a hand, thereby making their relationship closer and happier (something considered as having a higher or more pressing claim). Since he begrudged her the time, he didn't experience it as an offering, but as a loss to himself. Instead of giving them both a gift, he gave them both a loss.

One of the most well-known and well-ignored axioms in relationship lore is that, especially for women, little things mean a lot. Men, find something to do for your wife that won't put you out very much. Fix dinner one night, or pour her a glass of port after dinner and tell her you'll clean up the kitchen. Bring home a new tape or CD she'll love, or her favorite dessert from a bakery, or some fresh bread. Call her in the middle of the afternoon just to tell her you love her. Bring her a little sapling for the yard and tell her it's a love tree; as it grows, so does your love for her grow.

Gifts like these are what most women want more than anything else, small thoughtful gestures that show you are thinking about them.

Men appreciate little gestures like these too, women. But what men really want is to be acknowledged for what they are already doing. Thank your man for specific things he does and just for who he is in general. Let him know, often, how much you appreciate him.

The best story in all of literature about generosity and sacrifice is O. Henry's, "The Gift of the Magi" in which she cuts off and sells her long hair to buy him a gold watch fob, and he sells his prized watch to buy her a gorgeous comb for her hair. I know a woman who, I have always felt, gave up the equivalent of her long hair, though, fortunately, not with such an ironic end result.

Melinda and Marty met when they were both in their fifties and had been living on their own for many years. Their meeting was magical and transforming for both of them. Within months, they had bought a home that was right for the two of them, and within a year, they were married.

The home they found was big and gracious but needed a lot of fixing up. They each sold their previous homes to buy it: in Melinda's case, a lavish, quite stunning condominium. Melinda's style would have been to take out a loan and do extensive renovations to their new home before they moved in. But Marty felt anxious about doing it that way. He wanted to do some of the work himself; he wanted to take great care with how each job was done; and he felt they needed to live in the house for a while before they could know exactly what changes they wanted.

Melinda told me,

> I could have insisted on my way; we could easily have afforded it. But I quickly saw that my way would create enormous anxiety for Marty and a lot of conflict between us. We didn't get together to increase the conflict and stress in our lives. We got together to enjoy each other's love and companionship. Marty was okay with getting some projects completed before we moved in. So I let go of the major renovations for the time being. At first I was disappointed and frustrated. But the truth is, I was so happy to be with him, and we were having such a wonderful time, the house thing just faded for me. It would all happen eventually. Could I get on a different time schedule to adjust to what Marty needed? Yes. No contest.

Melinda was patient and would laugh about her "period kitchen" or her "phantom laundry room." She never saw her compromises as bargaining. She never said to Marty, "If I give in on this, you have to give in on that." But over time, Marty agreed to renovations he would never have agreed to in the beginning. Because of Melinda's instinctive decision to let go of her way of proceeding with the house renovations, she ended up with both a beautiful relationship and, after about two years, the gorgeous home she had envisioned.

Melinda was as attached to a beautiful, functional home as the woman in O. Henry's story was to her hair. But in both cases, their courageous and loving decision to *give* brought them greater happiness and fulfillment in the end than if they had carefully guarded their possessions.

Melinda solved a problem—by herself—through the use of generosity and good will. She proved once again the validity of the point Emerson makes so eloquently in his essay on Compensation: If you want more, give more.

Are we on the verge of a Decade of Generosity? I doubt it. Don't wait for it. Create a Decade of Generosity right now in your own relationship. If you start to pay attention to it, you will be amazed at how many opportunities you have every day to do something thoughtful and generous for your mate.

In my college dorm, we exchanged names and became Holiday Angels for each other. For the whole month of December, you were supposed to think up all manner of little surprises and gifts for the person whose name you had drawn. We went to elaborate lengths to keep our identities secret, even after it was all over with. Yet we all tried to outdo each other with imaginative gifts and favors. You couldn't spend more that $10 for the entire month, either.

We had so much fun with this, I can't begin to describe it. What a concept! Imagine becoming a year 'round angel for your mate!

EXPERIMENT #35

Think Generosity

For specific ideas about how you might be generous to your mate, I refer you to Chapter Five, which is full of ideas. Or, simply brainstorm ideas yourself. You might want to keep a page in your journal to list ideas you want to remember to use in the future.

We have now discussed six affirmations designed to help you cultivate good will in your marriage.

This is not a problem, but a fact of life.
My partner is not wrong, just different.
This has nothing to do with me.
She is doing the best she can.
OR
He's doing the best he can.
My partner was wrong; I have a choice.
How can I be generous to my mate today?

Don't try to tackle them all at once; choose one that seems most relevant to your situation, and focus on it for a while. If you are someone who already operates with a great deal of good will, it may be far more important for you to work first on taking care of your own needs in your relationship.

Good will is its own reward. If you have not already figured this out in life, and particularly in your marriage or intimate partnership, may you have a rich journey of discovery.

CHAPTER NINE Loving Leadership: Self-Care and Good Will As a Blend

As we have seen, you are an individual who has needs, desires, dreams, habits, a history and a future. You need autonomy, space to be yourself, independence. You need support, love, attention. You need to figure out what you want and need, and give time and attention to fulfilling your desires.

In addition, you have an intimate partner, this person you have decided you want as a lifetime companion. Your partner also has needs, desires, dreams, habits, a history and a future. He or she also needs love, support, and attention—in this case, from you.

As a partner in a loving relationship, you have to keep putting "gold nuggets" on each side of the scale to try to keep it balanced. It isn't easy because sometimes, when you add or subtract something on one side, it throws the whole scale out of balance. Often, the two sides are in conflict. That's marriage!

SELF-CARE/GOOD WILL: AN "ALLOY"

In real life, couples who are doing well together, whose scales are more or less balanced, often do not experience "I" and "we," giving and taking, or assertiveness and acceptance separately. Much of the time they are not thinking, "Now I'm on one side of the scale, now I'm on the other." They don't experience themselves as *either* giving *or* taking, *either* asserting themselves *or* being accepting. What they experience instead is a blend: assertiveness *and* acceptance at the same time. They feel like they are taking and giving at the same time. The WE and the I work in rhythm with each other in a way that supports both the WE and the I.

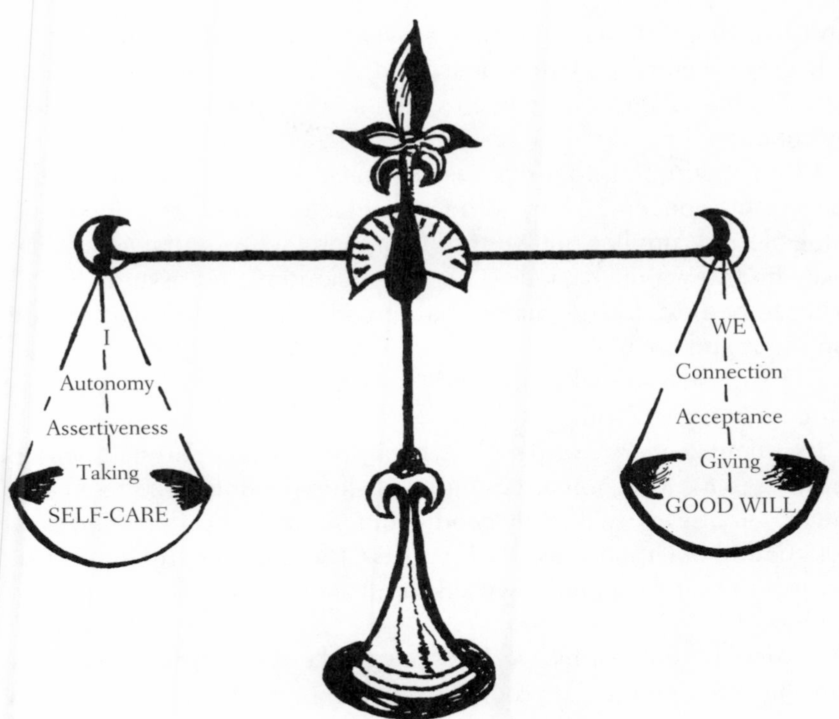

For example, when Mayer wants us to go to an antique show on Saturday afternoon and I want us to spend the afternoon with some friends who are going for a hike, if I "give in" and go to the antique show, I don't feel cheated or like I'm "losing" because (*a*) if I cared about the hike enough, if these were people we rarely see, or if they were hiking to a spot I probably wouldn't go to on my own, I could insist. I could even go on my own and let him go to the antique show. In other words, I'm aware I have other options, and I make a deliberate choice. (*b*) I'm aware that the highest priority for me is to spend Saturday afternoon with him. (*c*) There have been plenty of occasions when Mayer does what I want to do.

So I am actually taking care of myself and him at the same time. I don't experience them as separate. When you are trying to strengthen your ability to keep a balance between taking care of yourself and giving to your partner, you have to work on each skill separately, as we did in the last two chapters. But the goal is to achieve a *blend,* so that you experience yourself, not as assertive *or* accepting, but as "assertively accepting;" not as autonomous *or* in connection, but as "autonomously connected." The attitude we are after is a single stance. When you give, you are doing it in a context of having taken care of your own needs. When you take, you can do so freely, because you have been giving. Self-care and good will blend into one quality.

I find it stunning that our vast language has not a single word to convey this concept. The psychological-jargon word "grounded" may come close. It implies that your foundation is solid so that you cannot easily be thrown off balance. Out of this kind of self-assurance, it is easier to be flexible and giving. "Grounded" implies that you are both confident and open.

But I choose to call this blend "Loving Leadership," an "alloy" of self-care and good will.

Excellent leaders are people who inspire others through selfless devotion to a cause. You are free to be selfless and devoted to a cause only if you already feel really good about yourself. Leaders who don't feel good about themselves will subvert the goals of the enterprise, and use the other people involved to fill their own need for approval and love.

Leaders have two jobs: (1) They have to keep a constant vigil to be sure they are pursuing appropriate, uplifting, worthwhile goals. They have to keep looking at the big picture, and not get so lost in details that the enterprise loses its purpose, its direction. (2) In addition, they must support all the individuals who are involved with achieving the goal.

Every relationship needs a loving leader like this, someone who inspires both partners through selfless devotion to the cause of a mutually supportive and pleasurable partnership. Ideally, this leader will already have good self-esteem, so as not to subvert the goals of the relationship or use the other person to fill his or her own need for approval and love.

A strong, loving relationship leader will do both jobs: (1) Keep an eye on the big picture, the direction, purpose and goals of the relationship, and (2) support both of the partners involved.

Many relationships have two loving leaders and share the leadership responsibilities. But it is enough for a relationship to have one loving leader, the one of you who brings the two of you together. Many successful relationships operate with one leader, one person who gives more attention to the big picture, who feels fulfilled and is able to give out of self-strength and self-love. Either the leader or the partner might be the person who pays attention to details. If you are the leader in your relationship, rather than resenting that you have to play that role, view it as a privilege, an opportunity to do an excellent job and to make a valuable contribution to both yourself and your partner.

Loving leadership presents us with a strong image of what the ideal blend of self-care and good will looks like. In order to understand this blend better, let's plot these two qualities on a matrix: self-care and good will.

Some people have very little of either. Some have a great deal of good will for their partner but pay little attention to their own needs. Then there are those who are great at taking care of themselves, but who have little good will for others. And of course, some possess both self-care and good will: the balanced scale, loving leadership.

Here are all the possible combinations:

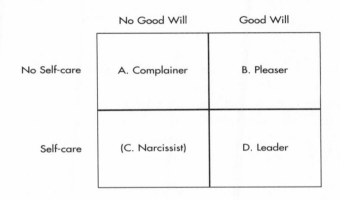

	No Good Will	Good Will
No Self-care	A. Complainer	B. Pleaser
Self-care	(C. Narcissist)	D. Leader

EXPERIMENT #36

Guessing at Your Type

Before reading further, take a moment to place yourself somewhere in this box. Draw the matrix in your journal, and put a dot in one of the squares or on a line between two squares.

Write a paragraph in your journal explaining the position you chose.

Most of us fall somewhere on the lines of this chart rather than smack in the middle of a box. Nevertheless, I will describe the "pure" types.

A. COMPLAINERS. Complainers have not learned how to take good care of themselves nor are they able to reach out to their partners with acceptance and good will. Complainers don't know what they want, or they know but do nothing to change their lives in order to get what they want. They experience themselves as victims. Because they don't feel good about themselves, they lack the capacity to reach out with good will to a spouse or partner, another deserving human being. Instead, they emphasize the negative parts of both their partner and their relationship. They blame, complain, and avoid action. Complainers are often passive-aggressive, that is, they don't express anger directly because they don't feel strong enough about themselves to do so. They express it indirectly by being hostile, cool, uncooperative, or apathetic.

Complainers need to work on discovering their true desires, beliefs, ambitions, and feelings. They need to concentrate on the six self-care affirmations in Chapter Seven. Only after they do that can they work on expressing good will, on being forgiving, understanding, and accepting, for only from self-love is it possible to offer genuine love to another person. If you have a poorly developed self to start with, you have little to give to another person.

B. PLEASERS. These are people who get their good feelings by meeting other people's needs. They are care-takers. Unconsciously, they want their relentless giving to compensate for the holes they feel in themselves, and they feel empty and resentful when their gifts are not appreciated.

To accommodate your spouse and fail to assert your own needs is to live in quiet denial. Pleasers are long-suffering victims who accept their powerlessness, usually because they believe they have no alternatives. Pleasers make an internal decision that it is more important to have a relationship than to have a self.

The most extreme cases of pleasers are victims of abuse who explain their bruises by telling the doctor they fell down the stairs. They may be so broken down from systematic and repeated abuse that they actually believe their abuse was a result of their own failure. But many men and women experience a less intense version of the silent pleaser syndrome. They simply give up their own desires and passively acquiesce to the demands and behaviors of their partner; they quietly lose themselves. As the nineteenth century Danish theologian Kierkegaard said,

> The greatest danger, that of losing one's own self, can pass off as quietly as if it were nothing. Every other loss—that of an arm, a leg, a wife, or five dollars—is sure to be noticed.

Mark, who let his wife decorate the house in a way that completely precluded his taste, was an example of a mild Pleaser. Without fanfare or conflict, he quietly acquiesced to his wife's strong desires and, without even noticing it, lost a part of himself.

Is there something you have quietly given up since you got into your relationship that you secretly wish you could have back?

Pleasers sometimes try to get what they want through a kind of emotional blackmail that says, "If I give to you, you *have* to give back to me." Their giving has a hook in it. Rather than doing the inner work that will enable them to love themselves, these Pleasers manipulate the people around them to return attention and approval. Pleasers tend to engage in magical thinking, fantasizing ideal resolutions of their unhappiness but doing nothing to bring these fantasies about.

The work Pleasers must do is to engage in self-exploration, to become better acquainted with what makes them happy and unhappy, with what gives them pain and what brings them pleasure. They too must concentrate on the self-care affirmations in Chapter Seven.

C. The Phantom Box. Although many of my workshop participants place themselves in box C (strong self-care, weak good will), there is (sorry!) no such thing as a pure "C." People who place themselves there say something like this: "I know what *I* want, but I have trouble feeling good will for my spouse, because my spouse behaves unfairly and is thoughtless and inconsiderate."

Here is the fallacy in such a statement: If you are taking care of yourself and have reached the point where you can lovingly say to yourself, "I'm doing the best I can," this means you have found compassion for yourself. You affirm and value yourself in spite of qualities you don't like. When you experience that kind of compassion for yourself, it almost always extends to other people, because you realize that they too have had to overcome hardships. They too are doing the best they can with what they have, which is all any of us can do.

So you see, self-care without good will is an unlikely combination, because compassion and good will follow naturally after genuine self-love.

Saying "I love myself but I don't feel good will for my spouse," comes suspiciously close to claiming that old booby prize, "I'm right. I know and like myself, but my spouse is out to lunch."

If you placed yourself in the "C" box, you may actually be closer to the "A" box, the Complainer, where you can still do more to uncover and express genuine compassion for yourself. When you can learn to forgive and tolerate yourself, you will naturally feel forgiveness and tolerance for others, because you will recognize that we are all in the same boat.

Or, you may be a pseudo "C."

Pseudo "C"s are Narcissists. They are precisely self-caring and without good will. But their self-care does not come from genuine self-love; rather, it is obsessive self-involvement that comes from a *lack* of self-love. Pseudo "C"s are preoccupied with themselves. Although Narcissists *appear* to know themselves and to act decisively, in fact their strong behavior conceals a deep-rooted inability to feel. Where other people have a sense of self, Narcissists have an empty hole. To compensate for their loss of true self, Narcissists throw a great deal of energy into building a powerful persona. Rather than being motivated by deep inner stirrings, they are motivated by the need to gain admiration. They depend on others to support the image they have of themselves, to substitute for an ability to give themselves support.

In order to get the attention they need from others, Narcissists tend to be ambitious, hardworking, and to have an inflated view of their own importance. When they don't get the admiration they seek, they can become almost insanely angry. Problems are virtually always someone else's fault, in their view.

Narcissists need to work on developing a strong inner self first, and then a capacity for good will toward others. They need to replace the pseudo-self-love of a glittering persona with knowledge of the real self that lies hidden beneath the appearance of success.

Ironically, because Narcissists believe and want others to believe that they are successful, important, and generally right about most things, and because they cannot afford to do anything that might tarnish or threaten their crucial image, Narcissists rarely engage in deep inner work. If they do, it is only because their image includes, "I'm somebody who does deep, inner work."

D. LEADERS. The "D" box represents the Loving Leader, the ideal blend of self-love and good will.

Imagine yourself as a wise, confident, caring, and cooperative Leader in your relationship. You care about the relationship and you offer ideas and initiate change from a position of both inner strength and good will toward your partner. You are cooperative, and you take initiative to work systematically and deliberately toward positive change. You show good will, understanding, and generosity and you are good at taking care of your own needs.

With which of the above types do you identify more, now that we have discussed them? If you were going to take a look at your own inner balance scales right now, what would they look like? It's the rare person who possesses the perfect blend of self-care and good will; almost all of us err in one direction or the other. Which side of your own inner scale is more heavily weighted?

Of course, how you fit with your partner is relevant too. If you tend to be a Pleaser and are married to a Narcissist, you aren't likely to get your own needs met very well. Your marriage may have little conflict, but it may be smothering you. Or, if you are both good at self-care and neither of you is especially compassionate, you may have a great deal of conflict.

Looking at the "fit" of your styles is interesting, but it is not where we should focus our attention when you are one person working to bring the two of you together. No matter where your partner is on the self-care/good will scale, you will change your relationship when you bring *yourself* into better balance.

THE "FEEL" OF BALANCE

One of the best ways to integrate new information is to experience it in your body. Talking about these boxes is not nearly so powerful as finding out what each box feels like in your body.

You can actually *experience* styles A through D in your body, and I encourage you to try it. Since the body and the psyche are inextricably linked, your body will feel different if you are in one box or another, and it will feel quite wonderful when you are balanced: firmly planted in your own self-love so that you can experience good will for your spouse. Experimenting around with your body can give you the physical feel of a balanced relationship. (Don't skip this experiment! It is one of the most powerful parts of our workshops.)

EXPERIMENT #37

Experience Each Type in Your Body

If possible, get together with a friend and do the exercises described below. Or just do them on your own. The advantage of a friend is that you can talk about your experiences which might add a dimension to the experience for you.

Be sure you talk with each other about what you experience *before* you read my explanations.

A. Stand up. Lock your knees. Lean back just slightly. Breathe very little, just enough so you are not holding your breath. Hold this stance for a minute or so.

How do you feel?

With your knees locked, you have little mobility or flexibility. Leaning, and with little breath, someone could knock you off-center easily.

This is your stance at times when you are afraid to connect either with yourself or with another person. You are disconnected from your self—not solidly centered knowing exactly who you are and what you want. Because of this, you have no strength or solidity with which to reach out to another, no capacity for good will. You can't love another until you can love yourself. Put another way, if you don't feel safe yourself, and you won't if you feel "off-center," dealing with another person's needs will only add to your own fear and anxiety. This is the feeling of the Complainer, box A.

B. Stand next to your bed or couch, facing it. Again lock your knees. Now reach out toward the couch with your arms and keep reaching until you fall.

How did that feel?

This is your stance when you are focused entirely on good will and have given up any attempt to look after your own needs. Classic "codependents" are in this category, along with many of the rest of us who bury our own needs and try to take care of everyone else. Of course, when you are denying your own needs, much of your caretaking behavior will be destructive. You will be depending on the person you are taking care of to take care of you—by coming through for you, in one way or another. This is convoluted caregiving. The other person will feel your "help" as a demand, and you will collapse, because you are not operating out of your own solid self-loving foundation. This is the feeling of the Pleaser, box B.

C. Stand just slightly up on your toes. Take a big breath in your upper chest. Wrap your arms around yourself in a self–bear hug. Set your lips firmly together. Hold this stance for a minute or so.

Talk about how this feels.

This is the pseudo "C," the Narcissist. In this stance, you are looking after your own needs and are not in touch with your good will or your concern about other people. You feel self-importance and safety. You are paying attention to yourself. But are you operating from deep self-love? No. Your confidence is a puffed-up, affected stance, an image you have to force, because you fear uncovering your real self. You feel confidence only from your waist up. You have little connection with your feet and are not solidly planted in the ground of genuine self-love. Instead, you are "hung up," with all your feeling in your chest, shoulders, and head, as though you were suspended on a hanger rather than standing on the ground.

This is the stance of people who operate from a pseudo "I'm okay" that requires so much of their energy to maintain, they have no time in their lives for the needs of others. They lack both self-love and good will.

D. Stamp your feet on the floor several times. Shake your body and loosen up. Take a deep breath way down in your belly. Now bend your knees as far as you can without taking your feet off the ground. Hold that position for thirty seconds, even if it feels uncomfortable.

Straighten up. Keep your knees slightly bent, and sink down into your feet. Puff your chest out just a little and hold your head high.

Breathe fully in a relaxed way.

Gently reach your arms out in front of you, slightly more than shoulder width apart, palms tilting upward. Hold this stance for a minute. Then, talk about how it felt.

This is the feeling of the relationship Leader, of both standing your own ground, being firmly planted in self-caring, and at the same time—in fact precisely because you are confident in your own self-love—being open to others.

Because these postures represent extremes, they are useful for getting the feel of these attitudes in your body. What is going on in your body has both a cause and an effect relationship with your psyche: Your body reflects what is happening in your life. But also, a change in your body can help to effect a change in your psyche. For example, try smiling and laughing and feeling depressed at the same time.

So practice the Loving Leader stance. Even for a few seconds or a minute or so, when you get up, before you retire, or when you are doing other exercise, assume the stance. Hold it for a full minute or longer. Feel how it feels to be firmly planted and open at the same time. Let the feeling sink into your body and your spirit. Make it into a small, private ritual, a reminder that you are striving for the "alloy" of self-care blended with good will in your marriage. When you get the feel of it in your body, you will begin to get the feel of it in your relationship also.

WHAT IS YOUR WORK?

If you saw yourself in the description of either "A" or "C," you may need to work on both identifying and meeting your own needs (Chapter Seven), and on being more understanding with your partner (Chapter Eight). You will benefit from working on both the "I" and the "we" in your marriage.

If you see yourself as a "B," you need to work on becoming more assertive, on taking better care of yourself and your own needs in your relationship (Chapter Seven).

And if you see yourself as a "D," you may need only encouragement and ideas like the ones in this book to become an even more powerful and loving Leader and change-agent in your relationship.

In a workshop, Linda told us with a great deal of excitement that she had purchased a pair of earphones and had them installed in her TV so that she could read in bed while her husband watched the news at night. We could see what a victory this was for her and congratulated her on taking good care of her needs.

But then, William spoke up feeling slightly bewildered: "I feel a little weird saying so, but I don't see what the fuss here is. So she bought a pair of earphones. What's the big deal? I don't see why she didn't do that years ago!"

We explained to William that Linda had been begrudgingly watching TV at night for years; she was used to letting her husband call the shots and was in the habit of acquiescing to him; that taking care of her own needs in this way was a very big step, a symbol, and a turning point for her. William was a person who took excellent care of himself, and couldn't imagine unwillingly watching TV for years with such a simple solution at hand. But when we pressed him, we found out that he had started vacuuming the dining room after dinner in the evenings, and that this was a pretty "big deal" for him. Why hadn't he been doing that for years? He had also brought his wife flowers twice since the beginning of our workshop, something he had never done before, while there was another man in the workshop who brought his wife flowers all the time and couldn't understand why bringing flowers was such a big deal.

At the end of our discussion, we decided we had discovered a new law of the universe: People have different "big deals!"

What sort of an action would be a "big deal" for you? What would stretch you out of your comfort zone? Would it be an action in which you take care of your own needs? Or one in which you offer a gift to your spouse out of love and good will?

The "I" vs. the "We"

For a moment, let's see how the matrix applies to us collectively.

As a society, our internal scales are woefully out of balance. A nation born of the quest for individual freedom and nurtured on the exhilaration of rugged individualism, we are far more concerned about individual rights than about social responsibility, about the "I" than the "we." Our culture is a giant pseudo "C."

We were founded on the principles of Loving Leadership: We affirmed individual freedom *and* our joint responsibility to provide everyone with life, liberty, and the pursuit of happiness. But we gave the individual freedom side of the scale all the weights, and let the social responsibility side become so light that it has virtually disappeared into the stratosphere. When you give attention only to "rugged individualism" and "every man for himself" [*sic*], and you don't temper this drive with good will, inevitably the individuals who are most self-involved and least caring will end up with all the money, power, and influence.

That's what happened, just like a marriage that will fall apart if the partners are focused only on their own needs. Those with the power in our culture justify their personal "success" by appealing to the "I" side of our Constitution: "I live in America; I'm free to do whatever I am capable of achieving." They conveniently forget that part of the American experiment was supposed to be that we would "provide for the general welfare." It takes imagination, creativity, and money to provide for the general welfare of all of our people. Most of our country's imagination, creativity, and money go to increase the size and power of large corporations, not the common good.

There is nothing wrong with this country that couldn't be cured by a dose of good will equal to the narcissism that has become our supreme operative value. We promote individual freedom at the price of the general welfare, "I" over "we," a scale out of balance.

Don't use our national values as a model for your marriage.

Instead, use as examples these reports from individuals on the journey to becoming Loving Leaders in their marriages.

> FRAN: In my former marriage, I never confronted my husband with what I didn't like. I just went along with things. I even moved when it was the last thing I wanted to do. I was preserving the marriage, but my soul was lost.
>
> In my new marriage, I'm different. Eddie was seeing a lot of this old girlfriend, now a close friend of his. To a point, it was okay, but I felt she was behaving inappropriately and that he was going along with it. An occasional lunch was one thing, but dinner on a Friday evening without me? Come on! So I confronted Eddie. It was hard, but I told him I loved him and that I had feelings I thought he needed to know about. In the end, he agreed with me, and my speaking up gave him the courage he needed to set limits with her. It was scary for me, but it worked out beautifully.

Fran's "big deal" was to pay attention to her inner voice, to the feelings she was having, and to express them. She found a way to do so with love and respect, which she also clearly expressed. She balanced her own needs with good will for her husband and regard for his needs.

Sybil, on the other hand, was an expert at being self-sufficient. Her "big deal" was to reach out to her husband with good will.

SYBIL (married three years): I had to admit to myself there are things I don't like about him. That was first. And that was a disappointment. My first instinct was to pull back into my disappointment: I was fine before I met him; I can be fine again. For a while, I felt like we were singles who happened to be married. We were friends, but I was pulling way back, taking care of myself.

After I started this workshop, I realized that attitude would never get me what I wanted. When I started to "think good will," and "act as if" I was a loving spouse, I saw, he is doing the best he can. He truly can't help it that he grew up in a family where he never saw people treat each other well. I feel like I have a bigger view than he does, not a superior view, but I can see that he behaves in ways that don't serve *him* very well, let alone me. I don't have to support the behavior I don't like, but if I can support *him* with my love, and show him by example what love means to me, then there is a chance he'll grow and change. And I want to support him, because I do love him. Hey, my parents stuck by me when I did some pretty awful stuff. It's kind of like that. I want him to know at all times that I love him.

It was hard for me to start doing this. I resisted it, I didn't get it. But when I did start reaching out and being generous with him in various ways, when I made the effort to be *understanding,* it really felt good *to me.* I could feel again that I love him. [She began to get teary.] I haven't said anything for weeks about the mess in the den, but last night he told me he will clean up the boxes in there this weekend. It was a real gift, because he knows how much this means to me.

Remember, what we are striving for ultimately is a blend, a way to be assertive in an accepting way, and accepting in an assertive way; to support our partners in a way that supports ourselves and vice versa. In order to achieve this blend, however, we often need to work on the two qualities separately. What is the area in which you might be able to improve?

Perhaps this affirmation will help you develop your capacity for Loving Leadership in your relationship:

I love myself, and I love you.

❤ ❤ ❤

After reading this far, are you still wondering whether you even *want* to take care of your spouse and yourself? Maybe your partner is

EXPERIMENT #38

Where Is Your "Area for Improvement"?

1. In your journal, draw the four-square matrix again. Now that we have discussed each box, locate yourself by drawing a little circle. You might not be fully in one box or another but somewhere near the edge or on the line between two boxes.

2. Generally speaking, which is your greatest strength: taking care of your own needs? Or taking good care of your spouse? In your journal, complete this sentence: "I am best at ______." Write a few sentences or a paragraph supporting your statement.

3. What is your "big deal"? Which kind of behavior—supporting yourself or supporting your spouse—is a greater stretch for you? In your journal, complete this sentence: "My challenge is to give more support to (my spouse/myself)." Write a paragraph supporting your statement.

4. Whatever your challenge is in No. 3, select one thing you might do to begin to work on this challenge. For ideas, go back to Chapters Seven and Eight, or brainstorm with yourself. How could you begin today, in some small way, to take better care of yourself or of your spouse, whichever you said was your challenge? Select an activity and then do it.

just not the right person for you. If you have that question, Chapter Ten will be helpful. If not, feel free to skip it and go directly to Chapter Eleven where you'll get to celebrate what you have with your partner.

Part Five

When You Set Change in Motion, Anything Can Happen

CHAPTER TEN

Evaluating Your Relationship

Through nine chapters now, you have tried this new approach to bringing the two of you together, but you are still unhappy and uncertain. Having read this far and completed some experiments, you remain ambivalent about whether the relationship you are in is the right place for you to be at this time in your life. Maybe some of the experiments you did even brought unexpectedly unpleasant results.

You are aware of deficits in your partner and in your relationship, and you are not sure whether these are serious enough for you to consider breaking up. Part of you worries that they are, whether that part is ten percent of you, or ninety percent. You just aren't sure in which direction to move.

When is it time for you to *stop* tolerating and accepting your partner? When does offering good will turn into being exploited? When does taking care of your own needs mean that you need to get out of a relationship that will never give you back enough, no matter what you do? How unhappy is too unhappy?

As one woman I interviewed said,

> I have only one life to live, and I don't want to waste it! Could I find someone new and be much happier? Is the heartache and trauma of divorce worth what I'd gain if I started over? Or am I a fool to give up the good things I have now?

The important questions are, *how* do you make a decision if you aren't sure whether or not to end your relationship? And *what* should you decide? This chapter will provide you with answers to both questions.

HOW TO DECIDE

Before we discuss whether you should stay or leave, we need to look at how you make such a decision. *"How do I decide?"* comes the anguished question so often when I address audiences, or appear on radio and TV talk shows.

Here is how:

1. Gather and review information.
2. Consult your inner wisdom.
3. Create an action plan with a deadline.

Step One—Gather Information

You can't figure out what to do by thinking about your relationship—the mistake most people make, sometimes for years. Thinking about your relationship will keep you mired in ambivalence forever, because the information you already have *isn't enough* for you to make a decision. Otherwise, you would already have made one. Running the same information through your brain over and over is a dead end. You need new data.

Remember a time when you were engaged in some creative endeavor. It could be planning a meeting, organizing an event, painting, sculpting, writing, gardening, sewing, building—anything that meant coming up with ideas or shaping something. Once you began to work, new ideas emerged, because you were immersed in the process. One new development led to another, and the shape of the project changed from its original. You could never have imagined your later improvements before you started working on the project; they emerged out of the process you were in.

Consider your marriage a creative endeavor. New information and ideas come while you are taking part in the relationship, not while you are thinking about it.

In other words, you must try something new in your relationship in order to get new data about it. If you keep behaving the way you have always behaved, you'll never get the new information you need in order to make a decision about what to do.

You have to experiment.

The experiments in this book are an ideal place to start. You may have read right through them because you were certain how they would turn out anyway. But, as we've said, until you actually do an experiment, you cannot know whether your prediction is right or wrong. And you can't know what other unexpected changes might ensue from whatever you set in motion. If all that happens is that you have now tried something new and you got the same old result, even that is useful information. But the chances are great that you will get some unexpected results, and that those results will lead to other unanticipated changes.

If you set change in motion, you have no idea what may happen. You can control the action, but never the outcome. Whatever does occur, this is the information you need to move beyond your indecision.

A big part of the data you are trying to obtain is information about your own feelings, your motivation to make your relationship work, and your own deepest desires. You are trying to make an assault on your own ambivalence. So as you conduct your experiments, it is as important for you to take note of your own responses and those of your partner.

Let's say you try one of the experiments in Chapter Four, in which you create a loving atmosphere in your home, or one of the ones in Chapter Eight where you are invited to be generous and loving to your spouse—or to *act* generous and loving, even if you don't feel that way. How do you feel as you do these acts of loving generosity? Do they make you feel loving? Do you feel resentful and bitter? Can you barely bring yourself to do them? You can't find out if all you do is think about doing an experiment. You must actually *do it* to find out.

In addition to gathering data about yourself, you will get information about your spouse. When you act as if you are a loving spouse, how does your partner respond?

If you are serious about resolving your ambivalence about your relationship, choose five to ten experiments out of this book, maybe one or two from each of these chapters: Three, Four, Five, Seven, and Eight. Or, design some experiments of your own.

Now, over a period of several weeks, formally conduct each of these experiments. Be a little scientist. Write down your plan; then write down your results. Record your own feelings, your spouse's words and actions, and any changes in your relationship that you become aware of.

Consider repeating experiments or doing them over a period of time. Often you will not get much in the way of results the first time or two. You may get more information by repeating the same experiment over and over than by doing more experiments only once.

Avoid the phrase, "It didn't work." If you use this, it means you were expecting a certain outcome. You may hope for a certain outcome, and you may be disappointed if you don't get it, but whatever the outcome, the experiment "worked," because you learned something.

Family members will fight back against your experiments. *You* may resist doing them; your mate may have all sorts of reactions. Anticipate this. Do not see resistance as a sign of "failure." Obstruction and blocking are an inevitable part of many of the experiments you will try. All of this gives you information.

Just as inevitably, you will make mistakes. You will do the experiments imperfectly. You will discover weaknesses and vulnerabilities you didn't know you had. Good! As Tallulah Bankhead said, "If I had to live my life again, I'd make the same mistakes, only sooner!"

If you are like most people who are ambivalent about their marriage, you will resist the idea of doing any experiments. You'll say they feel dumb. You have already tried everything. There is nothing new to learn after all these years.

What is probably going on is that *you are afraid that your relationship will change in a way you don't want it to change.* You may fear, either that you will start feeling better about your mate, or that you will make the situation worse. If you can figure out which fear you have, that in itself will be important information for you. At your deepest level, what do you *hope* will happen when you make a change in yourself? What do you wish the outcome would be? Do you want the experiments to show you that the relationship should continue—or end?

Maybe you fear that any change at all will be a change for the worse, no matter what happens. Your ambivalence is comfortable and familiar. If you leave things as they are, you don't have to make any painful choices, take any risks, or make any permanent decisions. You get to keep all your options open, and you don't have to give anything up. Maybe you just really *like* that booby prize of feeling "right" about who's at fault in your marriage.

But you pay an enormous price if you remain on the fence forever, comfortable and safe but unfulfilled, because you don't get to experience your life fully. You are not participating fully in your relationship, and you are not freeing yourself up from it to experience something new. This is your life we are talking about!

Perhaps the saddest epitaph of all is "I waited."

In a book that has awakened creativity in many people, *The Artist's Way,* Julia Cameron says,

> We change, and the universe further expands that change. Leap and the net will appear.

Experimenting with new behaviors in your relationship and then taking careful note of the results is the only kind of data gathering that has any value. Getting the opinions of other people won't be relevant, because you are the one who must decide. Talking with your spouse about your relationship when you have complaints about it requires a certain amount of skill and even luck. It is too easy to exacerbate the tension between you when you do this and to keep yourself stuck.

Some couples, when one or both parties are unhappy, enlist the services of a professional counselor as a way to gather data. That in itself is an experiment, and will almost certainly be useful, because you are doing something new. Besides, what the counselor will most likely ask you to do is—experiment!

So, in response to the question, "How do I decide?" Step One is, do something different in order to get new information. Using suggestions in this book, designing your own, or using the suggestions of a skilled therapist, experiment. This data-gathering stage can go on for anywhere from six weeks to six months, but probably not longer than that. When you set up your experiments, set up a maximum block of time. You may obtain the data you need earlier, but by that maximum deadline you should be ready for Step Two.

Step Two—Consult Your Inner Wisdom, Your Intuition

A decision about whether to stay in your intimate relationship or to leave it cannot be made in your head, although that's where most people try to make it. Your mind has an unlimited capacity to think thoughts and can churn out pros and cons, theories and advice, obligations and desires, and possible scenarios forever and ever. You don't have to invest yourself in every thought your mind thinks up; but the trouble is, which thoughts should you follow and which should you dump? More thoughts will try to answer that thought, and you will finally drown in a morass of thoughts so thick that you can't breathe, let alone think.

To make a final decision about your relationship, you must set aside your thoughts, quiet your mind, and go deep inside. Where you *feel*. Whereas your mind is capable of staggering amounts of self-deception, denial, and confusion, your body, where your intuition lives, will never lie to you. Most of us get clear messages from our inner wisdom all the time, but we don't listen. We let our minds lead us astray, and then much later on, we say, "I knew better!" or "Something told me I wasn't doing the right thing." You may know *right now* what you need to do deep down inside. But you may be obscuring that clear message with a lot of thoughts. Or you may still be gathering the courage to act on what you know you need to do.

There are two steps involved in consulting your inner wisdom. First, as much as possible, you have to clear away all those thoughts in your mind.

Get a big, blank piece of paper and divide it into four squares. At the top of the left column write "Stay." At the top of the right column, write "Leave." In the top boxes write "Pros," and in the bottom boxes write "Cons."

Stay	**Leave**
Pros	Pros
Cons	Cons

Now let your mind have a field day. Fill in those boxes to your mind's content. Review the notes you made during your experiments. For this part of the exercise, you may even talk things over with a friend who might think of factors you forgot.

If you like you may go one step further and weight each pro and con according to its importance to you. For example, you may have twelve pros that are each only a 3 in importance, and only one con; but the con is a 10 in importance—or a 50 in importance.

Work on your pro and con boxes until you feel there is nothing left to say.

Then, put them aside.

Usually it is a good idea to wait several hours, or a day, before doing the second part of Step Two.

Now you will need a quiet place and uninterrupted time. Calm yourself with gentle, deep breathing. Sink down into your body. Relax every muscle. Put your focus on each part of your body separately and notice how each part feels.

Now, tell yourself you have already made the decision to stay in this relationship and commit yourself to it wholeheartedly. Imagine this in as much detail as you can. What will mornings be like? What will evenings be like? What will be different around your house? What will you say to your mate? What will you do differently? Think about each day, each week. Imagine the present and the future. Think in details.

As you throw yourself into this fantasy of staying, feel what it feels like to you. Do you feel relieved? Do you feel happy? Do you feel scared, anxious, sad? Get into the fantasy that you have wholeheartedly committed yourself to this relationship, and see how you feel about it.

After thirty or forty minutes, come back to the present and move around a bit. Now, move to a different place in the room and repeat the entire process, this time imagining that you have made a firm decision to leave your partner. Imagine it in every detail over the next days, weeks, and months, and notice how you feel.

A variation on this experiment that some find even more useful is to do it over a period of several days or even a week. Go through an entire week pretending just as thoroughly as you can that you have made the decision to stay. Let all your thoughts, words, and behaviors flow from that pretend, all the while noticing *how you feel.* Then, for an equal period of time, pretend you have made the decision to leave and let everything flow from that, noticing all the while *how you feel.*

By the end of one or the other of these experiments, you may have a clear message—or you may not.

If you now know what you need and want to do, you are ready for Step Three.

If you still have no resolution and remain steeped in ambivalence and confusion, then let yourself off the hook. Congratulate yourself for all the effort you have put into these experiments. Make a deal with yourself that you will simply live in a state of ambivalence for a while longer. Then, when you feel ready, repeat Steps One and Two.

You may never feel as certain as you would like to feel—in your mind or your gut. All important decisions are made on the basis of insufficient data, because one thing you can never know is what will occur after you make the decision and act on it. If you had perfect data, you wouldn't need to make a decision; the decision would make itself.

At some point, you will need to take a risk and make a decision based on the information you *do* have. If you wait until you have no doubts and no fears, you will wait forever. Decide to commit yourself fully to quality in this relationship—or decide to leave. Let your deepest inner wisdom show you the way.

Step Three—Create an Action Plan with a Deadline

Many is the person who has made a decision to divorce or leave a long-term relationship years before the split actually occurs. Sometimes there is a valid reason for this, like waiting until the kids are out of the house. (Although I recently read a "Dear Abby" column in which a reader advocated *divorcing* for the sake of the kids! And I heard of a couple who divorced at age ninety-five because they wanted to wait until the kids had all died! Remember, the worst epitaph of all is, "I waited.")

But so often the delay relates more to a lack of courage. If you decide to break up your relationship, you may have a monumentally difficult task on your hands. But just because it is hard is no reason not to do it—if it is the right action for you to take.

If you know clearly what you have to do, this may be one case where you need to feel your fear, brace yourself for a hard time, find some supportive friends, gather together all your courage, and make your leap. Remember, when you take the leap, the net appears.

Once you have come to a decision within yourself about what to do, whether it is to commit yourself to your relationship or to end it, the kindest thing you can do for everyone involved is to make an action plan with a deadline, and then carry out your plan.

WHAT SHOULD YOU DECIDE?

Of course only you can know in the end what is right for you. I can't tell you what to do, and neither can anyone else, though people may try.

However, I can offer you some factors to consider.

First, as we explained fully in Chapter One, if you commit yourself fully to *quality* in your relationship, your chances of success are high. Most troubled relationships will benefit enormously from experiments like the ones in this book, or the ones that would be suggested by a competent marriage counselor. If there is even the tiniest spark of willingness on the part of either partner, one of you *can* bring the two of you together, or the two of you working together can renew your relationship. We know for certain that hundreds of very troubled couples have turned their relationships completely around and have found pleasure and fulfillment with each other when one or both of them made an effort to make changes.

Is Divorce a Solution?

We also know that divorce often causes more problems than it solves. The setbacks it causes can be horrendous, and they go on forever: financial pressure, psychological devastation, and endless emotional turmoil, even when there are no kids involved.

According to divorce mediator Joel Edelman, divorce is not the end of a relationship but a restructuring of it. He identifies four divorces in every family breakup: the legal divorce (paperwork); the economic divorce (dividing up the property and the children); the social divorce (managing friends and relatives); and the emotional divorce (truly letting go of each other, a process that can take years). While divorce is supposed to free the parties, more often it ties them up for years with feelings of anger, despair, loneliness, and the fear of risking love again.

With divorce, you may simply exchange your present problems for worse ones: A thirty-three percent decline in your standard of living (if you are a woman); financial loss and obligation (if you are a man); loneliness (ask several single men and women how much they really enjoy the singles scene); and the pain of a lost dream.

Even with all your pain and loss, the big losers if you divorce are your children. Years after your actual separation, your children continue to live out the emotional scars of your lack of motivation to work on becoming a happier couple.

"But if we are miserable, should we stay together for the sake of the kids?" you may ask.

This question itself traps you in a pseudo-dilemma. For even though you may have convinced yourselves that your only two options are (1) being miserable together for years or (2) divorcing, this is not at all the case. At least one other option is to become loving toward each other again, to make your marriage work—for yourselves and for your children. This may not feel possible to you right now. But according to the experience of many who have gone before you, it is.

You will almost certainly be amazed at the positive changes you can make in your marriage if you are willing to experiment, to defy your stereotypes and beliefs about your marriage, and to dare. Most people think that happy couples have a good marriage because they got lucky and they are simply right for each other. But as I know from my study of couples who thrive, the causal connection usually goes in the other direction: Happy couples seem right for each other because they *do what they need to do* to make their marriage happy. Thriving couples start out with the same incompatibilities, power struggles, dissatisfactions, and conflicts that beset most marriages. But—*because* they believe in their relationship and want it to work—it does. It is not the raw materials they have to work with, but what they *do* with the raw materials that makes them happy.

It may be easy for you to believe that divorce will give you the opportunity for personal growth, the chance to see where you went wrong and do it differently the next time, but realize this: If you don't make any *personal* changes, you will take your same old self with you into your next marriage and very likely repeat your self-defeating pattern. And if you are prepared to make some personal changes, how much more sensible and rewarding it is to change within your present marriage, to build upon the history you share and the family and community you are a part of, especially if you have children.

On the other hand . . .

There certainly are situations in which ending a relationship could very well be the best decision for you. Let's look at several of them.

A Word to Singles

I believe you should consider ending your relationship if you are not yet married or committed to the person you are with, you still want a lifetime partner, and you have a lot of uncertainty about the relationship you are in. While I have emphasized that good will and self-care can bring about excellent results in a wide variety of relationships, nevertheless, while you still have the opportunity to choose the person who will be your lifelong companion, *choose carefully!* Don't make the mistake of staying in a relationship you are less than enthusiastic about, or that has significant problems, just because you aren't paying attention!

The most important quality to hold out for, when you are still looking for a life partner, is a feeling of certainty deep within you that this is the right person for you. You want to be with someone who feels like a true peer: an emotional peer, an intellectual peer, and a "consciousness" peer.

You probably won't find the exact person you have dreamed up in your fantasies, right down to the last lock of hair. As virtually all the thriving couples I interviewed concurred, love always shows up in the form you least expect. Keeping your standards high means that you hold out for someone you feel completely enthusiastic about, and who feels the same way about you, even if some of the "desirable qualities" you thought you wanted are missing.

How did you get into the relationship with this partner? Did you more or less blunder into it, or did you make a conscious choice: This is definitely the person I choose to be with? When you look at the qualities in your mate that you are working to "tolerate" and "accept" in a spirit of good will, are they qualities that are an annoyance for you, whether a little annoyance or a big one? Or are they problems that are more like fatal flaws, irreconcilable differences, or insurmountable obstacles? When you are still single and have the opportunity to choose a mate, don't force yourself to tolerate anything in your partner that you can't respect or live with.

It may be hard to end a relationship that feels comfortable and that is meeting some of your needs. But if you seriously doubt that this is your soul mate or your lifelong companion—and you know you want such a partner in your life—then the difficulty of splitting up is not a good enough reason to avoid doing it.

One of the most common mistakes singles make is to spend months or years in what I call "BTN" relationships: Better Than Nothing. BTNs keep you out of circulation for finding the true love of your life, and they lower your self-esteem. I have written extensively about BTNs in my book, *If I'm So Wonderful, Why Am I Still Single?* and about exactly how to keep your standards—and your spirits—high as you search for your soul mate. Here, suffice it to say that, if you are looking for a committed relationship but are not yet in one, that in itself might very well be a reason for you to end your relationship. Save your skills as a Loving Leader for a relationship that you are certain you want very much to be a part of.

No Children, No Money, No Property

Another circumstance in which it might make sense for you to take the risk of ending a relationship, even if your partnership is not a disaster, is if you have been together a short time, you have no children together and no complicated financial or legal entanglements like co-owning a home or a business, and you recognize that you simply used poor judgment or made a mistake. You may discover sides of your partner that were completely hidden early in your courtship.

This is dangerous territory, because virtually every relationship goes through some period of fall from the honeymoon, disillusionment, and disappointment, and most relationships that weather those tough, painful times go on to flourish for many years. But if you are discovering what, for you, is simply unacceptable behavior in your partner, if you discover no willingness on the part of your partner to negotiate, if you see that the commitment you thought your partner made simply isn't there at all, then you may be doing yourself an enormous favor by viewing this relationship as a stepping stone, learning all you can from it, and having the courage to move on.

Sarah met a lovely young man, Juan, while she was studying in England during her junior year in college. She stayed in England an additional six months so Juan could finish his degree program, and then they came to the States. One evening over coffee, Sarah said to me, "I know this seems hasty, and I feel like I am young to get married, but I adore Juan! He has so many wonderful qualities. (She cited a long, well-thought-out list of them.) I feel certain I want to be with him the rest of my life. I think we can make a wonderful life together."

They married and set up housekeeping. But Juan didn't adapt well to his new job and their isolated city life. He became depressed. One night at 1:00 A.M., Sarah called me, quite distressed and frightened. Juan was engaging in bizarre behavior and saying crazy things to her. I persuaded her to call the police who took Juan to a psychiatric unit.

In the next few days, Sarah learned that Juan had carefully hidden from her a history of manic-depressive episodes, and that he had consistently resisted medication. Juan's own family decided to fly him back to England for treatment, and in the ensuing months, Sarah reevaluated her decision and—after many difficult phone calls and anguished conversations—decided that she did not want to sign up at her tender age for a lifetime of managing a mental illness. Their divorce was uncomplicated and clean.

Bob, on the other hand, was sixty-four and had been alone for eight years when he met Barbara, also sixty-four, through a personal ad and fell passionately in love with her. The two were like teenagers in the height of bliss. For two years, they traveled together, spent time with their families, and made a lovely home together in the big city they both loved. But Barbara kept putting off a discussion of marriage. And she began spending more and more time away from Bob on her own trips, traveling with women friends, or spending extended periods with her sister in a distant city. Bob was tolerant and patient, though he told Barbara clearly that these separations troubled and upset him. Then, Barbara decided to spend a week with an old boyfriend of hers. The week became ten days. Bob reluctantly admitted the facts: that Barbara simply didn't have the commitment to this relationship that she claimed to have. He saw years of Barbara's capricious behavior stretching out in front of him, and though it broke his heart, he moved out of their apartment and asked her not to call.

A therapist in her forties, Glenda, told me, "I knew when I got engaged at age twenty that it was a terrible mistake, but I was simply so weak and impressionable back then, I didn't realize I had the choice to say no. I was caught up in the strong influence of Nick and literally didn't know how to get out of it." Glenda and Nick were together for seven years, but they never had children, and their finances were simple. After Glenda joined a women's group, began keeping a journal, and focused directly on building her self-esteem, she liberated herself from a relationship that was never right to begin with. The divorce was uncomplicated, and the break with Nick was total. Glenda's was a decision that brought her much inner peace, joy, and freedom.

You deserve a wonderful relationship in your life. You deserve a partner who adores you and wants to make you happy. You deserve to be with someone you respect and love. If you are absolutely certain that the person you are with now is not that person, and you can make a clean, uncomplicated break, maybe what you need is the courage to make the break.

BUT—even if you are going through the dark night of despair with your mate right now, if you have the tiniest corner of positive feelings, if you know you have felt love for this person before, if you can list your partner's positive qualities, OR if you have children or complicated economic entanglements, then you are almost certainly better off to pursue your relationship with great determination. You cannot even imagine the rewards that can be yours if you do—or the emotional roller coaster that may be yours if you don't.

Verbal or Physical Abuse

If you are in an abusive relationship or one that is completely toxic for you, leaving may, again, be your best option.

Abuse can be in the form of physical battering, or it can be verbal abuse. According to Patricia Evans, author of *The Verbally Abusive Relationship,* the effects of verbal abuse are as devastating as those of physical abuse, and the wounds—to your self-esteem and ability to trust—can take much longer to heal.

Physical abuse is always preceded by verbal abuse. If your spouse is abusing you, *you are the only person who can take the initiative to end the abuse*. You must do something about it yourself. If you suspect that what is going on in your relationship might be considered abuse, without delay call your local shelter for battered women; or your rabbi, minister, or priest; or the Employee Assistance Program of your employer; or a therapist, listed in the yellow pages under "Psychologists," "Psychotherapy," or "Marriage, Family, and Child Counselors."

With the support of experienced volunteers and professionals, you will be able to take the two vital steps that will turn your life around and get you out of your abusive situation. Your first step is to recognize and identify the abuse clearly and to admit to yourself that you are the victim of abuse. Your second step is to begin to set limits with your partner—that is, to stop tolerating the abuse—and to remove yourself from the abusive situation and possibly from the relationship altogether.

Both of these steps are almost impossible to accomplish by yourself. Fortunately, virtually everywhere in this country, knowledgeable professionals stand ready to help. But you have to make the first phone call.

Your spouse is abusing you if he (I'll use "he" for convenience; women do abuse men too, but far less often) becomes angry with you several times a week over issues that completely surprise you—and then denies that he is mad, or blames you for starting the fight. He refuses to acknowledge your feelings of pain or hurt, so that you never feel you have resolved anything with him. An abusive spouse will blame you for *everything,* put you down, and refuse to listen to your point of view or to recognize your needs. When you try to discuss a recent fight with him, he will act as though he has no idea what you are talking about, and will simply get angry and blame you again.

The goal of an abusive spouse is to *control* you. He will try to control your *time* by showing up late, refusing to schedule anything ahead of time, and changing plans by himself at the last minute. He will try to control your *relationships* and isolate you from a supportive network by refusing to pass along phone messages, and becoming angry every time you see a friend. He will try to control your *mind* by interrupting you, and using confusing and inconsistent arguments that wear you down. He will invade your *privacy* by disturbing you when you want to be alone, and depriving you of sleep. He will open your mail, listen in on your phone calls, and demand to know exactly where you are going or where you have been. He may even hit or beat you. He will try to control your *money.* He will even try to control your *reality* by claiming that you said, or did, or saw, something other than what you remember. He will try to keep you feeling confused, insecure, and powerless.

Patricia Evans identifies fifteen categories of verbally abusive behavior, like withholding, discounting, diverting, blaming, criticizing, trivializing, name-calling, and so on. She also offers her readers specific verbal and behavioral responses to each category of abuse, to thwart the abuser's attempts to control you and begin to restore the balance of power.

Identifying abuse and the tools you need to escape it is beyond the scope of this book. I simply want to make the point here that an abusive relationship could be one that you would be better off ending.

You might want to try working on your relationship first. When you become aware of the methods of abuse your spouse is using and you find ways to stop tolerating the abuse, your spouse may respond positively. Some abusers actually are capable of change, once their abusive behavior is pointed out to them. The program outlined in this book will be useful to you, though my work has not been with partners in abusive relationships, and I strongly recommend that you work with professionals or volunteers who have had specific training in working with abusive partnerships.

If you are being abused and your partner does not respond to your attempts at change—as wrenching as it might be for you and your children, financially and emotionally—divorce could actually be a positive option for you.

In addition, divorce might be your most productive option if your spouse is hopelessly addicted to drugs, alcohol, gambling, or any dysfunctional pattern that makes a normal relationship virtually impossible for the two of you. If your spouse has not an ounce of good will anywhere, is completely uninterested in your relationship, or is consistently untrustworthy—these, too, are circumstances in which taking care of yourself may well take precedence over taking care of a relationship that is destroying rather than supporting you.

I rarely advocate divorce. However, you have only one life to live. If you are in a partnership that is genuinely toxic for you, breaking free of it could give you a whole new self and years of productivity and happiness that might otherwise be lost to you—lost in adapting to a person who will never be able to love and nurture you, and who is beyond your reach to help.

Are you unhappy with your relationship and uncertain what to do?

We've looked at how to go about making a decision and presented some ideas about what to decide.

The real question is, do you want to be in this relationship? Do you want to resolve the problems you have so that you and your mate can be happier? Or have you crossed over to the other side where you really don't believe in your marriage anymore, and deep down inside you don't want it to work out well?

If you have the desire to make your relationship work and the willingness to experiment, you can resolve your conflicts and reignite your love. If you have lost your desire and willingness, and nothing in this book has helped you get it back, then it is possible that one of you *can't* bring the two of you together, and that you should move instead to the formidable task of finding a way to say good-bye.

CHAPTER ELEVEN The Good Marriage, The Good Self

A great relationship is like a fine heirloom. It may have tattered corners or a missing part or two. But it is prized and treasured far beyond its counterpart that's shiny and new. You cherish an heirloom because it has been a part of your history for so long. It conjures up a feeling of belonging, of continuity and security. An heirloom had to have quality to begin with, for it has endured countless traumas to get to where it is now; but it has survived!

Just so with your relationship. Its worn edges and comforting familiarity were not easily or quickly come by.

Cherish it.

And by the way, don't be timid about telling the world that you are in a thriving relationship. The negativity that surrounds marriage in our culture is overwhelming. You can help counteract the pervasive wisdom that marriage is hard work and that the most you can hope for if you labor at it for years is moderate happiness with each other. I believe this doomsday scenario becomes a self-fulfilling prophecy for many couples, the ones who laugh at you, or make a cynical comment if you tell them you are happily married. The world needs to know that thriving marriage is not an unobtainable dream, but a reality—some days more than others, to be sure, but nevertheless a reality—that many of us are happily living.

YOUR RELATIONSHIP AS A SPIRITUAL PATH

According to psychologist and spiritual writer John Welwood, a thing is sacred if it "brings us into greater alignment with who we are."

Since your effort to achieve a blend of self-care and good will in your relationship will do exactly that, your relationship presents you with a unique opportunity for spiritual growth.

When you love someone, when you expand your own world to include the welfare of another person, you are automatically on a journey. If you go on that journey with even the least bit of consciousness, it will bring you into greater alignment with who you are. And your loving relationship may help to bring others into greater alignment with who they are. If we could only expand love enough, we could achieve a world that is in greater alignment with its true nature, for the only impediment to universal peace and happiness, to the Garden of Eden, is actions that are inconsistent with love.

Though it may not feel like it day in and day out, your love is a spiritual journey, a path to greater wholeness, a sacred pilgrimage. The ultimate destination of your pilgrimage is your true self, not a separate self, as it turns out, but a self wrapped in unity with the person you love and with everyone who loves, everywhere. Just as a drop of water becomes a part of the whole ocean, the clouds, the rain, and then the ocean again, your love is not isolated, but is a part of the universal experience of love.

What does it mean that your relationship "brings you into greater alignment with yourself"?

Each of us consists of an essential being made up of (*a*) inherited physical characteristics, (*b*) basic personality tendencies, and (*c*) an intangible, hard-to-define inner self that we might call a vital spirit or breath of life. Some call it a soul, or a motivating force, or consciousness itself. That vital spirit is the deepest essence of each of us, the pith around which the body and the personality drape themselves.

From the moment a baby is conceived, outside influences begin to modify the person who is emerging. Family, economic conditions, complex relationships, weather, social conditions—layers and layers of extrinsic material surround and shape the essential being.

A spiritual journey, whatever form it takes, is about moving back through the layers of added-on life experience to discover what these layers are and how they have influenced the essential being, and to recover and free up the essential self. The more you can discover about the forces that shaped who you are today, the more choice you have about who you truly want to be. For even though your family, your friends, your home town, your education, your travels, and all of the experiences that were uniquely yours growing up have had an enormous impact on who you are, as an adult you still have an extraordinary amount of choice about who you want to be, what you want to do with your life, and how you want to treat other people. A spiritual journey is simply the process of recovering your essence, of reclaiming your inner self, of finding the self that you yourself can truly love and that you most want to express in your life.

The most spiritual question you can ask yourself in any situation, whether it be painful or joyful, is, "What is the lesson in this for me? What can I learn about myself?" Usually, we'd rather ask, "What is this other person's problem?" or "Why did this happen to me?" But if you can make yourself look for it, you are bound to discover some new nuance on who you are.

Self-discovery virtually always leads to, or may be motivated by, a feeling of connection to other people and to the force of life itself. We do not exist on this planet as lone organisms but are linked in numerous ways to each other and to a process and purposefulness that is beyond ourselves. We have a desire to be in rhythm with nature and with the laws of goodness, meaning, and value, rather than setting up our lives to be at odds with these ideals. So, as we search, along with uncovering our own true essence, we discover a reality larger than ourselves, a meaning or alignment that holds our world together and binds us to each other. Great teachers who devote their entire lives to spiritual practice report that the highest spiritual achievement is the experience that we are not actually separate from each other but are all aspects of one being; that is how tied we are to each other.

Viewed according to this model, evil is not a separate army that has set up a war with goodness, using humans and planet earth as the battlefield. Instead, evil is actually ignorance. "Evil" people are those who are still at the mercy of the forces that have smothered their inner self. As the world assaulted the tiny flame that is their essential being, these people developed layers of fear, anger, and hate. It is out of these layers that they now operate, unaware that a beautiful, loving ember still glows deep within, gasping for air, nearly burned out by all the layers of "protection." Anyone who begins a spiritual journey of any kind will become conscious of the layers, will become aware that they are added on, that they are not the self's true essence. That is how evil, selfish people come back to a spirit of goodness sometimes after years in jail, or at the end of their lives. They re-connect with the inner flame of goodness that was their true, essential self all along. They come into greater alignment with who they are.

A religion or specific spiritual tradition is simply a vehicle for taking this journey of discovery. Many, many such vehicles exist. The great world religions can be vehicles for a spiritual journey. A regular practice of meditation can be a vehicle. Personal growth workshops and self-help books can open up a spiritual journey or make a contribution to it. An intimate relationship with a skilled psychotherapist is a spiritual vehicle for many people, providing perhaps one of the most direct routes to self-discovery; to the deep, permanent release of old layers; and to the ecstasy of re-connecting with one's true inner self, free of the burdens it has been bearing for so many years.

And certainly, your relationship is a vehicle for a spiritual journey. Working on your relationship by yourself according to the guidelines in this book will make you aware of some of your "layers," will lead you in the direction of your essential being, and will "bring you into alignment with who you are."

Your relationship is "spiritual" in another way also.

For thousands of years and still today, the great spiritual traditions teach the same core ideals: love, forgiveness, generosity, and truth. It is astonishing how little of the world, still, lives by these values. But people whose source of life is the layers of fear, greed, anger, and hate that cover their true selves are simply not motivated to look at timeless spiritual values or to make choices about them.

The program laid out in this book offers you practical, easy-to-implement techniques for behaving in accord with the great spiritual principles. Everything we have suggested grows out of love, forgiveness, generosity, authenticity, and reverence for life.

I'm quite well aware that some of what I have suggested asks a lot of you. Accepting qualities in your mate you don't like, acting as if you are happy when you are angry. These endeavors aren't easy. But you don't have to be a master to *understand* spiritual principles and to live by them to the best of your ability. Indeed, that is probably what you are already doing. The ideas in this book are simply a boost. They suggest specific ways that you can *behave* like a spiritual master without actually being one.

Some of the strategies we have discussed are the kind that take a minute to learn and a lifetime to master. But that doesn't mean that you can't experience great progress—and wonderful changes in your relationship—right away. The suggestions in this book are ways to practice spiritual principles in simple, concrete steps. At the very least, these approaches will set you off in a useful direction, one that is rooted in the great spiritual teachings of many centuries.

Of course, you may be a reader who is already on a spiritual path and already well-acquainted with spiritual teachings. I hope this book is giving you practical suggestions for putting to work in your relationship the spiritual principles you are already striving to achieve.

REVIEW

Let's take a moment to review and summarize what we have said in this book. Without all the lists and steps, here's the essence of the message:

A spirit of generosity and good will toward your partner is likely to bring you a happy, peaceful relationship faster than if you focus on solving your problems. The more you can find ways to take care of yourself and your own needs in your marriage, the more you can let go of having to get your partner to change to meet your needs, an exhausting and futile effort. Focus on what you like about your partner, and take advantage of everything you enjoy about your relationship.

Take charge of your own happiness. Don't wait for your partner to change. As much as you can, accept all that you have, just as it is. Count your blessings, and don't let yourself dwell on what you wish were different. Some specific ways to focus on happiness are these:

- "act as if" you feel the way you want to feel
- think "good will"
- focus on what you like, not what you don't
- change "incompatible" to "complementary"
- create relaxing, fun time for the two of you
- try out the "Seven Steps to Bring the Two of You Together" (at the end of Chapter Four)

Try not to judge or blame your partner. Look behind the behavior you don't like to the person who is there, and have compassion. Your partner is probably doing the best that he or she can, given all the circumstances. Remember all those circumstances, and be understanding and forgiving, as much as possible. Your partner is far likelier to respond to love than to criticism.

When you are angry or hurt, let yourself feel angry or hurt, but then, use your creativity to find a change *you* can make to fix the problem. Don't let the situation that is making you angry continue indefinitely. Do something that you have control over doing. Problem-solving ideas we discussed in detail include these:

- act on your own: try to take for yourself as much as you give to your spouse
- deliberately do the opposite of what you have been doing
- depolarize your power struggle
- make the problem *yours* and enlist your partner's help in solving it
- express empathy out loud to your partner
- accept what you can't change
- ask for what you want in a way that is likely to bring positive results
- Men, "space in"; Women, stop coaching

Intimacy and the pleasure of companionship will follow naturally from your generosity and creativity. Don't try to force these qualities in your relationship. Be aware of what your partner wants, too, and, as always, try to take care of both of you. Appreciate the everyday pleasures of being with your partner. Relax and let them in, just as they are.

Taking care of your relationship by yourself boils down to balancing these two skills: take care of yourself, and take care of your spouse. The affirmations that will help you take care of yourself are these:

I'm doing the best I can.
If I don't take care of myself, who will?
I can do this.
Things take time.
My desires are reasonable.
I can take a stand.

The affirmations that will help you take care of your partner are these:

This is not a problem, but a fact of life.
My partner is not wrong, just different.
This has nothing to do with me.
She is doing the best she can.

OR
He's doing the best he can.
My partner was wrong; I have a choice.
How can I be generous to my mate today?

When you are able to achieve a reasonable balance of self-care and good will in your relationship, you will experience it as a blend which might be thought of as Loving Leadership. It is possible to experience the feel of Loving Leadership in your body: a self-confident, firmly grounded inner core from which you are able to reach out and give without feeling threatened.

Finally, if you are trying to decide whether to get out of your present relationship, quiet down your thoughts and consult your intuition, your inner wisdom. Assume that deep down inside, you already know what you should do; you just have to pay attention to that knowledge. And don't take forever to make your decision.

IN CONCLUSION

As I was in the throes of writing the final chapter for this book, I attended a conference where Dallas radio personality Suzie Humphreys was the keynote speaker. She is one of those presenters whom audiences completely adore. She relates her stories so that her own setbacks and triumphs seem like your very own. We were in tears of sadness one moment and laughter the next.

Imagine my shock when the final portion of her speech was a story about the exact principles I had been writing about for months. She couldn't have provided a better testimonial for good will and self-care if I had prearranged it and paid her a million dollars. With her gracious permission, I would like to share her story, just as she told it to us. Try to imagine this warm, completely unpretentious, delightful, funny redhead—with a fabulous Texas drawl.

> I have to tell you up front, I'm nuts about my husband. I didn't think I'd ever be, 'cause he certainly wasn't the first one.
>
> Or the second one. I'm not going to tell you which one he was, 'cause it doesn't matter.

But I'll tell you he's the only one! But boy, I didn't know it back then when we met. I didn't know how to love anybody. I was always lookin' for somebody to love me! And I always figured I could change him. I don't like the way he dresses—I can change him. I don't like the way he talks—I can change him. The only standard I had was, he had to be breathing!

Then I met Tom. He and I went to marriage lessons. You know how we all are at the beginning. We don't like certain things. I don't like the way he snores. I don't like the way he dresses. He doesn't earn enough money. I don't like the way he doesn't remember my birthday. I don't like the way he forgets our anniversary. I don't like the way he's always workin' on that airplane. I don't like the way he's always going huntin' in the winter—what am I supposed to do while he's gone?

Finally, Tom and I looked at each other one day, realizing all that friendship we had, we took each other's hand and we said, "Ya know? For whatever moment of friendship or love or affection we ever had, we need to get this right. We need to either get it right or get goin'."

So we decided to take marriage lessons. We went to the marriage lesson lady, and I did all the talking. She said, "I'm going to put you in a group."

I said, "I don't do groups. Groups are for crazy people."

She said, "Well you need to be in one!"

So I went in there every Wednesday night and carried on about "I don't like the way he . . . He never . . ."

Finally this big lawyer in my group, six foot seven inches tall with feet about this big and huge cowboy boots, propped those elbows on those knees, leaned across to me and said, "Ya know? I been listenin' to you for one solid year talk about him. And I'll tell you what I think you ought to do."

I was interested! I said, "Whaaaat?"

He said, "I think you ought to leave him."

I said, "Leave him? *Leave him?*"

He said, "Yea! 'Cause if you can't accept him exactly as he is, you need to get going!"

I said, "Accept him? Accept him exactly as he is?"

He said, "Exactly as he is. Now why don't you think about this tonight and let somebody else talk for a change—and you come back here next week and tell us what you've decided to do."

I went away that night and I thought about it all week, and

I'll tell you something, my friends. You know a moment in your life when everything changes. You know that moment. You can recall it, you can sense it, you can remember it. It's with you every day. That big six-foot-seven-inch lawyer made me think about something that I'd never thought about before because he made me focus on losin' Tom. And when I focused on what I was losin'—I focused on what I like about him.

I love the way he fills a room. I love the way he walks. I love the way he walks with purpose and the way his head bobs, and I love the way he has passion in everything he does. I love the way he's buildin' a deck, fixin' a fence, sellin' real estate, reading—he's got fifteen projects going on and they've all been goin' on for four years. I love the way he can't stand to go to sleep at night 'cause he doesn't want to miss anything. And I love the way, regardless of what's goin' on in his world, he puts his feet on the floor every morning and says, "I got another shot at it." I love the way he takes his kids—all the way from forty down to our Josh who's eighteen—and kisses them on the head and stands proud—he's so proud of them—and doesn't try to meddle in their lives or tell 'em what they should or shouldn't do. I love the way, when I have no makeup on and it's this ruddy face and freckles and no eyebrows or eyelashes, just two blue holes, he takes my head in his hands and he says, "You are the cutest girl. I'd love to get in your skivvy drawers."

I went back that next week and that big lawyer said, "What's it gonna be?" and I said, "I can do it! I can do it!"

He said, "What if he doesn't earn enough money to suit you?"

I said, "The money doesn't matter. I didn't marry him for his money. I can make money. We can all make money. We just don't know it."

He said, "What if he's always goin' huntin'?"

I said, "I'm going to stand at the door when he goes out and say, 'Have a great time!' "

You know what happens to a man when you send him off and tell him to have a great time? He's home two days early!

I call him John Wayne. You know what happens to a man when you call him John Wayne—instead of Jerk?

We been married twenty years. And Tom hasn't changed a bit. I have. I changed the way I looked at him. I looked at what was right and not what was wrong.

So there I was at the radio station, with a great marriage, livin' in a house I adored. I loved this house. We did a lot to fix it up.

The house was my roots. When I'd drive in the driveway, my soul sang.

Well, about five years ago, John Wayne comes in to me and says, "We need to leave Dallas."

I said, "What for? Leave Dallas?"

He said, "Yeah, let's go do something new."

I said, "Like what?"

He said, "Like go to the hill country, the Texas hill country. Got lots of live oaks and rivers. Let's go build something."

I said, "What? Why would I want to leave Dallas? I'm in radio. Everybody knows me. I'm someboooody."

He said, "Let's just drive down there and take a look at it."

So we did. We drove down there, and I said, "Yeah, it's beautiful man! Out here in the wilderness. You get up every morning and breeeeathe in the fresh air—*and then what?!!*"

He said, "Let's just think about it."

So I started goin' with it, you know, trying to like it.

But I *didn't* like it. There wasn't anything to do there. No people. No committee meetings.—But then we came on a little town called Fredericksburg. I liked it! It had little German buildings. Everything was pristine, and it had a lot of shops! I said, "I could live here. Let's do that, Tom, *some day!*"

Tom said, "No, let's do it now."

I said, "I don't want to go now."

He said, "Well, let's just get used to it. Let's just go down there and visit." And we did that over the next year or two.

January 1993. John Wayne wakes me up in the middle of night—doubled over. He said, "I'm in trouble." We got in the car. I tried so hard not to be afraid. He could see the fear in me, and he has the most arcane sense of humor. So as we pulled up to the hospital, he said, "You s'pose we could pull over and make love one more time before we go in?"

So we go into the hospital, and we're laughing. We felt a lot better going there laughing! I was asking him, "Where is the will. Who are your six best friends? What kind of music do you like?"

After they looked him over, they said he'd be okay but he had a lot of stress. When he was comin' around, I went over to him and I said, "Listen, John, you know you and I've been given a wake up call here."

He said, "I know it."

I said, "What is it you really want to do with your life?"

He said, "I want to move to Fredericksburg."

I said, "Well let's do it."

He said, "We don't have any land!"

I said, "Well, I got a surprise for you. I rented a bed and breakfast for you for the whole month of February. Go down there and find your rainbow."

So he takes off with his black lab dog. Two days before the B&B expired, by following his inner voices, he found the exact piece of property we'd been looking for. Right down to the last detail.

He called me and said, "I'm gonna make a run at it."

I said, "Go for it!"

He said, "I got one question. How are we gonna put anything on the land?"

I said, "We'll sell the house."

I said that? My precious house?

I said that. Because happiness is not a state of location; it's a state of mind. There'll always be another house.

And mostly I said that because of the realization that love is not an emotion. It's an action. It's not something you get. It's something you give.

Thirty-three days later, we had sold our house. I gave my resignation at the radio station, and we moved down to the hill country where we have a runway for his airplane and an electric gate and greenhouse and a kennel and a hangar and an office and a bedroom for our son. We live in an old general store. It's a two-room house. Our Dallas friends come in and say, "Oh what a darling cabin. It's so cuuute!"

It's our *home!* Because what had to change was our perception of, what is a perfect life? What is a perfect house? Ask me now, and I'll tell you it's a two-room house!

Let me tell you why I think this happened for us, my friends. Goethe said it. He said, "Begin it now." Once you commit yourself to something, once you see it in your mind, there will occur in the universe all sorts of things to make a way for it to happen for you. But you must first begin it now. *Begin it now!* Don't let fear get in your way. Don't let doubt come in your way.

And the main thing you have to do is be good to yourself. Treat yourself special. If you're treatin' yourself special, then you're not waitin' for somebody else to do it for you.

So you've taken him every Christmas for four years to the jewelry store and showed him that bracelet. And every year for four years, he still hasn't gotten it. So buy it for yourself and put his name on the card! It lets him off the hook, and you're happy.

Or if you're waitin' for her to buy you that fly rod. She's not good at that. Buy your own fly rod.

I found that out when I was thirty years old and I was married to one of those husbands, and he wasn't going to give me a surprise birthday party. And I'd always wanted a surprise birthday party. Women want that! We give 'em to you guys!—You neeever do it back! You think a single rose from the grocery store is gonna cut it.

So I decided to plan my own surprise birthday party. We were at a dinner party one night and I said, "Mark down the 24th on your calendar. I'm givin' myself a surprise birthday party. Everybody laughed—just like you are—until the invitation arrived in the mail. It invited them to the First Annual Suzie Humphreys Surprise Birthday Party. It had the time and place, and it had a little map to show you where to park your car so I wouldn't get suspicious. Then it charged 'em twenty bucks a couple.—Well why should I pay for the food, I was cookin' it!—And then it said, "Don't waste your money on a silly gag gift; put it all together and buy me something real nice. I'd like a silver chafing dish!"

Come the night of the party, I blew up 350 helium balloons, painted signs that said "We love you Suzie! You're the greatest!" I assigned my two best friends to take me out to get a drink so everybody'd have time to get in there and hide. Seven o'clock, I walked into a pitch black room and twenty-four people yelled, "Surprise!"—And I cried!

The point is, who can plan your surprise birthday party better than you can! And if we do it for ourselves, we are not waiting for someone else to make our lives exciting. We can live together in marriage or friendship and know we have all within us to do what we need to do. We don't have to look to someone else because, "My life didn't turn out like I wanted it."

Suzie Humphreys got it! (If you'd like to hear one of her extraordinary presentations in person, call her at 210/997-9721.)

What worked for Suzie will work for you!

Take care of yourself, and take care of your partner.

Begin it now.

Bibliography

BECK, AARON T., M.D. *Love is Never Enough.* New York: Harper and Row Publishers, 1988.

BORYS, HENRY JAMES. *The Way of Marriage.* Kirkland, Washington: Purna Press, 1991.

BUGEN, LARRY A. *Love and Renewal.* Oakland, California: New Harbinger Publications, 1990.

CAMPBELL, SUSAN. *The Couple's Journey.* San Luis Obispo, California: Impact Publishers, 1980.

EDELMAN, JOEL and MARY BETH CRAIN. *The Tao of Negotiation.* New York: HarperBusiness, 1993.

GRAY, JOHN. *Men Are from Mars, Women Are from Venus.* New York: HarperCollins, 1992.

HENDRICKS, GAY, Ph.D. and KATHLYN HENDRICKS, Ph.D. *Conscious Loving.* New York: Bantam Books, 1990.

KIPNIS, AARON, Ph.D., and ELIZABETH HERRON, M.A. *What Men and Women Really Want.* Novato, California: Nataraj Publishing, 1995.

ODEN, THOMAS. *Game Free: The Meaning of Intimacy.* New York: Harper and Row, 1974.

O'HANLON, BILL, and PAT HUDSON. *Love Is a Verb.* New York: W. W. Norton and Co., 1995.

PRANSKY, GEORGE S. *Divorce Is Not the Answer.* Blue Ridge Summit, Pennsylvania: Tab Books (McGraw-Hill), 1990.

TAVRIS, CAROL. *Anger: The Misunderstood Emotion.* New York: Touchstone (Simon & Schuster), 1989.

WEINER-DAVIS, MICHELE. *Divorce Busting.* New York: Fireside (Simon & Schuster), 1992.

WELWOOD, JOHN. *Love and Awakening.* New York: HarperCollins, 1996.

Index

Abuse
deciding on separation in cases of, 276–78
forgiveness vs., 238–39
setting limits in cases of, 208–12
Acceptance
as component of good will, 220
of current situation, 47–49
of partner's differences, 223–26
as starting point for change, 48, 147, 222, 225, 232
of what cannot be changed, 143–48
of yourself, 188–93
"Acting as if"
adopting opposite behaviors as, 123, 125
on changing incompatibility to complementarity, 104
experiment on, 95
in role of loving spouse, 90–96
Acting on your own for problem resolution, 116–22
Action, goals and, 200–202
Action plan, decision-making about relationship and, 270–71
"ADD: Acknowledgment. Don't Get Defensive," 76–80
Addictive behaviors, deciding on separation in cases of, 278
Advising and assisting
problems associated with, 10
stopping coaching behavior, 160–62
working on discontinuing criticism and, 46
Affirmations
confidence and self-, 208
on good will, 220–45, 284–85
on self-care, 188–212, 284
Amen, Daniel, 201, 235
Anger, 50–83
ERAP technique for using your, 53–76, 81–83
partner's, 76–80
personal style of, 51–53
Anger eclipser, 51–52
charging anger energy by, 54–56
Anger expresser, 51–52
discharging anger energy by, 56–58
Anger: The Misunderstood Emotion (Tavris), 59–60
Artist's Way, The (Cameron), 267
Asking for what you want, 149–55
ineffective ways of, 8–9
problem of not, 9
Assertiveness, building self-, 208–12
Assess step (ERAP), 63–66, 81
Attitudes. *See* Belief(s)

Balance. *See* Inner balance
Behavior(s)
"acting as if," 90–96
adopting opposite, 123–27
brain dysfunction and, 235–36
changing beliefs and changing, 88–89
changing feelings by "acting as if," 90–96
changing your own, 6–7, 81–82
your role in causing partner's, 36–40
Being right, letting go of, 29–34, 171
Belief(s)
both partners required to work on relationship as faulty, xi, 4–26
changing behaviors by changing, 88–89
changing your own attitudes and, 6–7, 103, 182
"Big person" in relationships, 22–25, 141, 213
Blend of self-care and good will, 246–53
BNT relationships (Better Than Nothing), 273–74
Body
balance between good will and self-care felt in, 253–56
charging/discharging anger in, 53–58
inner wisdom about relationship felt in, 267–70
Booby prize of relationships, finding problems and assigning fault as, 29–34

Borys, Henry James, 68–69, 96–97, 159, 162, 238, 240
Brain dysfunction, 235–36
Brainstorming, 69–71, 75
Bribery, emotional, 9–10
Bugen, Larry A., 13

Calming, strategies for self-, 61–62
Cameron, Julia, 267
Change, 20–21
acceptance as starting point for, 48, 147, 222, 225, 232
accepting impossibility of, 143–48
in feelings by changing behavior, 90–96
learning curve for, 46–47
in yourself, 6–7, 33–34, 45–47
Children, effects of divorce on, 272
Choice(s)
coming up with third, 128–29
in favor of forgiveness, 237–39
in problem solving, 68
in your emotional response and feelings, 40–42
Chopra, Deepak, 130–31
Closeness, 15. *See also* Intimacy
Coaching
problem of advising and, 10
stopping behaviors of, 160–62
Codependency, working alone on relationship vs., 18–19
Compassion, cultivation of, toward partner, 230–36
Complainer personalities, 249, 250, 254
Complaints about relationships. *See also* Problems in relationship
being right and your, 29–34
partner's, 35–36
Complementarity, changing views from incompatibility to, 101–5
Confucius, 237
Conscious Loving (Hendricks), 12–13
Control
in abusive situations, 277
managing partner's, through good will and detachment, 214–15, 227–28
Counseling for couples, xiii, 5–6, 37–38
Courage, building personal, 199–202
Covey, Stephen, 89–90
Cozy time, creating, 105–6
Criticism
asking for what you want without, 152–53
discontinuing, 46

"Date," planning surprise, 112
Decision-making about relationships, three-step method of, 264–71
Defensiveness, avoidance of, 76–80
Depolarization of power struggles, 128–35, 164
Desires for relationship, 43–44
asking for your, 8–9, 149–55
as reasonable goals, 206–8
Detachment from partner's behavior, 227–30
Disclosure, intimacy through self-, 178–80
Division of labor in relationships, 16–18
Divorce, deciding for or against, 271–72
Divorce Busting (Weiner-Davis), 12
Divorce Is Not the Answer (Pransky), 90
Doormat, practicing good will vs. becoming a, 218–19
Dreams, 207

Edelman, Joel, 271
Effectiveness
of good will, 217
of working alone, 4–10
Eight Essential Traits of Couples Who Thrive (Page), xi, 17, 96, 213
Einstein, Albert, xvii
Emotional bribery, 9–10
Emotions. *See* Feelings
Empathy for partner's point of view
acting on your own after expressing, 118–19
developing, as means of reframing power struggles, 129–30
expressing, for problem resolution, 138–43
Enchanting Evening, An (game), 107, 113
Energy
charging, for anger eclipsers, 54–56
discharging, for anger expressers, 56–58
ERAP (Emergency Resentment Abatement Procedure), 50–83
anger styles and, 51–53

Assess (mind) step in, 63–66
Express (body) step in, 53–58
Perform (relationship) in, 66–76
Relax (spirit) step in, 58–62
spouse's anger and, 76–80
using method of, 81–83
Evaluation of relationships, xiii, 11–14, 263–78
deciding on divorce or separation following, 271–78
three-step method of, 264–71
Expectations for relationship, 20, 43–44
Experiments, xiv
"acting as if," (#8) 95
acting on your own, (#13, #14), 121, 122
beginning personal journal and calling upon supportive friend (#1), xvi
changing "incompatible" to "complementary," (#11), 104
closing intimacy gap and reigniting love, (#21), 181
confidence and self-affirmation (#28), 208
courage (#26), 202
creating time together (#12), 106
cultivating acceptance (#30), 223
cultivating compassion (#33), 236
cultivating detachment (#32), 230
cultivating tolerance (#31), 226
determining areas of improvement for self-care/good-will blend (#38), 260
discontinuing criticism (#5), 46
doing opposite of usual (#15), 127
enlisting partner's help (#17), 137
experiencing good will and self-help in your body (#37), 254
expressing empathy (#18), 143
finding booby prize (finding problems and assigning blame) (#3), 30
finding gold (your role in relationship) (#4), 35
focusing on positive qualities (#10), 101
getting to know inner self (#22), 190–91
gracefully accepting what can't be changed (#19), 148
guessing your type of self-care and good will blend (#36), 249
identifying personal style of anger (#6), 52
looking at long-term anger (#7), 60
perseverance (#27), 206
reframing power struggles (#16), 135
self-care (#24), 196
self-love (#23), 192–93
spacing in (for men) (#20A), 158
stopping coaching (for women) (#20B), 161
taking a stand (#29), 212
taking care of yourself (#25), 199
taking inventory of partner and relationship (#2), 11
thinking generosity (#35), 244
thinking "good will," (#9), 97
working on forgiveness (#34), 239
Express step (ERAP), body charging and discharging of anger in, 53–58, 81

Fact of life, problems vs., 220–23
Fairness
practice of good will and issues of, 217–18
working alone and question of, 14–15
Family therapy, 37–38
Fault
being right and finding, 29–34, 171
family interactions and finding, 37–38
Favors, doing unexpected, 110–11
Fear, 131
Feelings
of anger, 50–83
changing, by "acting as if," 90–96
of hopelessness, 13–14
of intimacy, 163–64
about your partner and your relationship, 40–42
Fights, 80
Forgiveness, cultivation of, toward partner, 233, 237–39
Friend, calling on supportive, xv, xvi, 209

Gender
men: "spacing in," 155–59
relationship work and, 16–18
self-neglect related to, 195
tolerating differences in, 224–26
women: stop coaching, 160–62
Generosity
cultivating, toward partner, 240–44

good will as, 213 (*see also* Good will, cultivation of)
Gerzon, Mark, 38
Gifts, 110, 242
Goals
courage to accomplish, 199–202
dreams and, as reasonable desires, 206–8
focusing on true, 89
of leaders, 248
Godek, Gregory, 109
Good will, cultivation of, 96–97, 213–45
acceptance and, 220–23
blend of self-care and, 246–53
compassion and, 230–36
as critical factor, xi
detachment and, 227–30
forgiveness and, 237–39
generosity and, 240–44
possible objections to, 217–19
tolerance and, 223–26
Gray, John, 12

Hansberry, Lorraine, 231
Harmony, creation of, 87–114
"act as if" you are loving and, 90–96
brainstorming for creative problem solving and, 69–71
changing "incompatible" to "complementary" for, 101–5
creating relaxing times together for, 105–6
focusing on positive qualities for, 98–101
seven steps for togetherness and, 107–13
thinking "good will" for, 96–97
Hendricks, Gay, 12–13
Hendricks, Kathlyn, 13
"He's Doing the Best He Can" affirmation, 230–36
Hopelessness, feelings of, 13–14
House Divided, A (Gerzon), 38
"How Can I Be Generous to My Spouse Today?" affirmation, 240–44
Hudson, Pat, 13

"I Can Do This" affirmation, 199–202
"I Can Take a Stand" affirmation, 208–12
"If I Don't Take Care of Myself, Who Will?" affirmation, 194–99
If I'm So Wonderful, Why Am I Still Single? (Page), 204–5, 274
"I'm Doing the Best I Can" affirmation, 188–93
Incompatibility, changing views to complementarity from, 101–5
Individual rights vs. social responsibilities, 257–60
Information-gathering step of relationship evaluation, 264–67
Inner balance
body experience of, 253–56
personal needs vs. partner's needs and, 117–20, 187–88 (*see also* Self-care)
between self-care and good will, 246–53
working on, 256–60
Inner conflict, 131–32
Inner power, 14
Inner self, getting to know your, 190–91
Inner wisdom, decision-making on relationships by relying on, 267–70
Intention, 130–31
Interactions in relationships, 37–40, 45
Intimacy, 163–83
creating, 177–83
defined, 177, 178
"gap" of, in relationships, 164–70
methods for closing "gap" in, by yourself, 170–75
one or two partners working on, 15
word to women on, 175–77
Intuition about relationships, 267–70

Jonas, Barbara and Michael, 107

Keller, Helen, 202
Kennedy, Rose, 202
King and I, The, 90–91

Lao Tsu, 214
Law of Intention, Deepak Chopra's, 130–31
Leader personalities, 249, 253, 255–56
Leadership in relationships

- becoming the "big person" as, 22–25, 141, 213
- blend of self-care and good will linked to, 246–53
- body feel of balance and, 253–56
- identifying areas of improvement for, 256–60
- working alone as opportunity for, 25–26

Learning, 20–21
- anger and, 68–69
- changing relationships and curve of, 46–47

Letting go
- of being right, 29–34
- perseverance in relationships and, 204–5
- self-acceptance and, 190

Limbic system, 235
Limits, guidelines for setting, 209–11, 276
Love, finding imaginative ways of expressing, 107–8
Love and Renewal (Bugen), 13
Love Is a Verb (O'Hanlon, Hudson), 13
Love letters, sending, 108–10
Loving leadership. *See* Leadership in relationships

McGinnis, Alan Loy, 201
Marriage. *See* Relationships
Marriage counseling for couples, xiii, 5–6, 37–38
Maturity, 189
Men Are from Mars; Women Are from Venus (Gray), 12
Men in relationships
- mentoring of, in relationship skills, 17
- problem resolution by "spacing in" by, 155–59

Millman, Dan, 95
Mini blow-ups, 67–68
Mitchell, W., 201
Moods, "acting as if" and changing, 93
Motivation, 4–5
"My Desires Are Reasonable" affirmation, 206–8
"My Partner Is Not Wrong, Just Different" affirmation, 223–26
"My Partner Was Wrong. I Have a Choice" affirmation, 237–39

Nagging, 10, 160–62
Narcissistic personalities, 249, 251–52, 255
Nash, Ogden, 224
Needs. *See* Personal needs in relationship
Neuro Linguistic Programming, 91

Offering, sacrifice vs., 242
O'Hanlon, Bill, 13
1001 Ways to Be Romantic (Godek), 109
Opposite strategies as problem resolution, 123–27
Outings, planning for two, 111–12

Pain, maturity and managing life's, 189
Partner
- acceptance of, 47–49
- actions for bring yourself closer to, 107–13
- anger coming from your, 76–80
- attention given to, 174–75
- compassion for, 230–36
- complaints about you from, 35–36
- deciding to divorce or separate from, 263–78
- detaching from behavior of, 227–30
- empathy for viewpoint of, 129–30, 138–43
- enlisting help of, in problem resolution, 135–37
- finding fault and assigning blame to, 29–34
- focus on positive qualities of, 98–101
- forgiveness for, 237–39
- generosity toward, 240–44
- needs of, vs. your needs, 117–20
- power struggle with, 128–35
- response of, to your acting on your own, 120–22
- style of, as contribution to relationship, 173
- tolerance of, 223–26
- your expectations toward, 20, 43–44
- your feelings about, 40–42
- your role in behavior of, 36–40

Passion, goals and, 200–202
Patience, perseverance and, 203–6
Peal, Norman Vincent, 201
Perform step (ERAP), 66–76, 81

Perls, Fritz, 132
Perseverance, 203–6
Persistence, 203–6
Personal needs in relationship
  partner's needs vs., 117–20
  problems with denying, 10
  taking care of, 172–73 (*see also* Self-care)
Personal role in relationship, 34–49
  acceptance and, 47–49, 143–48
  anger and (*see* Anger)
  asking for what you want, 149–55
  attachment to being right, 29–34
  empathy and, 129–30, 138–43
  expectations toward relationship, 43–44
  feelings about partner and relationship, 40–42
  learning curve on, 46–47
  partner's view of you, 35–36
  power struggle with partner and, 128–35
  self-care and, 187–212
  your role in causing partner's behavior, 36–40
Physical abuse
  deciding on separation in cases of, 276–78
  setting limits to stop, 208–12
Pleaser personalities, 249, 250–51, 254–55
Positive qualities, focusing on partner's, 98–101
Power, inner, 14
Power of Optimism, The (McGinnis), 201
Power of Positive Thinking (Peale), 201
Power struggle
  intimacy gap as classic, 164–70
  reframing, for problem resolution, 128–35
Pransky, George, 90
Prayer, 188
Problem resolution, 115–62
  acting on your own and, 116–22
  anger and creative, 68–71
  asking for what you want as, 149–55
  enlisting partner's aid in, 135–37
  expressing empathy for partner's position in, 138–43
  gracefully accepting what can't be changed and, 143–48
  for men only (spacing in), 155–59
  reframing power struggles and, 128–35
  reversing directions and, 123–27
  as symptoms, 87, 102
  for women (stop coaching), 160–62
Problems in relationship
  being right and assigning blame for, 29–34
  discussion and focus on, as failed strategy, 87–88, 115–16
  facts of life vs., 220–23
  finding your role in, 34–49
  resolving (*see* Problem resolution)
  as symptoms, 87

Quality time together, 105–6

Raisin in the Sun, A (Hansberry), 231
Ram Dass, 222
Relationships, 279–90
  benefits of this book on, xii–xiv
  creating harmony in, 87–114
  cultivating good will in, 213–45
  division of labor in, 16–18
  evaluating, xiii, 11–14, 263–78
  experiments on, xiv (*see also* Experiments)
  finding fault and assigning blame in, 29–34
  finding your role in problems of, 34–49
  fostering intimacy and closeness in, 163–83
  S. Humphries on her, 285–90
  leadership in (self-care and good will), 246–60
  managing anger in, 50–83
  options for using this book on, xiv–xvi
  problems in (*see* Problems in relationship)
  resolving problems in (*see* Problem resolution)
  review of author's message on nurturing, 283–85
  self-care in, 187–212
  as spiritual path, 279–83
  structure of this book on, xvii
  taking care of yourself in, 187–212
  working alone on, 3–26

Relaxation time together, 105–6
Relax step (ERAP), 58–62, 81
Reliance, strengthening self-, 194–99
Requests
  ineffective ways of making, 8–9
  making specific, 149–55
  problem of not making, 9
Reverse direction as problem resolution, 123–27
Right, letting go of always being, 29–34, 171
Role models, 198
Romance, intimacy and, 181
Romantic evenings, planning surprise, 112–13

Sacrifice vs. offering, 242
Sainthood, practice of good will vs., 219
Self-acceptance, 188–93
Self-assertiveness, 208–12
Self-calming strategies, 61–62
Self-care, 172–73, 187–212
  balancing your needs and partner's needs as, 117–20
  blend of good will and, 246–53
  building assertiveness, 208–12
  building perseverance, 203–6
  building personal courage, 199–202
  building self-confidence, 206–8
  experiment on, 196
  strengthening self-acceptance, 188–93
  strengthening self-reliance, 194–99
Self-confidence, 206–8
Self-disclosure, intimacy through, 178–80
Self-love, experiment on, 192–93
Self-reliance, 194–99
Separation, deciding for or against, 273–76
Seven Spiritual Laws of Success, The (Chopra), 130–31
"She's Doing the Best She Can" affirmation, 230–36
Singles in relationship, deciding on separation for, 273–74
Social responsibilities vs. individual rights, 257–60
Soul, 280
"Spacing in" by men in relationships, 155–59
Spiritual path, relationship as, 279–83
Spouse. *See* Partner

Taking care of yourself. *See* Self-care
Tassajara Zen Buddhist Center, 41
Tavris, Carol, 57, 59–60
Therapy for couples, xiii, 5–6, 37–38
"Things Take Time" affirmation, 203–6
"This Has Nothing to Do with Me" affirmation, 227–30
"This Is Not a Problem. It's a Fact of Life" affirmation, 220–23
Time
  fostering intimacy by spending, together, 178
  perseverance and allowance for, 203–6
  spending quality (cozy), 105–6
Timing, intimacy and, 180

Urgency of your position, relaxing, 130–32

Value judgment, choice in, 41–42
Venting vs. mini blow-ups, 67
Verbal abuse
  deciding on separation in cases of, 276–78
  setting limits to stop, 208–12
Vision, goals and, 200–202

Waiting
  relaxation and, 59–61
  as step in reframing power struggles, 132–35
Wants, asking for, 149–55
Way of Marriage, The (Borys), 68–69, 96–97, 159, 162, 238
Way of the Peaceful Warrior, The (Millman), 95
Weiner-Davis, Michelle, 12
Welwood, John, 279
When "I Can't Help It" Is for Real (Amen), 235
Women in relationships
  emotional work done by, 16–18
  fostering intimacy by, 175–77
  problem resolution by coaching stopped by, 160–62

Working alone on relationships, 3–26
codependency and, 18–19
effectiveness of, 8–10
evaluating worth of relationship and, 11–14
expectations on results of, 20–22
experience of, 19–20
fairness of, 14–15
intimacy, closeness, and, 15
as leadership opportunity, 25–26
methods of, 22–26
objections to, 3
principle of working together vs., 4–8
by women, 16–18

ABOUT THE AUTHOR

Susan Page is a Protestant minister and the former Director of Women's Programs at the University of California, Berkeley. She has a background in both theology and psychology.

To contact Susan Page regarding lectures and workshops, or to share with her your response to the ideas in this book, write to her at 1941 Oregon Street, Berkeley, California 94703.